GHOST OF A CHANCE

GHOST OF A CHANCE

A Memoir

PETER DUCHIN

WITH

CHARLES MICHENER

RANDOM HOUSE

NEW YORK

Grateful acknowledgment is made to The Anita Loos Trust
for permission to reprint an excerpt from *Cast of Thousands*
by Anita Loos (Grosset & Dunlap, New York, 1977).
Copyright © 1977 by Anita Loos. Reprinted by permission of
Ray Pierre Corsini, agent for The Anita Loos Trust.

Library of Congress Cataloging-in-Publication Data
Duchin, Peter.
Ghost of a chance : a memoir / Peter Duchin with Charles Michener.
p.   cm.
Includes index.
ISBN 0-375-75131-9 (alk. paper)
1. Duchin, Peter.   2. Musicians—United States—Biography.
I. Michener, Charles.   II. Title.
ML422.D8A3   1996   784.4'8'092–dc20
[B]   95-46748

Random House website address: www.randomhouse.com
Printed in the United States of America on acid-free paper
Book design by J. K. Lambert
9 8 7 6 5 4 3 2

First Paperback Edition

For Brooke

CONTENTS

1. Make Someone Happy 3

2. A Soothing Hum 9

3. The Best American Girl 21

4. Dad 35

5. The Forests of Arden 53

6. Ma 63

7. Ave 79

8. Stormy Weather 99

9. "Who's Playing Clarinet?" 125

10. Youthful Improvisations 147

11. Paris 165

12. Advanced Harmony and Counterpoint . . . 195

13. A Glockenspielist in Panama 203

14. Society Beat 215

15. At Home in the St. Regis 233

16. Ports of Call 259

17. View from the Bandstand 279

18. The Private Sport 295

19. Losing Ma 309

20. Pam 319

21. Endings 331

22. Second Time Around 341

23. Piano Rolls 355

   Afterword 361

   Acknowledgments 365

   Index 367

GHOST OF A CHANCE

MAKE SOMEONE
HAPPY

"When a young man kills his first stag," our Scottish gardener used to say with great seriousness, "the older hunters smear the animal's blood on the lad's forehead. It's called *blooding*." I must have been almost ten when I heard that story, but, weirdly, I started thinking about it fifteen years later, as I stood in the bathroom of a suite in the St. Regis Hotel, staring in the mirror at a small shaving cut on my neck. It was the night of September 25, 1962, and the older hunters were all downstairs, dressed in black tie, waiting for me to attend to the stag.

I stuck a piece of toilet paper on the cut, splashed cold water on my face, and tried to fix my tie to hide the red spot on the collar. The guy looking back at me was scared to death. I had just turned twenty-five, and I was about to make my professional debut as a bandleader, not in some out-of-the-way dump where nobody would notice but right at the top: the Maisonette in the St. Regis, one of the classiest supper clubs in New York. The audience was a killer, too—several hundred celebrities, newspaper columnists, and people from café and old society.

A pair of ivory-backed hairbrushes that had belonged to my father—the old-fashioned kind with hard badger bristles that fit together—was lying on the edge of the marble sink. I slicked back my hair with them, then pulled up my suspenders, clamped on the cummerbund, put on my dinner jacket. I checked my watch, a gold Omega with a black alligator band. It had also belonged to my father. Dad's ghost was all over this event. The Maisonette was exactly the sort of place he had "owned" in the thirties and forties, when the Eddy Duchin Orchestra was one of the most famous bands in the country.

Out in the sitting room, I poured myself a drink. On the wall above the little bar was a mezzotint of a Scottie dog that looked just like Kilty, the pooch that had belonged to my maternal grandmother, "Mammy" Oelrichs. Mammy had lived at the St. Regis for years, or at least for as long as Dad had paid her bills. When I was a kid, I'd occasionally visit her for tea. She'd draw me into her bosom, which reeked of Chanel, and my blazer would get smeared with her white face powder. I remembered wonderful pastries arriving on a silver tray from room service after we'd taken Kilty out for a sedate walk in Central Park.

Tonight there were no tea and cakes, although César Balsa, who owned the St. Regis, was throwing a little warm-up downstairs—a cocktail party for the press and a few old friends. I finished off the Scotch and checked myself one more time. The blood had dried. Gingerly, I removed the toilet paper.

The first person I ran into at the party was Dorothy Kilgallen from the *Journal-American:* no chin, pounds of pale makeup, big doll eyes. She whipped out a notebook. "How do you feel?"

"I can't believe this is happening to me," I said, gamely.

She had her quote, for what it was worth, and moved over for the next guy, John McClain, the Hearst columnist. John had been a friend of Dad's and one of the hosts, along with Cary Grant and Jimmy Stewart, of a legendary party they'd all thrown in L.A. in 1946, when I was nine. "I got tears in my eyes, kid," John said. "If only Eddy were here."

Next came Popsie Whitaker of *The New Yorker,* a wonderful heap of a fellow who reminded me of a crumpled newspaper. I mumbled some inanities, then turned toward the tall Dorothy Lamour look-alike who was smiling at me: Chiquita, my stepmother. A couple of years earlier, when I was sweating it out as a glockenspielist in the Army Band in the Canal Zone, Chiq had invited me to Mexico City for a little R and R. One night we went to a restaurant called Uno, Dos, Tres, and after too much to drink I started playing the piano. When the owner heard that the kid fooling around was Eddy Duchin's son, he'd handed me his card and murmured, "Call me when you're back in New York." He was César Balsa.

As Chiq was saying how proud—at last—she was of me, all three hundred pounds of Toots Shor glided over. I'd known Toots most of my life. Back in the twenties and thirties, he was a bouncer at Leon & Eddie's, the speakeasy on West Fifty-second Street. When he wanted to open his own saloon after Prohibition, Dad gave him a blank check. Toots never cashed it. He didn't even tear it up. He called it "visual collateral."

Toots was family. Everything at his place was "on the house" for me and my pals. Toots had made sure I wasn't alone at the screening of *The Eddy Duchin Story,* the Hollywood tearjerker about my father's life. Watching Rex Thompson, the brat who played me in knickers, I'd wanted to hide under the seat, and when the movie was over I'd felt pretty beat up and confused. As we were leaving the screening room, Toots put his big paw on my arm.

"Pete, when were you born?"

"July twenty-eighth, 1937."

"What was it in the movie?"

"Some day in December."

He punched me gently on the shoulder. "See what I mean? It's all a load of crap."

Now he punched me again.

The couple right behind Toots were more family, and I kissed each of them in turn. First, "Ma," my godmother, Marie Harriman, looking sexy behind her dark glasses. Then her husband, Averell, the former governor of New York and ambassador to Moscow, now a big deal in the Kennedy State Department. Ave wore a dinner jacket that had undoubtedly been made by the little Italian tailor who came twice a year to his house on East Eighty-first Street.

Ma was dragging on a Viceroy in a white plastic cigarette holder. "This is the night we've been waiting for, kiddo," she said.

Ave beamed his all-purpose smile. "You'll do *just* fine, Petey."

Ginny Chambers, my other godmother, sailed up. "I never lost hope, darling. Though you certainly pushed it." Ginny's whiskey baritone crackled through a wreath of cigarette smoke. "Do you believe it, Marie, after all this kid's put us through?"

There was a soft voice at my elbow.

"Eees time, Peter," said César Balsa.

≡

The Maisonette's backstage was a cramped area behind the bandstand with ten lockers and a closet-size changing room that was being used by our vocalist, Nancy Manning, a buxom brunette who sang in the vanilla style of Jo Stafford and Kay Starr. Otto Schmidt, my manager and tenor saxophonist, was chatting with the musicians.

"The boss is here, fellas," Otto said.

Boss?

One by one, they filed through the door to the bandstand. Nancy emerged from the closet, gave me a peck on the cheek, and joined the parade.

I felt my knees turning to jelly. The lights dimmed, and I actually heard myself saying "Don't blow it" out loud. Then Otto was rapping on the stage door. They were ready to go.

As I stepped into the spotlight there were cheers, whistles, applause. A friend had suggested, "Before you sit down and play, stuff a handkerchief up your sleeve. It's what Horowitz does to calm himself."

To hell with Horowitz. I sat down and positioned my fingers over the keys, then glanced up at Otto. He raised his sax. I nodded the downbeat.

By the beginning of the second chorus of "Make Someone Happy," everybody was up on their feet, dancing.

My second Christmas, in Studio City, California.

2

A SOOTHING

HUM

My arrival in the world was a disaster. For the details I rely on Anita Loos, or "Neetsie," as I came to know her. In *Cast of Thousands,* a memoir of her days as a Hollywood screenwriter, she recalls that she took a two-week leave of absence from MGM in the summer of 1937 to be with her friend Marjorie Duchin, who was pregnant with me.

I found Marge in great form, buoyed up for the forthcoming ordeal by our mutual friend, Marie Harriman, whose husband Averell was in Washington, holding a high post in the Roosevelt Administration.

Dominating the situation was Marge's mother, "Big Marge." She had been a reigning belle during the Gay Nineties, and nothing could convince her that those snooty days had come to an end.

Marge was her only child, and to Big Marge she had never ceased to be "Baby." So her greatest concern was that Little Marge should have the most fashionable obstetrician in New York and that the baby would be born in a stylish hospital.

That hospital was located above the Colony Restaurant. . . . The majority of its clientele were either alcoholics bent on sobering up, hypochondriacs pampering their egos, gourmands trying to reduce, or middle-aged beauties hiding out for a facelift. The hospital was noted for its lenient house rules: patients could order gourmet meals sent up from the restaurant below; nurses would look the other way when dipsomaniacs sent out for booze, or the overweight phoned down . . . for a few crêpes Suzette. There were no restrictions against visitors, who used to drop in at all hours to enjoy cocktails or nightcaps with their pampered friends.

Just as my mother was about to be admitted to this stylish fun house, Anita was called back to MGM.

I was very disappointed not to be around when the baby came, and when Marge saw me off at the station, it was a pretty melancholy goodbye, which I put down to the war clouds that overshadowed everyone's personal affairs in those dark days. While waiting for train time, Marge said a little uneasily, "Going into that rowdy old hospital to have a baby doesn't seem to make very good sense, does it?"

"Good sense" wasn't the phrase for it; "tragic" would have been a better description. I boarded the train, waved goodbye to Marge through the window, and that was the last time I ever saw her.

Hearing that my mother had gone into labor, my father flew to New York from Chicago, where he'd been playing at the Palmer House Hotel. Everything seemed fine, and he flew back to Chicago, only to turn around the next day when he heard that things weren't so fine. He was at my mother's bedside when she died at 6:30 A.M. on August 3, 1937, six days after my birth. Her chic obstetrician couldn't be found. According to Anita Loos, he'd gone off hunting in the wilds of Canada.

Two years earlier, my parents' marriage had made headlines. "A romance between Broadway and Park Avenue," they called it. My mother had just redecorated their apartment at 2 East Sixtieth Street in anticipation of my arrival. Now her funeral was being held there. According to *The New York Times,* "More than three-hundred floral tributes" were delivered, including "two heart-shaped floral pieces made up of sweetheart roses, Mrs. Duchin's favorite flower." My father received 4,000 messages of condolence, including one from President Roosevelt, for whose inaugural ball he and the band had played in 1933.

===

Not long after I was born, I developed severe respiratory difficulties, and I was not expected to live for more than a few weeks. I was put into an oxygen tent, a germ-free environment. Recently, I asked Dr. William Cahan, an eminent New York cancer specialist and an old friend of my father's, to describe what an oxygen tent for a newborn would have been like in those days. He explained that it would probably have been a reinforced cellophane cube suspended from rings on the ceiling, with vented openings to let doctors' hands through.

I asked Bill how the air got in.

"A motor blew in oxygen and cool steam, for moisture."

Did the motor make a sound?

"A continual hum. It would have been very soothing."

The other soothing factor at this point in my life was my nurse, Chissie. Until her death in 1994, Chissie and I stayed in touch through birthday and Christmas cards. She lived in Virginia, and a few years ago when I found myself playing a gig in Roanoke, I called her up and invited her to lunch. Then in her seventies, Chissie still had the ramrod straight back of an immensely competent woman. Her hair was black and worn in a bun, and she had an air of calm, levelheaded kindness.

"You know, Peter," she said, "leaving you was the saddest thing that ever happened to me. I thought of you as my own child." Chissie remembered our life together very clearly. A few weeks after the lunch in Virginia, I received a manuscript of seventeen neatly typed, double-spaced pages. The title page said, " 'Peter Duchin's Early Childhood' by Rita C. Chisholm." It took me a long time to sit down and read it, but when I was finally able to take Chissie's manuscript out of the drawer where it had lain undisturbed for months, I couldn't put it aside.

Chissie, then a private nurse in New York specializing in newborn babies whose lives were endangered, had been summoned by my pediatrician, Dr. Schloss, who told her about "a critically ill seven-day-old infant who had been born in a small private hospital that was inadequate for the care of small babies." She agreed to take on the case—me—and went over to New York Hospital, where I had been transferred.

Chissie found me "very listless," with "extremely labored respirations." The problem was "atelectasis," a malfunction of the muscles that raise and lower the rib cage. The strategy, she recalled, was to keep me alive long enough for me to outgrow my abnormalities. Since any infection could have been fatal, it was essential that I be kept in isolation.

I made good progress. At three months, I was alert and gaining weight. I was, recalled Chissie, "happy, responsive, and increasingly active within the small area of the oxygen tent." By nine months, I'd learned to pull myself upright by holding on to the side railings of the crib. According to Chissie, during those first nine months in the hospital my father came to see me only once.

In the spring of 1938, New York Hospital was filling up with polio victims, and a new home had to be found for me. Various of my mother's friends offered to take me in, and, as Chissie wrote, "It was decided to accept the Harrimans' invitation since their mansion, Arden House, was in the country and surrounded by many acres of land. It was about forty miles from New York City, near enough for Dr. Schloss to visit. Tanks of oxygen were available in a nearby community."

Since I was becoming more active, I graduated to an adult-size tent. Chissie and I were installed in a suite consisting of a large bedroom, a sitting room, and bath. We were given a special nursery maid to cook, clean, and do the laundry, so as to minimize my risk of infection from contact with servants.

To mark my first birthday, I was photographed in one of the gardens at Arden House, standing on a chair, naked except for a white bonnet and a harness to keep me from falling off. I seem to have been extremely pleased with myself. Among the gifts I received were a baseball and bat from my father. They arrived along with a telegram that read: HAPPY BIRTHDAY SON SORRY UNABLE BE WITH YOU LOVE AND KISSES—DADDY.

Winter was coming, and it was decided that I needed a warmer, drier climate. Marie Harriman consulted Neetsie, who came up with a house in one of the warmest, driest spots in southern California, Palm Springs. On November 8, 1938, Chissie and I boarded the Twentieth-Century Limited for the great trek west.

The logistics were extraordinary. So I wouldn't have to change trains in Chicago, it was arranged for our New York Central car to be hooked up to a Southern Pacific train. Chissie and I were given adjoining compartments, one for the accommodation of four oxygen tanks. A special battery-run tent was devised that could fit through the doors. A vast supply of ice was ordered for the tent's cooling mechanism, to be delivered at stops along the way. All this was thanks to Averell Harriman, whose father had built up the Union Pacific Railroad. Averell was chairman of the board of directors until he entered politics.

Chissie and I were seen off at Grand Central Station by the Harrimans and other friends of theirs. The group did not include my father, who was playing somewhere out of town. He did, however, monitor our progress via Western Union. At every stop along the 3,000-mile route, Chissie got telegrams from him and Marie Harriman, asking how things were going.

Everything was fine until we pulled out of La Salle Street Station in Chicago, whereupon I developed a fever and ear infection. At the next station, we were met by a pediatrician who advised immediate hospitalization. But Chissie insisted we press on, and the engineer was dispatched to a pharmacy with a prescription for the ear infection. Two days later we arrived in Los Angeles. We were met by Neetsie and an ambulance that whisked me off to Cedars–Mt. Sinai Hospital.

I was given two weeks to live, but within a few days my temperature had dropped to normal, and Chissie and I soon set off for Palm Springs. There, in a tiny, nondescript bungalow suitable for Dillinger on the run, Chissie and I hid out for the next eight months. Our only regular visitor was Neetsie, who drove three hours every Sunday from Santa Monica just to see how I was doing. On Christmas Day, she arrived with Aldous Huxley and his wife. Huxley and I apparently hit it off, so much so that he came back to see me several more times.

"Palm Springs in 1938–39 was a small community," Chissie recalled. "To prevent any possibility of infection to Peter, I also had to be isolated. My only outing was going to the Post Office to collect our mail. Since the Post Office was a mile away, I bought myself a bicycle so I could get there and back quickly."

My father was touring with his band, and he was apprised of my progress in letters Chissie sent to his office in New York. He sent us, she recalled, "a couple of typewritten letters which said very little." Later Chissie learned that these replies had been written by his secretary over his signature. In the spring of 1939, my father came to Palm Springs on a visit to friends and stopped by to see me. He said to Chissie, "What a great friend you turned out to be." It was, she recalled rather bitterly, "the first compliment I had ever received from him."

In early summer, the temperature soared past a hundred degrees, and Neetsie came up with another, cooler home—a little ranch-style cottage in Studio City, just over the Hollywood Hills in the San Fernando Valley. There I made my first friend, Yvonne, the granddaughter of Neetsie's black chauffeur, whose wife, Hallie, was taken on as our housekeeper. Hallie and Yvonne lived with us.

A snapshot of me and Yvonne shows us holding hands in front of the cottage, both dressed all in white. That spring my father dropped by again, this time with two tricycles—one for me, one for Yvonne. Then he took us to a photographer's studio where the three of us were posed. He held me on one side of him, Yvonne on the other. The "family portrait" ended up on a Christmas card, signed "Peter, Eddy, Yvonne," and was sent to thousands of Eddy Duchin fans. I can't imagine what they made of that beautiful little black girl with my father's arm around her.

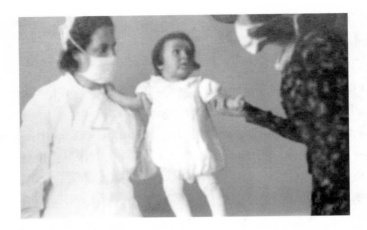

I was a fragile baby, and spent my first nine months in
New York Hospital with my nurse, Chissie.

Two remarkable women took care of me for the first three years of my life.
Chissie, left, treated me like her own child, and Anita Loos, right, looked out
for me in southern California, where I was taken for the climate.

Apparently, I had a "keen" sense of music, as demonstrated by the interest I showed in my father's recordings, which Chissie made a point of playing for me on a little phonograph. I soon learned how to operate the machine myself, and I always, recalled Chissie, knew exactly what music I liked.

By then my lungs were functioning normally, and I was allowed out in the open air all day long. But I didn't give up my tent easily. After Chissie would tuck me into bed, I'd insist that she lower the tent over me with the motor humming. Only then could I fall asleep.

The next spring, we prepared to leave California. My breathing was fine, and Chissie thought it was time I develop a relationship with my father. In June 1940, we boarded the train for the trip back east.

This time, my father met us at Grand Central. We all checked into a suite at the Plaza Hotel, and the next morning I was taken to hear him rehearse with his band in the Persian Room. According to Chissie, I could stand only about ten minutes of it. "I don't like all that noise," I said. "Let's go." The next day, Chissie and I left for the Harriman estate—Arden. Dad left for a gig in California.

It is clear from Chissie's account of our three years together that there had been friction between her and my father for some time. She wrote that she gave notice that summer after being told by Dr. Schloss that she was "no longer appreciated." In September 1940, this amazing woman, who had been my lifeline, said good-bye. "I packed my bags," she wrote, "promised Peter I would come to visit him, and departed, feeling very sad." Several months later, she returned to Arden for a last visit:

We had a delightful day. . . . A few days later I got a telephone call from your father, who was very angry. . . . I remember him saying, "Stay out of Peter's life and don't ever see him again." Naturally, I was crushed and did not visit you again. . . . [Later] you sent me a letter with your picture taken at the local school. . . . I kept this picture with me throughout my years of duty in the Army aboard a hospital ship.

Chissie's disapproval of my father's absences may have been obvious, which could only have rankled him, but her abrupt dismissal is mysterious. When I called her up to ask her about that, she said she'd give it some thought. A few days later she sent me another letter:

Dear Peter,

I felt [your father] was very self-absorbed, unpredictable, quick-tempered, unappreciative, always concerned about expenses. But he could be thoughtful and charming when he wanted to be.

It is not unusual for a father whose wife died during or shortly after childbirth to reject the baby, subconsciously blaming the baby for her death. In addition, your father had the problem of a baby who was critically ill with little hope that he would survive. I was told that he was very depressed for several months after your mother's death and was discouraged from becoming interested in the baby, since—if the baby died—it was feared his depression might increase to dangerous proportions. His manager was purposely keeping him out of the New York area as much as possible.

Therefore I was not surprised when your father did not come to see you the first few months or even telephone the hospital. What did surprise me and annoy me was that his lack of attention to you lasted so long. . . .

[After our return to Arden,] Marie convinced your father that he should call me every Sunday evening between 8:00 and 8:30 P.M. when he was away from New York City. He was to call on her private line by her bed so it wouldn't cost him as much as using the regular Arden House number and having to wait for me to be summoned to the phone. I would sit in Marie's bedroom from eight o'clock until your father called. He did call every Sunday between eight and nine o'clock. I remember one Sunday he hadn't called by ten-thirty, so as I thought he was not going to call, I left the bedroom. About eleven o'clock he called on the regular Arden House number and was furious with me for having left Marie's room.

About four months before I left Arden, I was talking to your father's secretary, and she said, "Don't you realize they want you to leave because you know too much about the affair going on with Mrs. Harriman?" I was shocked and didn't believe it was true. They were certainly very discreet about it whenever they were at Arden.

The most unpredictable thing your father did as far as I was concerned was to enlist in the Navy. Had his affair with Marie terminated? I've wondered if that influenced his decision to enlist.

I can only wonder as well.

My mother, Marjorie Oelrichs, photographed by Cecil Beaton,
with the silhouette of my father behind her.

3

THE BEST
AMERICAN GIRL

When I was about three or four years old, I would ride my tricycle along the upstairs corridors of Arden House, past rows of photogravures of American Indians. They had been taken by the great nineteenth-century photographer Edward S. Curtis, and there were dozens of them: fierce, painted faces crowned by feathers. Pedaling past the Indians, I would imagine that we were warriors together, racing silently through the woods.

The first painting I remember being drawn to was Picasso's *Woman with a Fan,* which hung over the couch in various Harriman living rooms and now hangs in the National Gallery in Washington. The woman in the picture sits in Egyptian-like profile, with an upraised hand that seems to beckon an unseen person from beyond the frame. I wanted that unseen person to be *me.* When I got a little older, and when Ma and Ave weren't at home, I'd sneak downstairs in the middle of the night, flick on the picture light, and float toward the woman. She was always welcoming.

I was told that the beautiful woman in the photographs in the silver frames on Ma's bedroom dresser was my mother, but that was all anybody said about her, at least within earshot of me. The photographs had been taken by Cecil Beaton, a great friend of my mother's in the thirties.

When I was five or six, Zellie, the French governess who had replaced Chissie, took me into the city to see *Bambi*. When Bambi's mother was killed, I cried so hard I had to be taken out of the theater. Zellie didn't think it was a good idea to talk about whatever connection I might have made between the death of Bambi's mother and the death of mine. Nor did anyone else. My mother's death was such a closed subject that in my scrapbooks of news clips and photographs, all references to how she died have been either blacked out or cut away.

The newspapers called her a "New York and Newport socialite," but her background was more complicated. On her paternal side, Marjorie Oelrichs was descended from a shipping family that had arrived in New York from Hamburg in 1780, prospered in the merchant marine business, and made their way into the upper echelons of New York society. By the time my great-grandfather Charles DeLoosey Oelrichs came of age, things were falling apart. He had aristocratic Austrian forebears on his mother's side, but he was a ne'er-do-well—a failing broker on the New York Stock Exchange.

Charles's older brother was something else. My great-great uncle Hermann Oelrichs had married one of America's wealthiest women, Theresa Fair, a daughter of James Graham Fair, who was a partner in the Comstock Lode in Nevada, the largest silver deposit ever unearthed. Theresa and Hermann Oelrichs hired Stanford White to build Rosecliff, a palatial summer "cottage" on Bellevue Avenue in Newport, Rhode Island, that rivaled The Breakers, the Vanderbilts' cottage, for gilded, turn-of-the-century opulence. A forty-five-room replica of Louis XIV's Grand Trianon at Versailles, Rosecliff was the setting for the Roaring Twenties parties in the 1974 film of *The Great Gatsby.*

Uncle Hermann was a man-about-town whose philandering cost him his marriage. Shortly after the building of Rosecliff had been completed, in 1902, he left his wife. Out of loneliness, Aunt Theresa threw herself into entertaining on a scale matched only by that of her two Newport rivals, her sister Virginia Graham Fair, who was married to William K. Vanderbilt, Jr., and Mrs. Stuyvesant Fish. On August 20, 1904, she gave a bash that is still remembered on Bellevue Avenue.

She called it the White Ball. White dresses were required of all the ladies, many of whom powdered and puffed their hair à la Madame de Pompadour. A hundred attendants and waiters were clad in white, head to toe. The grounds were lit by thousands of white electric lights—in those days, a real novelty. Out on the back lawn, white swans glided around the white marble fountain. Tables were set in white pavilions, dripping with white roses and white hydrangeas. The crowning touch lay at anchor out in the ocean: twelve full-size models of white-sailed racing sloops—backdrop for the all-white, midnight fireworks.

=

All this I learned only recently when I went up to Newport. I had arranged a tour of Rosecliff with a historian from the Preservation Society of Newport County. As we wandered through the great mirrored rooms, I learned that Aunt Theresa had not been your typical grande dame. Perhaps because she'd grown up in a mining camp, she had had a mania for cleanliness, which meant that every bed in the mansion's twenty-two bedrooms had to be changed every day, regardless of whether it had been slept in or not. The morning after one of her great parties, she could be found on her hands and knees, scrubbing the marble herself. She was not without a sense of humor about it. "When I die," she once said to a friend, "bury me with a cake of Sapolio in one hand and a scrubbing brush in the other. They are my symbols."

My guide at Rosecliff knew all about my branch of the family—the "poor Oelrichs cousins." In fact, he said, the house that had belonged to my great-grandfather Charles Oelrichs was still there. "It's down on Kay Street," he said. "No doubt your mother spent time there as a girl."

The house on Kay Street could have been dropped into Rosecliff's ballroom. A much-gabled, yellow-painted frame structure with white gingerbread trim, it sat on less than an acre in a modestly comfortable part of town. I had not called the owners in advance, and I didn't know what to expect when I rang the front doorbell. But once she heard who I was and why I was there, the woman who came to the door invited me in. Her husband was a doctor, she said, and except for the room downstairs that had been turned into his office, the house was just the way it had always been.

I was shown into a classic center hall that opened into a parlor on one side and a dark-paneled library on the other. Upstairs, I walked into four bedrooms and looked out the dormer windows, glimpsing the same views my mother would have glimpsed after spending the night at her grandparents'.

The woman who was showing me around handed me a book she said would be helpful in evoking what life used to be like in the house. I didn't recognize the title—*Who Tells Me True*—but I rec-

ognized the name of the author. Michael Strange was the pseudo-
nym of my great-aunt Blanche Oelrichs, a celebrated beauty of the
twenties and thirties, political radical, occasional actress, and
writer of dreadful, flowery poems. She had been married three
times, most notoriously to the actor John Barrymore. They had
battled on an internationally stormy scale and produced a notoriously stormy daughter, Diana, who later wrote the first *Mommie
Dearest* memoir, *Too Much, Too Soon.* I had once heard someone
describe the marriage between Aunt Blanche and Barrymore as a
"tennis match made in hell, with nobody missing the ball."

I had always assumed that my great-aunt had to have been a
model for her niece, my mother. Opening the book to a marker on
page 17, I found this description of the Newport from which
Blanche Oelrichs—and, by extension, Marjorie Oelrichs—had
rebelled:

I loved the dear yellow wooden house in which I lived from baby-
hood until my marriage, with its old-fashioned gables painted in
white, its shaky tower up which I hopefully climbed through thousands of cobwebs on each Halloween of my childhood and girlhood,
a candle in one hand, and a mirror in the other—upon which I
might but never did—receive the glint of my lover's face. . . .

There was a cozy library where the chairs suddenly got comfortable, and I could stare up at dozens of pictures lining the walls, to
ask my mother, the eternal storyteller, why Mrs. Lorillard Spencer
wore a coronet in her hair, like the goddess Diana, why the plumes
in Mrs. Belmont's hat were half as big again as Mr. Belmont, and my
mother never failed me, with brilliantly stimulating replies about
Mr. Belmont's appearance in armor at the Bradley Martin ball, and
of how the beautiful Mrs. Lorillard Spencer had a great sorrow, and
had gone to nurse in the Philippines. Then she would sigh and put
away her sewing to go off and dress for some five o'clock cotillion

with my father, who at that incredible hour would be all dressed up in a tall hat and frock coat.

My mother's childhood was not so idyllic. Her father, Charles Oelrichs, Jr., turned out to be no more financially astute than his father. When my mother was thirteen, her parents were divorced. Her mother—my grandmother Marjorie ("a Turnbull" from Morristown, New Jersey)—was forced to support herself and her only child by going into "trade," selling dresses and perfume in a Madison Avenue shop.

At a young age, my mother became an entrepreneur. After graduating from the Spence School for Girls in New York and "coming out" as a debutante, she scandalized her mother by lending her name and face to ads for cigarettes and beauty aids. In the campaign for Lucky Strikes, in which she was featured along with other debs of the twenties, cigarettes were called "torches of freedom," implying that if nice girls smoked, it was OK for bad girls to smoke.

My mother traveled a lot in Europe, supporting herself by selling real estate in Paris. In New York she opened a dress shop and did interior decorating for friends. The biggest job she landed was for the ski lodge in Sun Valley, Idaho, the winter resort developed in the early thirties by the Union Pacific Railroad and its chairman, Averell Harriman, who had married my mother's old pal from Spence, Marie Norton Whitney. According to accounts of the lodge's opening in 1936, my mother's decor consisted of light orange walls; navy blue, leather-covered oak furniture; and blue net hangings. Sun Valley soon became the most fashionable winter resort in America.

A couple of years ago, I ran into Charles Baskerville, the New York painter, who recalled the time he'd encountered my mother in a camel market in Marrakesh. "It must have been the early thir-

Rosecliff, the Newport mansion built by Stanford White for my mother's great-uncle Hermann Oelrichs. It was the setting of the parties in the film *The Great Gatsby*.

In the early thirties, my mother lived in Paris. This photograph was taken at the club of her friend Brick Top, who gave it to me. Brick Top is the woman sitting down. The inscription on the back says that the "lady with her arm around Mabel [Mercer] is Miss Marjorie, your lovely sweet Mama, God rest her soul in peace." It's signed "Your Auntie Brick Top."

ties," he said, "and Marge was with a Polish conductor whose name I've forgotten. She was wearing a blindingly white duck caftan and a sort of Panama hat that was very unusual for a woman to be wearing in a place like that. She was very paintable."

Another old friend of my mother's, Cordelia Biddle Robertson, gave me this haunting picture: "Margie and I were really something in the thirties. We'd get dressed up in men's suits and ties, hit the bars, smoke on the streets, and swear like sailors. Was she fun!"

From time to time my mother wrote for popular journals. She was only nineteen when she published her first article, an essay in *Liberty* magazine with the headline "What's the Matter with American Men?" The layout featured her in a tight turban—very twenties—and a sleeveless dress with a skirt well above the knees—very sixties. Her views on love and marriage were both naive and worldly, romantic and sophisticated:

"The reason I prefer foreign men to American men," she wrote,

is that they have learned that love is among the fine arts. . . . A European man genuinely in love with a woman is a gallant lover. He does not tell her of his success in the business world or of his prowess on the polo field. He talks to her about herself. . . . Once married to such a man, she will probably be taken to live on one of his family's estates. She will find it dull there—if she is incurably American—as there will be no night clubs or any gaiety of the kind she has been used to. Instead, she will find a simple, healthy life: riding, shooting, golf, tennis, and cards, and conversation in the evening when his relatives and friends from nearby estates come over for dinner and linger until bedtime—say half-past ten, sometimes eleven if the talk is especially animated. . . .

If she should take herself a lover, she will find that her husband will meet the situation like a man of the world. He will do one of two things: order her from his house and refuse ever to see her again, or find himself a mistress by way of counterbalance, and let their domestic arrangements otherwise run on as if all were well.

I like this viewpoint in foreign men. They understand that love can not always last forever. So if it should transpire that the wife takes a lover and the husband a mistress, there is no unseemly commotion.

Whether it was because the editors found this all too radical or because my mother had suffered last-minute qualms, she ended with a disclaimer:

Understand me, I feel profoundly that no irregular affair should ever be begun. Such affairs are essentially impractical and makeshift and too often unfair. Except in the rare cases of blind and unquestioning love, they must always burn out. . . . Whatever the American girl is who tries a foreign marriage, I hope she will be happy. I do not expect to try it. I have told only why I prefer foreign men to American men. I do not say I expect to marry a foreigner.

She didn't marry a foreigner, but she did marry a man whose background was a long way from hers: a first-generation American whose parents had arrived without a dime in this country at the turn of the century, along with the great wave of other Jewish immigrants from Russia and the Ukraine.

In a newspaper account of my father and mother's marriage, which took place on June 5, 1935, in her mother's apartment at the Hotel Pierre in New York City, it was reported that the bride wore flowered taffeta instead of virginal white. And when a reporter asked how she felt about being kicked out of the Social Register for marrying Eddy Duchin, her answer was "Who cares? It's only a telephone book."

Among my boxes of memorabilia is an album of photographs by Cecil Beaton, showing my parents as they were during their Fitzgeraldean romance. I've always been haunted by one photograph: It shows my father—sleek black hair, dinner jacket, white cuffs studded with gold cuff links, wide, Ipana smile—gazing at my mother as though she's the most wonderful creature in the world. Dressed in a light silk dress with puffy shoulders, she's a flawless blonde with strong, Nordic features, not unlike Garbo's. Judging from the way she's leaning into him, they're completely in love. But there's something odd: Her amused, adoring gaze is directed not at my father but at the man behind the lens.

Recently, I received from Beaton's biographer, Hugo Vickers, two extracts from the photographer's diary, both written in the thirties. The first is dated "Summer 1937." It was written on the day that Beaton, then on holiday in Capri, learned that his great friend Marjorie Oelrichs had just died:

It is as if all trees had died, all skies, all fruit, all music—so essential a part of existence was Marjorie. One couldn't think of her as being ill. . . . She was so healthy and serene and big and alive, and although often depressed and things went wrong, she seemed so infinitely capable of looking after life.

She had a hard time with her mother's extravagance, her own extravagance and unending financial difficulties. She had worked to make money. She had been in states of indecision lasting years about her affairs, her beaux, her interests, and at last all had seemed smoothed-out serenely. She had been bold enough to marry the pianist Eddy Duchin and it had worked like a charm, for he turned out to be everything she hoped him to be and everybody else adored him. And she had giggled and said, "Well you know I'm not really the mother type, but you know a girl must go through with this sort of thing and it'll be fun and it'll be all right." And that this should have happened baffles one. It takes all confidence in existence. It is shattering.

Marjorie was one of my best friends in the most serious sense of the word. . . . She would criticize me when I behaved poorly. She would say, "Now really!" . . . With her, there were more laughs than with anyone. Her sense of humor was extraordinarily acute and of a wide range; the subtlest jokes she was as susceptible to as the broadest. If only for her sense of humor alone she was a remarkable American. For her integrity, loyalty, courage and sensibility, she was the best American girl I have known. She had none of the common feelings of her compatriots. She was incapable of snobbery and sham. She was completely unaffected by extraneous conditions. She never changed. One returned to her after no matter how long an interval to find her as intimate and considerate, as deeply friendly as ever before. . . .

She really cared for my welfare. She really put herself out for my benefit. When I had confided to her my lack of sex life and that I had never been to bed with a woman, she volunteered her services in my first experiment—and if this sounds comic, it was done from the best motives. . . .

She came to tea and took off her shoes and twiddled her big ring round her little finger and smoked too many cigarettes and combed her long pageboy's hair and flung back her head and with a sweet smile that was almost a sneer would say in a dry, crackly voice, "What's noo?"

I am haunted by her smile.

The second extract is from October 1, two months later. It was written after Beaton had come to New York and stopped in at my parents' apartment. And it contains what is probably the earliest vivid description of me:

My mother and father in Santa Monica with Anita Loos and her husband,
John Emerson, and Leopold Stokowski.

I went to see Mrs. Oelrichs and Eddy in the apartment that [Eddy and Marjorie] had just found and were in the process of furnishing. It is the loveliest I have ever seen in New York, for the ceilings are so high, the rooms have personality, and the view, overlooking Central Park with ducks swimming on the ponds, trees like Paris, like Japan, and the colonial lights and turret silhouettes of the skyscrapers, is unique. Marjorie furnished the rooms with great taste, *recherche* and a certain individuality, and the big room with two pianos and so many books is really one of the most livable, sympathetic and interesting rooms I have ever seen in New York. It is the room for two alive, alert people to live in, and I felt more dreadfully shocked at the terrible thing that has happened. Marjorie's personality was so strong that it was awful to realize she would not come into the room any moment, but was lying dead. Eddy looked very gray and aged and his smile flashed so much less brightly, but Mrs. Oelrichs seemed to bear up very well.

I morbidly looked at all the photographs and objects I have known so well, and when [a picture of] the baby was shown, my sensations were fierce. I loathed the little beast that is wickedly ugly, lying on its back, wriggling, farting with over-long body, dark hair and pig-snouted. I loathed this pig devil that together with the doctor was the cause of the death of one of the strongest, most courageous and sympathetic friends I have ever had.

≡

One recent rainy morning, I pulled off the Major Deegan Expressway a few miles out of New York City and drove through the iron gates of Woodlawn Cemetery, stopping at the gatehouse for a map. Although Woodlawn is situated in the middle of the Bronx, it might be a beautiful stretch of Connecticut, with its winding roads, towering old trees, even a pond or two. I passed mausoleums in every style: Greek, Egyptian, Gothic. Many bore the names of famous old New York families: MILLBANK, VAN CORTLANDT, STUYVESANT, HITCHCOCK. Spotting the name of a recently buried old friend, I slowed down for a closer look: MILES DAVIS.

At the sign for the section called Arbutus, I stopped. Across the way was a gardener, gathering leaves.

"I'm trying to find a grave."

"Whose grave would that be?"

"Marjorie Oelrichs . . . Duchin."

He nodded. "It's right over here."

I followed him up a hill and down the other side.

"There she is." He pointed. "Right next to her mother."

Set into the soft, damp ground, a few inches apart, were two flat stones, each about eight by ten inches. Grass curled up over the edges. I could just make out the inscription on my mother's stone: MARJORIE OELRICHS DUCHIN, WIFE OF EDWIN FRANK DUCHIN, 23 JUNE 1908–3 AUGUST 1937. I turned to thank my guide, but he had disappeared over the hill.

I knelt down and brushed away the dirt and ran my hand over the cool, rough surface of the stone. I wondered why I had never come here before.

4

DAD

During the thirties, the era of Big Bands, my father and his orchestra appeared in the best hotels, the best casinos, the best dance halls. His records were played constantly on the radio. His distinctive piano style was widely imitated, and it spawned an industry of sheet-music arrangements, featuring his trademark smile and slicked-down hair on the covers. Dad was a star.

All this I took in only obliquely when the Philco radio in the kitchen at Arden was turned on and I would hear a voice say, "And now, ladies and gentlemen . . . Eddy Duchin and His Orchestra coming to you live from . . ."

My scrapbooks are filled with letters Dad wrote to me, along with snapshots of him posed at the keyboard in white tie and tails or standing on the bridge of a Navy destroyer in his officer's dress uniform. I have all the cards that came with his birthday and Christmas presents, everything carefully pasted down by Chissie or Zellie. Most are signed "Wish I could be with you—I love you, Dad." Underneath is Chissie or Zellie's description of the gift: a drum, a stuffed dog, red earmuffs with a metal band.

After Dad went off to war in 1942, the radio would be turned on in the late afternoon for the news from overseas. Somehow I understood that he was connected to the reports that would make Frances, the Irish cook, grow quiet or Zellie suddenly stiffen. I was told my father was "in danger." Zellie was convinced the Germans would be landing "any day on the beaches of Montauk Point," and she would tell me how brave Dad was. "He's protecting us from the enemy, but he can't write us what he's doing because it's *censored*." I loved that word.

The times he visited Arden before he shipped out, Dad would greet me with a big smile and a kiss and pick me up in his arms. I liked his officer's hat and his brass buttons, but I could feel he wasn't at home in the country, and I knew he wouldn't stay long. We would walk hand in hand through the woods to the lake, and I would be bursting to tell him about the fish I'd glimpsed the day before, but I knew he'd only pretend to be interested, so I kept it to myself. He looked nervous, climbing into the green rowboat, worried he'd get his clothes wet. I don't remember what we talked about, but I remember feeling uncomfortable.

=

A couple of years ago, when my band and I were in Florida for a gig, I took the opportunity to explore two parts of my past. One I had known well. The other I had never investigated.

Marie Harriman, me, and Dad at Sands Point.

I had been hired to play for a dinner dance at the yacht club in Hobe Sound. The hostess was an old friend, Toddie Findlay, the daughter of Dwight Deere Wyman, the Deere & Co. heir who produced a lot of Rodgers and Hart musicals in the thirties. Toddie had rescued me after my first marriage came apart by letting me stay at her house in New York. At her request, I had played for the funeral of her first husband, Gubby Glover, out in Moline, Illinois. It was one of the more surreal gigs of my career. Toddie had made a list of Gubby's favorite songs, and I had played Gershwin, Porter, Berlin, and Rodgers, tears running down my face in a church full of equally tearful nostalgists.

All through my childhood, I spent most of my Christmas and spring vacations at Hobe Sound, staying in Ma and Ave's big, white oceanfront house on Jupiter Island. A forty-five-minute drive north of Palm Beach, the island had been developed back in the twenties as a winter place by Joseph Verner Reed, a cultivated, wealthy businessman from Denver, and his wife, Permelia Pryor, sister of Samuel Pryor, one of the founders of Pan Am. Over the years, several hundred rich families with sufficient background and character to pass the Reeds' muster had bought land on the island and built large, discreet winter houses. When I was a child, they were hidden at the ends of long, pebbled driveways bordered by high hedges of hibiscus and sea grape. There was the Yacht Club, the Jupiter Island Bath and Tennis Club, the golf course, the boat docks, the liquor store, and the old movie house, the Tangerine, with Spanish moss hanging from the ceiling. That was it, except for the occasional wildcat prowling about, herons and ospreys fishing, and gulls and pelicans sailing up and down the beach.

Hobe was Never-Never Land. I'd wake at five in the morning and head out across the lawn with my fly rod. At sunrise, I'd be standing in my sneakers, knee-deep in the warm inland waters around the golf course, casting my popping bug for redfish, snook, or sea trout feeding in the shallows.

Ma and Ave had a butler named Hollingsworth—a name Ave could never get right. He'd call out "Hollingshed!" or "Hollington!" or—Ma's favorite—"Hollywood!" I remember being awakened one morning by a knock and the sound of Hollingsworth's discreet voice saying, "Sir, the blues are running." I felt I had died and gone to heaven.

When I was six and had come to Hobe Sound for the first time, my godfather Brose Chambers told me not to pick up anything in the sand that resembled a bracelet with red, yellow, and black bands on it. "That's what a coral snake looks like, Peter," he said. "If it bites, you die in less than a minute!" For days I combed the dunes, poking at lizards, crabs, and fragments of turtle eggs, looking in vain for coral snakes.

I doubt if anyone has spotted a wildcat near Hobe Sound in years, except maybe during the summer, when the place is deserted. But when I arrived at the yacht club for Toddie's party and saw everyone standing around on the sloping green lawn that stretches along the waterway, I thought the only thing that had changed was that the same old people had gotten older. There were the same old tiny lights twinkling in the distance, the same old palms swaying in the breeze, the same old wicker furniture and chintz. One of the old waiters spotted me and said, "Nice to see you back, Mr. Duchin, it's been a while."

Standing around with their whatever-and-tonics and munching cheese puffs were people I'd known all my life. Old Joe's son, Nat Reed, who kind of runs the island, came over and said, "Got any time to go fishing, Pete?"

I embraced Douglas Dillon, President Kennedy's secretary of the treasury, and Nelson Doubleday came over to chat about our school years at Eaglebrook. All the men were in blue blazers, linen trousers, and tassel loafers. The women wore various shades of pastel and little jewelry.

Shortly after midnight, the band packed up and Toddie and I kissed good night. As I drove slowly down the island, past the little white signs at the ends of driveways saying, "Half Moon Under," "Faces East," and "Harlequin," I felt as comforted as I would have been in the kitchen at Arden, smelling burnt toast.

The next morning I drove fifty miles south to say hello to my father's younger sister, Aunt Lil. Since the death of her husband, my uncle Ben, a decade before, Aunt Lil had been living in a con-dominium near Fort Lauderdale. It was a faded, peeling, cinder-block complex where life revolved around the golf course and a swimming pool. There was a golf bag in the corner of Aunt Lil's living room. Now in her early eighties, as big boned and earthy as my father had been thin and refined, she was doing fine.

As a kid, I hadn't seen much of Aunt Lil and her family, who lived in Cambridge, Massachusetts, but I always associated my visits to them with a kind of earthy comfort. Uncle Ben was a doctor, and there were two children, Susan and Lester, both of whom were about my age. My grandmother Tillie lived nearby, and she would bustle around her kitchen in a loose, flowery dress, preparing the special meatballs I loved. Under a clear plastic hood would be a thick-frosted vanilla or chocolate cake.

My grandmother Duchin was a peasant: gray hair in a bun, rugged, deep-lined face, slightly Oriental features. She was a woman of few words, and she was totally at ease with children. I was fascinated as I watched her big hands kneading and shaping the dough for matzoh balls. My favorite place for a late-night snack is still the Carnegie Deli on Seventh Avenue in New York. I can't think of anything better for a good night's sleep than matzoh-ball soup.

Now, over iced tea—"made just this morning"—Aunt Lil reminisced about how the Duchins had come to America. Following in his brothers' footsteps from the Ukraine, where he was one of eleven children, my grandfather Frank Duchin had gotten off the boat at Ellis Island in the late 1880s and gone to Boston to become a custom tailor of men's suits. In 1906, he had married my grandmother, Tillie Baron (born Barashevsky), who had also just arrived from the Ukraine. My father, the first of Frank and Tillie's two children, was born on April Fools' Day, 1909.

Frank Duchin prospered and eventually expanded his business into a retail haberdashery that supplied many of the uniforms for the Boston cops and firemen. But he suffered from chronic kidney ailments and was often forced to go into a hospital for months. Despite these problems, Aunt Lil remembered a happy, secure childhood. "We never wanted for anything," she said firmly. "Dad's condition was diagnosed as a very rare one—leukoplakia. His doctors told him he needed a salt-air climate, so we moved out to Beverly on the North Shore."

I asked how my father had taken up the piano.

"Our grandmother on Mother's side had been a piano teacher in Kiev. And there was always a ton of classical music on the radio. Eddy loved it. When he was seven, he took his first lessons from a Mr. Scoville. At thirteen, Mr. Scoville said there was nothing more he could teach him. 'Take him to Felix Fox in Boston,' he said. So Eddy went twice a week for a couple of years to Felix Fox. He and Mother always took the streetcar—an hour each way. She waited for him during the lesson. Then she took him home."

"A real Jewish mother."

"She knew Eddy had talent. He had perfect pitch. He could hear something once and go right to the piano and play it. But he was lousy with lyrics. His singing was a disaster."

Me and my cousin Susan with my father's parents, Tillie and
Frank Duchin, in New York in the early forties.

Dad tries out a 1935 Terraplane convertible. He bought his
first car, a Peerless sedan, when he was eighteen. He paid for it
by playing the piano at Bar Mitzvahs.

"Did he like to practice?" I asked, remembering how much I'd hated it.

"No! He'd rather shoot pool or play basketball. Anything but practice."

"When did he get serious about a music career?"

Aunt Lil laughed. "When he discovered he could make money from it. By the time he was fifteen, Eddy was playing bar mitzvahs. For his sixteenth birthday, my parents gave him a baby Steinway grand. At eighteen, he was making ninety bucks a week!"

"What did he do with it?"

"Buy a Peerless automobile, that's what. But Mother and Father didn't think a musician's life had any security in it. Since there were a couple of pharmacists in the family, they pushed him in that direction. So right after high school, Eddy went off to Massachusetts College of Pharmacy."

After a year in pharmacy school, my father organized his first band—piano, violin, and alto sax. That summer he composed the only song he would ever write. It was inspired by a girl he was in love with, and it was called "Don't Forget About Tomorrow, Though Today May Be Gray." There were no signs that he was much of a wordsmith. In 1928, between his junior and senior years in college, he was hired for the summer as a rhythm pianist by Leo Reisman, whose band was booked at the Waldorf-Astoria in New York. He returned to college in the fall, got his degree as a pharmacist, and never filled out a prescription. As soon as he graduated, he was back with the Reisman band, this time at the swankiest nightspot in New York, the Central Park Casino.

Designed by Calvert Vaux in the late nineteenth century, the Central Park Casino was situated on the east side of the park, 400 yards off the Sixty-fifth Street transverse. The building had been dark for years when in 1929 Mayor Jimmy Walker and his Tammany Hall cronies decided that the city needed an exclusive night-club. Walker commissioned Florenz Ziegfeld's theatrical designer, Joseph Urban, to give Vaux's building a massive Art Deco face-lift. The renovation featured a spectacular crystal ceiling over the dance floor. Gold murals paneled with black glass lined the ball-room walls. The dining pavilion was done up in maroon and silver. The Casino was an instant smash, and everyone in New York who was anyone came there to be seen and to dance. Mayor Walker and his friends were entertained in private rooms, where many of the city's business transactions were also said to take place.

≡

On my way down the coast to Aunt Lil's, I had stopped to have breakfast with Herbert Bayard Swope, Jr., and his wife, Betty, at their waterfront house in Palm Beach. Ottie Swope was named after his father, the famous editor of the old *New York World* who had made a deal with the financier Bernard Baruch. In return for his making Baruch famous, Baruch made him rich. Ottie had grown up in a huge Gatsbyesque mansion in Sands Point, Long Island, just down the beach from where I'd spent many of my childhood summers in the far more modest Harriman house.

The Swope property was often the setting for one of Ave's favorite sports, croquet. While he, Ottie, and their friends were engaged in titanic, savage battles with mallets and wickets (Ottie is still one of the country's premier croquet players), I'd find the Swope grandson, Bayard Brant. The two of us would wander down to the brackish stream leading to the Sound to poke at fiddler crabs or search for eels.

This was in the tail end of the period when the Swope mansion was weekend headquarters for Robert E. Sherwood, Dorothy Parker, Ring Lardner, George S. Kaufman, Moss Hart, Deems Tay-

lor, Alexander Woolcott, Robert Benchley, and the rest of the Algon-
quin crowd. A principal attraction of the Swopes' hospitality was
their staff—three shifts of servants, on duty around the clock to answer every guest's need, whether you were playing in an all-night
poker game, taking part in an epic croquet match, or just thirsty.

Ottie had been a young man-about-town when my father was
starting out at the Central Park Casino.

"Your father," he recalled, "seemed to me a very strange character, particularly in the early days, when he was only the rhythm pianist. He would sit there silently at the keyboard, looking very
self-absorbed. He wasn't terribly kempt, at least when he was starting out. He had a faint bluish-blackish five-o'clock shadow. He was
the kind of man about whom you created a fantasy. For example,
was he on drugs? I think one of the things that got him so famous
was that he seemed neurotic and indifferent to the room."

"A touch of Gatsby."

"Something like that. There was another thing. He didn't smoke.
While the rest of the band went out for a cigarette break, he'd stay
at the piano and take requests. All the girls lined up. Your mother
was at the head of the line."

=

Before long, my father was the Casino's biggest draw. He wore
white tie and tails, with a red carnation for a boutonniere, and was
dubbed "the Cocktail Casanova." His piano style bridged the
sharply syncopated music of the twenties and that of the slower,
more melodically romantic thirties. By 1931, when he was only
twenty-two, he had inherited Reisman's job, and that year Eddy
Duchin and His Orchestra opened the Casino on Labor Day. He
had acquired some important fans and patrons. Early on, Averell
Harriman had donated a pair of black shoes, John Wanamaker of

The Central Park Casino in 1929, when it reopened as the most
exclusive nightclub in New York. It was the favorite hangout of
Mayor Jimmy Walker and his Tammany Hall cronies. My father was
the headliner there in the early thirties.

Dad and his orchestra in 1935, two years before I was born.
Dad had one of the top dance bands in the country and a
string of hit records by then.

the Philadelphia department-store family had given him his first dinner jacket, and John's sister, Mary Louise, gave him a pair of studs. George Gershwin helped him set the seating arrangement for the musicians.

John Wanamaker later presented Dad with a Bechstein baby grand. One afternoon as he was walking home from lunch, my father was astonished to see a crane hoisting it through his living room window. The note attached to the piano said,

> Dear Eddy, I hope you enjoy playing it as much as I enjoy listening. P.S. Please use the piano-tuning department at my store. Business is lousy!

Today, the Bechstein sits in the living room of my New York apartment.

In those Depression days, show business was one of the few businesses that wasn't lousy. My father launched his first radio show on NBC in 1933—Pepsodent's Junis Face Cream program. Two years later, he and the band were signed for the Texaco program, hosted by the comedian Ed Wynn. By then the Casino had been closed down by New York's park czar Robert Moses, on the ground that it was too elitist to occupy city property.

And by then the Eddy Duchin Orchestra—an eleven-piece ensemble of lead piano, three saxes, a trumpet, a trombone, banjo, fiddle, a second piano, bass, and drums—had become one of the top dance bands in the country. My father and his musicians introduced twenty new songs a month—Gershwin, Rodgers, Berlin, Porter, Arlen (among them, "Stormy Weather," "I Concentrate on You," and "Brazil"). Hollywood beckoned, and Dad led the band in Paramount's *Coronado* and Republic Pictures' *The Hit Parade*. He made one hit record after another. His biggest was "Ol' Man

Mose," a swing spiritual written by Louis Armstrong. What sent it to the top was the way the vocalist, Patricia Norman, fudged the line "Ol' Man Mose kicked the bucket/ Yeah, man, buck-buck-bucket . . . ," making the *b* sound like *f*. Today, I play "Ol' Man Mose" at every gig, and it never misses.

My father's keyboard style was instantly recognizable. He was one of the first bandleaders to take the piano out of the percussion section, where it had been used to pound out the rhythm, and make it the star attraction. His right hand was smooth, rippling, classical in tone. (His signature number was a paraphrase of Chopin's Nocturne in E-flat.) He favored big, squashy chords—his hands were enormous—that gave an orchestral richness. His left hand was driving and always on the beat.

When my father tried out a new song, he first talked his way through the lyrics so that he would have them firmly in mind. His playing had a nervous intensity, as though he were making the arrangement up as he went along. In 1935, George Simon, a writer for *Metronome* magazine, gave this description of the Duchin style: "The essence of Duchinesque piano playing [was] 'whatever he happened to feel.' Duchin's piano is one of moods. As he puts it: 'I close my eyes, hum to myself, and then play whatever I happen to feel inside of me.' I think it's the first time that any dance orchestra pianist has adopted that formula—playing what he feels rather than what he sees. It's inspirational rather than mechanical."

The reason he played with his eyes closed, my father explained, was for concentration, not effect.

One of his most distinctive trademarks was to switch the melody to the bass clef, crossing his hands and outlining it in dark single notes. He amplified the effect by installing a mirror behind the keyboard to reflect what his fingers were doing—an innovation that later became standard for television pianists. He explained that because he couldn't sing, he phrased the way a singer like Helen Morgan or Libby Holman "breathed." In 1934 he told a reporter: "My theory was that vocalists sounded different from one another because they breathed differently—their inflections were different. Therefore, I thought, why couldn't that be applied to a solo instrument? I began to hum on the melody with a singer's inflections—I breathed with the piano as I would with my voice. I played louder and softer, just as I interpreted the song through my humming."

Playing with the inflections of a vocalist, he said, made the listeners want to sing: "And when you've done that you've won them over, because then they want to dance." Another of my father's innovations was his freedom with tempos, which he changed according to the mood and abilities of the people dancing to his music.

By the end of the thirties, Dad was known as "the Magic Fingers of Radio." His hands were insured for $150,000. Sergei Rachmaninoff once told him he was good enough to play classical music. But how much money did he make playing in a band? the great virtuoso asked. When he heard my father's answer, Rachmaninoff said, "Forget classical. Stick to what you're doing."

=

I asked Aunt Lil whether Dad's personality had changed when he became a star.

Her reply was fierce: "No! Eddy was a marvelous son. When he started to make it big, Father got sick again. Eddy said, 'No more work, Dad, this is it!' From then on, he put them on an allowance."

"Did he have a problem being Jewish?"

"Not that I ever saw. We were all crazy about Marjorie—she was so sweet on him—so there was no problem from *us*. The only time it ever came up was when he got married again, to Chiquita, who was Catholic. The wedding was in St. Patrick's Cathedral, and at the last minute my mother refused to go. Eddy tried to change her mind, but she wouldn't budge. She gave her blessing, but she and Dad stayed in the hotel."

"Was Eddy embarrassed about his parents?"

Aunt Lil paused. "For only one thing. Did you know your grandmother never learned to read or write?"

I didn't—and was astonished I didn't.

"It was the family secret. She was very ashamed of it. I'll never forget when Eddy was playing the Persian Room and we all came down to New York. As usual he got us the best seats in the house, right up front. When the captain came over with the menus, Eddy jumped up and yelled, 'No menus! *I've* ordered the meal!' It was because he didn't want Mother to be embarrassed when she couldn't read the menu."

"I gather he had a bad temper."

Aunt Lil shrugged. "Most of the time he was *charming*. But once in a while he would snap. I don't know why. I once saw him throw a basket of rolls across the room because the waiter brought him white bread instead of Rykrisp. Another time, the hotel operator called while he was taking a nap, and he was so mad he jerked the phone out of the wall."

I remembered something that had happened when I was about three or four. Dad had come out to Arden one Sunday, and we were down at the boathouse: Zellie, Ma, her daughter Nancy, and the two English girls, Betty and Ninky, whom the Harrimans were boarding during the war. I was obsessed with a bowl of peanuts on the table. I loved biting the shells in two and getting the little nuts out of their hiding places. I had gone through most of them when I heard my father's voice: "Peter, I told you to stop eating those peanuts! You've left nothing for anyone else! You're to go back to your room right now and *stay* there! Mademoiselle, take Peter home!"

And so I was led away in tears, banished to my room in the cottage. Some time later, Nancy came in and found me clutching my favorite stuffed bear, the gray and white one with the ripped ear. She lay down beside me, propped my head against her soft arm, and opened my favorite collection of stories, Kipling's *Jungle Book*.

Before long, I had calmed down, transported into a world of my own by the tale of a wild, naked Indian boy named Mowgli who loses his parents and gets taken in by the Seeonee wolf pack, in whose protection he is taught by Baloo the bear and Bagheera the black panther how to hunt like an animal, how to speak to the wild bees, and how to master all the other "wind and water laws" of the magical jungle.

Arden, the Harriman family mansion, sat on a hill
on a ten-thousand-acre estate.

5

THE FORESTS

OF ARDEN

Today the New York State Thruway and Route 6 run right through
Arden, not far from the cottage where I lived during the war. You
can hear the trucks and cars whizzing by at all hours of the day and
night. The Harriman family says that the original plan put Route 6
on top of the stables and the cottage, and that Ave, who had been
governor of New York, had it moved. Nevertheless, the Thruway is
palpably close by, and relentlessly humming.

When I was a child, the only hum you ever heard was that of Bill
Kitchen's perfectly balanced and oiled manual lawn mower, neatly
slicing the grass. It might be joined by the growls of three or four
of Ave's Labrador retrievers playing with a ball, or the sound of
horses pawing the gravel in the driveway as they waited to be sad-
dled up for a morning ride. The sound of a car was a momentous

intrusion into our nonmotorized world of forests, meadows, lakes, and air back then, even after Ave gave the big house to the Navy for use as a convalescent hospital and he and Ma and I moved into two little white cottages near the stables.

But much about Arden is still the way it was, thanks to Ave's two daughters, Kathleen and Mary, and their children and grandchildren, who use it as a weekend retreat from the city. What I noticed when I visited Arden recently were the changes in scale. The two maples in the front yard outside the cottages are at least fifty feet taller than I'd remembered them. Inside, the rooms looked impossibly small. I couldn't imagine how all of us—Frances, the cook, Zellie, the two English girls, and I—had managed to squeeze into this dollhouse.

I drove up the hill—three miles of thickly forested, winding road. (Back in the thirties and forties, the estate comprised some ten thousand acres; today, it's been whittled down to roughly three thousand.) At the top sat the immense limestone and granite manor house built by E. H. Harriman, the construction of which had taken six years, from 1905 to 1911. It was the citadel of a completely self-sufficient world, which included a funicular railway to carry provisions up and down the hill, a power plant big enough to supply the surrounding area, and the largest private pipe organ in the country—plus a bowling alley. Now, the house belongs to Columbia University and is used as a conference center. From the outside, it is as awesome as I remembered it: a gray Valhalla perched on top of a world still unpolluted by the twentieth century. Inside, the wonderful Curtis photographs of Indians still line the upstairs bedroom corridors, but the baronial living and reception rooms downstairs have become institutional chambers with metal chairs and baize-covered tables and soft-drink machines in the hallways.

I headed downhill to Forest Lake, got out of the car with my fishing rod and box of flies, and walked through the woods. There was a green rowboat identical to the one I'd used as a boy, tied up at the dock where it had always been. I climbed in and shoved off, and with the first cast of my fly, I could see myself on that early summer morning in 1940 when I came to live in this enchanted kingdom.

As Chissie and I emerged from the car, there were Ave and Ma, flanked by a team of servants, a pack of Ave's salivating Labradors, and a strawberry roan, who was not just a pony but *my* pony, a gift from Ave and Ma for my third birthday.

In time, I would become completely familiar with Arden: the forty bedrooms, the stables, the polo field, the three lakes, the trout stream, the forests, the playpen with sand, the swing, built just for me. Before the word *ecology* meant anything, Arden was run as an ecosystem. There was no waste. Garbage went to the compost heap. The cows that provided our milk in the morning could be seen grazing in the meadows. You rode horses not only for fun but to get from point A to point B. Running alongside you were the dogs you'd trained for your shooting expeditions. If you bagged a bird, you ate it. Pheasant, grouse, woodcock, trout, largemouth bass, pickerel, perch, and sunfish: anything you killed you cleaned yourself. Then you brought it to Frances in the kitchen.

I came to regard Bill Kitchen, the caretaker; Alan Crawford, the riding master; Lionel Bond, the dog and gamekeeper; Dr. Dumbell, the local minister who christened me in the estate's little Episcopalian church; Frances; and all the sweet household maids as my family. I would learn to fish and shoot; to play polo, croquet, gin, canasta, and bridge; to plant and pick lettuce, carrots, radishes, and corn. I would learn how to muck out the stalls, to saddle-soap a saddle, to shoe a horse, to train dogs. Whenever Ma and Ave had guests, I was the only child in a roomful of great personages. I don't remember ever feeling lonely.

Thanks to Zellie, I became fluent in French. The first words I learned were *sales Boches*—"dirty Germans." Later, living as a student in Paris, I realized that Zellie was a classic Frenchwoman of the best type: absolutely correct in her manners, firm in her convictions and expectations, always in control. Whenever I did something really bad, Zellie wouldn't hesitate to take the ruler out of her desk drawer, tell me to take down my shorts and lean over the back of the wooden chair, and proceed to whack the living daylights out of me, hard enough to make me cry. Then she would send me to my room to "think about" the terrible thing I had done. After the appropriate time had passed, she would come in and announce the next activity: "There are weeds to be pulled." Or "Let's finish the new Babar," which she would read aloud to me in both English and French.

I dreaded the ruler, but I loved Zellie because she was so clear and so fair. And because I knew I could trust her. It comforted me to know that I was the focus of her life. She was *mine*. It was Zellie on whom I relied to mediate between me and the adult world, particularly the world of Ma and Ave and Dad.

In my fantasy life I was Mowgli, Kipling's wild orphan child in the woods. But in my real life I was a little person with a full schedule of chores to perform and skills to master—all under the strict, benevolent eye of Zellie. There was something so dedicated about her that I've always imagined she could have been a nun. Her bedroom was spartan in the extreme: a single bed, hardwood desk, white painted bureau. Her appearance was simple and functional: graying hair pulled back in a bun, never a loose strand; flower-print dresses, buttoned down the front; black, lace-up, low-heeled shoes.

Zellie was the first woman I ever saw without any clothes on. What a shock that was. One morning, when I was five, I made the mistake of walking into her bedroom without knocking. The sight that greeted me was Zellie, completely naked, standing on her head against the wall. After a moment that seemed like forever, she spoke without changing her position, raising her voice only slightly: "Peter, will you please leave the room."

I closed the door and sat down on the staircase to ponder what I'd just seen. Several minutes passed before Zellie appeared in her blue terry-cloth robe. Matter-of-factly, she said, "Peter, I was doing my morning exercise. Always remember to knock before you open a door." She never referred to the incident again.

=

The first thing that fascinated me about Bill Kitchen was his pistol, a .32 automatic in a leather holster he wore on his belt. When we lived in the big house, Bill wasn't around much, but when I was four or five and we'd moved down to the cottages, I saw him every day. During the war, our little corner of Arden was almost entirely populated by females. Several afternoons a week I'd be taken to play with the only other boy on the estate, Lionel, the game-keeper's son. But the only constant male figure around was Bill, who lived in a stone house on a hill just above the cottages.

Bill carried a pistol because he was a deputy sheriff, a position of which he was proud, though he was shy about producing the badge he kept in his wallet. He was a tall, thin, red-faced man with big ears, a big nose, and a really big Adam's apple. He dressed in twill or corduroy trousers, flannel shirt with a tie, and a tweed jacket with patches on the sleeves. On Sundays he'd have on his gray suit, and I'd see him holding the door of the Pontiac for Mrs. Kitchen in her best hat and veil and flowered dress, going off to the

For my third birthday, Ma and Ave gave me a pony
that I called Jenny Strawberry Roan.

I learned how to fish on Forest Lake, above Arden House, where Ma's son,
Harry Whitney, would take me out in a rowboat. My French nanny, Zellie, at right,
supervised all my activities. She was the first woman I ever saw naked.

Presbyterian church in Central Valley. After church I would be invited into their cozy living room for hot chocolate and Mrs. Kitchen's homemade shortbread.

One day, Zellie and I were taking a walk after lunch when I spotted Bill in the garage—a building big enough for twelve cars—rubbing a chamois cloth over the station wagon. I had been eyeing the pistol for quite a few days and hoping for a closer look, so I broke away from Zellie to find myself in the strange, dark domain of Bill, its air a good ten degrees colder than outside. Bill wasn't a man you barged in on. Whatever he was doing he did in smooth, deliberate movements, with great concentration. He spoke in a soft voice, using very few words. Until then, about the only thing I'd ever heard him say was "Good morning."

I stopped a few feet away from him, tongue-tied. He looked down, smiled, and said, "Hi, Pete."

I loved him calling me that. To the women and girls I was Peter or Petey.

"What's that?" I asked.

"That's my gun."

"Can I see it?"

"No. It's not a toy."

"Please?"

Slowly he unsnapped the holster and took it out and held it in his palm. I stepped forward and peered at it.

"What's it for?"

"It's for shooting. When you get old enough, I'll show you how to use it."

This was really something to look forward to. I felt Zellie's shadow. "Come along, Peter. Time for your nap. Say good-bye to Bill."

I watched as he put the gun back in the holster and listened for the sound of the snap. "See you later, Pete."

"Bye, Bill."

He threw me a wink.

Bill had power. He had the power to fix things: a blown fuse, a fallen tree limb, a flat tire. He had the power of transport: to take me over to Lionel's in his wood-paneled Pontiac station wagon with the chrome Indian on the hood; to drive the two of us up and over the hill to Forest Lake to fish, to Arden Dairy to fetch milk, or even to the village of Harriman to buy groceries and, along the way, be instructed in the art of spotting woodchucks. Ave had put a bounty on these creatures—a quarter a head—because they dug holes in the fields that might cause a horse to break a leg. When I was six, I was given my first .22 rifle, and whenever Bill would let me, I'd go out after the bounty. Bill showed me how to cut off the tails of the woodchucks I killed and put salt on them. We stored them in a barrel so that Ave could count the number we'd shot. He always seemed very pleased.

Now, more than fifty years later, I rowed the boat toward a patch of lily pads under which a huge bass might be lurking. I cast my popping bug to the edge of the lilies, played with it awhile, then cast again. For many years, the actual catching of a fish has been relatively unimportant to me. Even as a boy, I was one of the first at Arden to use a hook without a barb on it. It's always been the act of fishing I love, the psychological connection with the fish. Fishing heightens your perception of everything around you, forcing you to observe every stirring of a leaf, every ripple of the water, every movement of the bugs, the tugs and lessenings of the current. What comes over me is a profound feeling that the fish and I share something. I can sit and stare for hours at water, whether it's a flat lake or a rushing stream.

As I gazed at the earliest waters that ever hypnotized me, my mind drifted back to a day in the wartime forties—the most exciting day I ever had with Bill. I must have been about seven. By then he had taught me how to shoot and how to cast a plug and use an Ambassador reel. I'd learned to identify the different wildflowers, from salvia to skunk cabbage, to gather huckleberries and wild strawberries, to sit in the woods and wait for a deer or a fox to run by. Sometimes, when I was impatient to fish, Bill made me sit at the lake's edge and watch the muskrats, the otters, and the herons in total stillness. He told me there was always the chance of spotting a bear, but I never did. He taught me that there was nothing to be afraid of in all these miles of woods, that it was a place of beauty, adventure, and contentment, a place to feel at home in. By watching him do the things he did without ever taking a shortcut, I came to understand that there was a right and a wrong way to go about your business.

On that long-ago day, we had been out on the lake for a couple of hours. Dusk was falling.

"OK, Pete," Bill said. "Take a few more casts and let's go home for supper."

I cast to the edge of the lily pads. The moment the red and white plug hit the water, the biggest fish I'd ever seen surged up, grabbed the plug, and disappeared after a splash that sounded like a thunderclap.

"Good lord!" Bill said. "That's huge! We can't lose it. Give him as much line as he needs."

For fifteen minutes I played him, reeling him in, giving him line, absolutely petrified. Bill prompted every move: "Keep him away from that log or he'll get tangled and bust off. . . . Keep pointing the tip of the rod toward him. . . . Don't give him any slack."

When Bill netted the fish—an enormous largemouth bass—I experienced a rush of pleasure like nothing I'd ever felt before.

We got the bass into the station wagon and back down the hill. When we arrived at the cottage, I cradled my catch with both arms and ran into the kitchen. "Look what I caught!" I yelled.

Frances yelled, too: "Mary, Mother of God! What do you have there, Peter?"

Bill was right behind me. "Let's weigh it," he said. "I know it's a record."

I could hear the pride in his voice.

6

MA

Chissie and I had been at Arden only a few months when I was led one evening into the oak-beamed room where Marie Harriman was sitting with a couple of friends, drinking a martini.

I let go of Chissie's hand and approached the sofa. My face was burning. Marie looked up and said, "What is it, darling?"

I rushed at her, grabbed her knees with both arms, and cried, "Is it all right if I call you Ma?"

She set her glass down and pulled me into her. "Of course."

From then on, I never called her anything else.

Ma's arrival was always dramatic. It wasn't the motor you first heard but the crunch of the pebbles. Then the huge black Lincoln

Zephyr came into view and rolled to a stop in front of the cottages. I'd race over, nearly bumping into Walter the chauffeur as he held open the rear door. "Hi, Pete. How ya doin'?" he'd say in his gravelly Bronx voice. And out stepped Ma.

During the war, Ma would come up to Arden once or twice a month to get away from her USO duties and relax with friends. Her maid, Victoria, would arrive first. Everybody loved Victoria. She was a round French peasant with bluish white hair, a heavy accent, and a cackling laugh. She'd pull me to her, tickling my cheek with the little hairs that grew out of her nose, and then she'd announce, "I'm going to get the house ready for Madame!"

Ma was tall and chestnut-haired, and her great charm was in no way lessened by the thick, tinted glasses she wore after her operation in 1941 for glaucoma, a condition that made her nearly blind for the rest of her life. She would lean down and kiss me, and I would be thrilled by the softness of her skin, the silkiness of her dress, the scent of her perfume.

I always had so much to tell her: about how Alan Crawford had taken me out that morning on one of the polo ponies and we'd spotted two bucks fighting in the woods. I knew "Rikki-Tikki-Tavi" by heart. Did she want to hear it?

"Of course, darling!"

I loved the way Ma talked. She was totally direct, no bullshit. The daughter of a prominent Democratic lawyer, Sheridan Norton, and a wonderful old character of a mother, Beulah, who was part Jewish and part Irish, she had a mongrel's love of the unconventional. She spoke out of one side of her mouth in a sort of drawl through clenched teeth. It was one of the things that must have endeared her to a man she always said she'd found "immensely attractive"—Al Capone. In the twenties, when she was married to

Marie Harriman, "Ma," in the little Crosley at Forest Lake in 1939,
with her ubiquitous cigarette holder.

her first husband, Sonny Whitney, she'd gambled with Capone at the casino in Nassau.

Ma chewed gum and smoked Viceroys in white plastic holders that were scattered everywhere in china and silver cups. She had a habit of emptying the contents of one ashtray into a larger ashtray and carrying the whole mess out to the kitchen. It was the only time I ever saw her go into that room. After one of those journeys, she reappeared white-faced. "My God, Mado," she said to one of her buddies, Madeline Sherwood, wife of the playwright Robert E. Sherwood, "I've just seen the goddamn butler drinking straight out of a bottle of Black Label. What should I do?"

"Fire him immediately," Mado said.

Firing a servant was the last thing Ma could do, partly because of her kind heart and partly because she hated confrontations. The job of firing her boozy butler, along with other unpleasant tasks, was left to her faithful secretary and friend, Ann Sardi, sister of the restaurateur Vincent.

Ma could cut through any phoniness or stickiness, usually with a crack that began, "For Chrissake!" She loved talking about sex, and she swore like a trooper. She may have coined the expression "rat-fuck," which is what she called parties that were too big. I don't know what she had against the City of Brotherly Love, but she called a really terrible big party a "Philadelphia rat-fuck." Another Ma-ism: "Boston girls are staid. Newport girls are fun. And Philadelphia girls are easy lays." In general, I've found that she was right.

Once, just after the war, Ma and Averell were in Paris, where he had been sent by President Truman to set up the Marshall Plan. Ave and Ma were invited to lunch with Konrad Adenauer, the chancellor of West Germany, and on the way, Ave said, "For God's sake, Marie, don't get into anything political. Just keep quiet and listen."

Everything was going fine, but Ma got bored. She wasn't used to just listening. She became increasingly restless until finally, when there was one of those awful silences during which you can hear the knives and forks clicking, she found herself saying, "Chancellor Adenauer, I'm very concerned about my dachshund, Gary Cooper. He's in a bad way because I can't find a girl for him and I think he might have hard balls."

Ave's jaw dropped, but Ma sailed on. "I think what I should do is start a bordello for pets."

Adenauer roared with laughter. A week later, another dachshund arrived at Ma's hotel with a note from the chancellor: "Now you can start your bordello." Ma named her Fifi.

Gary Cooper—the dog—starred in another Ma story. One Christmas, Ma and Ave were down in Hobe Sound with their houseguests, including Madeline and Bob Sherwood. After the Sherwoods left, Bob wrote a thank-you note on a postcard and as a joke addressed it to "Gary Cooper, care of Marie Harriman, Jupiter Island, Hobe Sound, Florida."

When the local postmaster, who read everything, saw the name on the card, he immediately called up Fred Arborgast, the local realtor. "My God," he said. "You'll never guess who's staying at the Harrimans'. Gary Cooper!"

Fred, never one to miss a wealthy sucker for a property deal, jumped into his car that morning and careened up the Harriman driveway. An aged gardener was raking leaves outside the house.

"Fine day," Fred said, climbing out of the car.

"Certainly is, sir," the gardener replied.

"Uh, tell me, is Gary Cooper in the house?"

"Yes, I reckon he is, sir."

"Do you think I could say hello to him?"

The gardener looked at the realtor curiously, then said, "Well, sir, I don't think right now. I believe he's still in bed with the madam."

Fred got back into his car and fled.

Ma, who was having her morning massage upstairs, heard this exchange and nearly fell out the window. Needless to say, she did nothing to stop the gossip that had swept the island by lunchtime.

Ma was not a woman who screamed, but she lost it one morning as she watched Ave tie one end of a string around a baby tooth I was losing and the other end to the knob of an open door. He positioned me carefully and told me it might hurt for "a second." I was speechless with terror. When Ave slammed the door, out popped my tooth, along with a geyser of blood. Ma screamed.

In the early sixties, I was invited on a trip to the Philippines and Japan, where Ave, then undersecretary of state for political affairs, was sent to explain the Kennedy administration's policy in the Far East. I was to keep Ma company while Ave was working, which was most of the time. In Honolulu, during a twenty-four-hour stopover, Ma and I left Ave to hit the town. He had suggested we take in the "terrific hula show" in the hotel, but Ma had immediately vetoed that as "tourist crap." She ordered a limo.

No sooner had we climbed in than she tapped on the dividing glass and said to the driver, "Do you know how to find that stripper who can make the tassels on her boobs go in different directions at the same time?"

"What, Mrs. Harriman?" asked the driver.

Ma repeated the question in the same offhand tone.

"I don't believe I know who you mean, ma'am," the driver stammered.

"Last year," Ma said, "I went to a club with a fabulous stripper who had these huge knockers with blue tassels on them. She had terrific coordination. One of them went clockwise. The other went counterclockwise. You *must* know her."

"I don't think so, ma'am."

"Oh, for God's sake," Ma said. "Just drive us around. We'll hit all the joints if we have to."

A dozen clubs later, we still hadn't found the stripper with the ambidextrous boobs. Ma didn't want to give up, but we'd run out of clubs. There was nothing to do but tell the driver to take us back to the hotel. Ma gave me fifty bucks to give him for a tip. The driver said, "Thank you, ma'am. I've never had so much fun in my life."

≡

Underneath Ma's salty exterior, she was deeply vulnerable. I've often wondered whether this had to with the fact that neither of her husbands was sexually faithful to her. Her first marriage, to Sonny Whitney, a great-grandson of old Commodore Vanderbilt, was wrecked by his roving eye. Her second nearly came apart during the war when Ave's romance in London with Pamela Churchill, who was married to Winston's son, Randolph, was splashed all over the front pages.

Ma had stayed behind in New York, where she was recovering from her eye operation. She had known about the affair from friends and didn't seem particularly bothered, dismissing it as "one of those wartime flings." But when it hit the newspapers, she fired off a telegram to Ave with the ultimatum that he'd better stop playing around or he'd be facing the most expensive divorce "in the history of the Republic." Years later, laughing about it, she remarked, "I was very proud of the word *Republic*."

After the war, when Ave was Truman's secretary of commerce in Washington and Ma was mostly in New York, their marriage hit another rocky patch. Ave was having a fling with Kay Halle, a beautiful journalist and department-store heiress from Cleveland who, oddly enough, had been romantically involved with Randolph Churchill before he married Pamela. Ave proposed to Kay but was turned down. His marriage was saved when he was appointed to lead the Marshall Plan team in Paris, where Ma accompanied him.

I believe it was only when Ave ran for governor of New York in 1954 that he realized what an asset she was. With her warmth, utter lack of snobbery and pretension, and ease with all sorts of people, Ma was a great campaigner, especially in contrast to the candidate. Ave had stammered as a boy, and he was a stiff, dreadful public speaker. But Ma could wade through any crowd, looking absolutely thrilled to be there, making new friends wherever she went.

She hated having her picture taken, and with each passing year she got a little younger, according to the date of birth in her passport. By the last fifteen years of their marriage, when I was old enough to understand their relationship, Ma and Ave had settled their differences and forged a real closeness based on mutual dependency, deep devotion, and lots of kidding. Ave was well aware that he would never have become governor—and continued to be called Governor, which pleased him to no end—if it had not been for Ma's brilliant campaigning. He had also come to rely heavily on her judgments of people, realizing that in this crucial area she had far better instincts than he.

In those days, the world of grown-ups wasn't as open to children as it is today, and as a child I had no idea that behind Ma's exuberance she hadn't had it easy. Her near blindness was a terrible trial for her, especially since her greatest pleasure was art. In the thirties, she had assembled the world-class Harriman collection of Impressionist and post-Impressionist paintings. Her happiest years, she always said, were from 1930 to 1942, when she ran the Marie Harriman Gallery on East Fifty-seventh Street. There she had showed her favorite painters—among them, Picasso, Braque, and Gris—as well as such contemporary American artists as Walt Kuhn, Isamu Noguchi, and John Kane, whose careers she avidly promoted. She designed all the catalogs herself, and they were so striking that they were given an exhibition of their own at the New York Public Library.

As wonderful as she was with me, Ma was not very good with her own children from her first marriage, to Sonny. (She and Ave remained childless.) Ten years older than I, her daughter, Nancy Whitney, was the first girl in my life to whom I attached the idea of "beautiful." Soft, blonde, and exquisitely pretty, she was also immensely kind. As soon as I heard that Nancy would be coming to Arden for the weekend, I couldn't wait for her to burst into the cottage to give me a bath and snuggle up for a Kipling story.

Harry Whitney was the perfect older brother. Even though we were separated by thirteen years, he had all the time in the world for me, maybe because he refused to grow up himself. Harry was big in every way: six foot three, physical, loud, totally unpredictable. He was extremely handy with radios and cars, and he drove a Model T Ford called Annie, in which we'd race around Arden, looking for woodchucks. Later, he and Annie gave me my first driving lessons.

He also tooled around on a huge, shiny, black motorcycle. Being driven the four miles to my public school in Central Valley in Bill Kitchen's stately Pontiac was nothing compared with climbing on the back of Harry's Harley-Davidson and sending the gravel flying. One morning we roared into the schoolyard. When we hit the

Harry Whitney, top, Ma's son from her marriage to Sonny Whitney, was the closest thing I had to an older brother. He gave me driving lessons and let me ride on the back of his motorcycle. His sister, Nancy, was one of the most beautiful girls I'd ever seen. Harry and Nancy (below, in Sun Valley in the forties) had a tougher time as kids than I realized then.

parking area, Harry spun the Harley around and around, faster and faster in smaller and smaller circles. Before a bug-eyed audience of first- and second-graders, I felt like Lindbergh.

Exploring Arden on foot with Harry made the woods seem deeper, the sense of a bear or fox behind every tree more real. Harry sharpened my forest vision with fantastic stories. Once into the woods, we'd lie on the ground behind a thick bush to see how close a deer might come to us. While we waited, Harry in his hoarse, deepest whisper would describe the terrible monster with jagged teeth and long arms who was lurking behind that great beech. Not to mention the goblins, hairy and dwarflike, who would undoubtedly arrive the moment the sun went down. If I looked very hard across the stream, I might be lucky enough to glimpse the wood nymphs—"the most beautiful girls you ever saw"— cavorting naked in the morning mist. Lying there wide-eyed, I was sure that any perceptible shift in the light signaled the appearance of these wonderful creatures.

Later I learned that much of what fueled Harry's fantastic imagination was opera, especially *The Magic Flute* and Wagner's Ring cycle. Harry paid no attention to rules. One night he got thrown out of the Met for singing along with the soprano in his booming baritone.

But Harry, who died after a heart operation in 1985, was a tragic figure. Not until I became an adult did I know that he was manic-depressive. Nor, until recently, did I realize that my wonderful "older brother" had been constantly at war with the woman I found the easiest person in the world to be with.

≡

One recent bleak November day, I drove over to say hello to Harry's sister, Nancy, at her house in central Connecticut. She was recently widowed, and the loss of her husband was plain on her face as we sat by her kitchen window, looking out over a long meadow, now completely brown. A few weeks earlier, I had played for the wedding of her youngest daughter (and my goddaughter), Vicky. Once we got through the wedding gossip, I asked what it had been like to be Ma's daughter.

"There's no point in not being completely honest, is there?" Nancy began.

"Of course not."

"Well, I know you thought the world of her—and she did of you, Peter—but there was a time in my life when Harry and I would wake up every morning and wish she were dead."

"You're kidding."

"No. In fact, there were many times when Harry and I actually plotted to kill her. You know, she never had much time for us."

I said lightly, "Well, maybe you and Harry weren't the easiest kids in the world."

"God, we were difficult! I guess that goes with being a Whitney. But we wouldn't have been so difficult if she hadn't had that way of *erasing* us. I know Harry was furious when he was sent away at seven to a school in Arizona because of his asthma. He felt he was being thrown out of the family."

"Were you both rebels?"

"You could say that. Mummy would make us come into the sitting room when she had guests for dinner. I was supposed to curtsy, and Harry was supposed to bow. Instead he'd pee on the carpet."

"Amazing."

"He did it *repeatedly*. There were all sorts of scenes with Mummy. She couldn't cope with poor Harry. She'd wake me up in the middle of the night and say, 'You have to come and do something about your brother.' I'd walk into his room half asleep and he'd be sitting in bed, propped up with all these pillows, his little fists clenched with rage, his eyes narrowed, and screaming at poor Mummy, 'I hate you! Get out of my room!' I'd go over and sit by the bed and pat his hand and say, 'Everything's going to be all right.' Finally, he'd calm down and say to me, 'I'm going to blow up this house! I'm going to kill my mother! I'm going to kill Averell! I'm going to kill everybody!' You can't imagine what a relief it was for Mummy when you came into our lives. You were perfect. You were so easy. You were someone we could all feel sorry for."

I winced. "Did Ma and Ave know how ill Harry was?"

"No. In those days, nobody understood about manic depression. Do you know about the time Harry tried to kill me?"

"No."

"We'd all gone out west to a wedding, and Harry and I were staying in the same motel. He'd had too much to drink, and he locked himself in his room and wouldn't come out. I was in the hall, listening to him going on and on about wanting to kill himself and all sorts of crazy things, and I just stood there, pleading with him to open the door. Suddenly, he did open the door, and he pulled me inside. He put his big hunting knife up to my neck and said he was going to kill me. I knew he meant it. I'll never forget that feeling. Then it occurred to me that the only way to calm him down was to take him back to our childhood. I said, 'Remember the game of mumble-the-peg we used to play out in the backyard? You always beat me. This time, let me go first with the knife. Come on, Harry, let me go first.' He got very quiet, and he handed over the knife. I threw it out the window and ran like hell."

This was shattering. I had known and loved Harry and Nancy all my life. I thought of them as family—yet they had belonged to another family, one that I had known nothing about.

Nancy continued in her clear, quiet way: "Do you know what Sonny [Harry and Nancy's father] did to Harry over that girl he wanted to marry?"

"No."

"She was the first girl he ever loved—she was perfect for him. Harry went to Father to ask his permission to marry her, and Sonny told Harry the girl was a tramp, that he'd slept with her himself. Of course it wasn't true, but Harry believed him. I don't think he ever got over it. Here's something else you may not have known. I'm sure Ma was in love with Sonny all her life. She only left him because he was after some chippy. You know, when she died, she was wearing Sonny's wedding ring. Averell had it taken off before she was buried. After she died, Harry would go up to the family plot and sit on her grave and talk to her. If you asked him why, he'd say, 'Because I never could talk to her when she was alive.' "

"For me she was the easiest person in the world to talk to."

Nancy looked at me. "Well, you *do* know about her and Eddy . . ."

"You mean that they had an affair? Yes. Ma all but confirmed it."

"That doesn't surprise me. We all *assumed* it . . ."

It had been the summer after I'd finished Yale, and I was leaving in a few days for a blowout in Greece before going into the Army. The night before, Ma and Ave had thrown a party for my twenty-first birthday at Sands Point. That morning, Ave was up bright and early, out campaigning for reelection as governor of New York. Ma had made it out of bed around eleven, finished her breakfast, and had her massage. She was now breaststroking up and down the pool.

I was standing in the shallow end, nursing a filthy hangover, when I blurted: "Ma, did you love Dad as much as Ave?"

Marie Harriman and Dad. "For Chrissake! We were *very, very* close!"
she said when I asked about their relationship.

Ma stopped paddling. "I loved your father very much, Peter."

"Did you ever want to marry him?"

Pause, then: "I don't think I would have made a very good wife to a musician."

"Come on," I persisted, "out with it. Did you have an affair with Dad?"

Ma twisted her mouth the way she always did when she was trying to sound tough. "Darling," she said, "for Chrissake! I said we were *very, very* close!"

$$=$$

Now, telling this story in Nancy's kitchen, I said, "You know what? I was never so happy to hear anything in my life."

Nancy smiled. "I bet."

7

AVE

My earliest image of Ave is that of a tall, lanky man, moving purposefully and gracefully against the wintry landscape at Arden. Ave: remote but sharply etched, always off somewhere even when he was sitting right in front of you, poring over the morning newspapers.

During the war when he was running the Lend-Lease program in London, and later when he was ambassador to Moscow, I saw very little of him. But when he did drop in at Arden, I knew that "the boss," as Bill Kitchen called him, had arrived.

Suddenly, everything would speed up. Horses would be readied in their stalls in case Ave wanted to ride out into the fields. The old Pontiac station wagon would be brought out into the driveway, all cleaned up and polished with Bill's chamois. Ave would step out of the Lincoln Zephyr in his double-breasted suit, button-down shirt, tie, and shiny black shoes and would disappear into the cottage, only to reappear minutes later in his country clothes: a raggedy V-necked terry-cloth pullover of dark or light blue, creaseless tan corduroys, sturdy, rubber-soled brown shoes. The servants would be greeted with a smile and a brief hello. I would get a light kiss on the cheek and "Hello, Petey, how are you doing?"

In my scrapbook is a snapshot of me when I was five or six, sitting with Ave in a horse and buggy. It must have been one of the first times he and I went on an outing together. I'm wearing a tie, which means it was Sunday and we were on our way to Dr. Dumbell's service at St. John's, the Arden chapel. Ave is in country tweeds, wool tie, and jodhpurs. I look happy and proud: the little lord of the manor.

Whereas Ma's day would start around noon with her breakfast tray and the *Times* crossword puzzle in bed, Ave's would begin hours earlier with the morning news. I would have gotten up even earlier, and after I was dressed I'd rush over to his cottage. If the weather was fine, he'd be sitting on the screened porch at a plain, painted white table, listening to the radio and reading the New York dailies, one by one. He'd be wearing his tattered light blue bathrobe, leather slippers, and blue pajamas, all from Brooks Brothers. I'd enter without knocking and say, "Hi, Ave," give him a kiss, then go into the kitchen and ask the cook for an egg or—a special treat—Irish oatmeal with melted brown sugar on top.

Then I'd sit myself very quietly at the other end of the table. After a minute or two, during which I'd concentrate very hard on not moving a muscle or making the slightest sound, Ave would look up and say, "Good morning, Petey." Then he'd go back to his paper, one ear tuned to Quentin Reynolds or Edward R. Murrow, whoever was giving the news from Europe. The only break in his con-

W. Averell Harriman with Churchill and Stalin in August 1942. Ave was
representing President Roosevelt at a meeting called by Stalin to discuss the
war. He was made ambassador to the Soviet Union the following year.

centration would come when one of the Labs, sitting patiently at his elbow, growled or put a paw on his knee. Without taking his eyes off the paper, Ave would insert a piece of toast into the salivating jaws.

I would eat my egg in silence. Finally, the last paper would be folded together. Placing it on the pile to his left, Ave would glance up and announce his agenda for the morning. He always had an agenda. Then he'd say, "It'll take me an hour. After that, why don't we go for a ride?"

=

I was probably six or seven when I began thinking of Ave as the father I wished I had. I knew I had "Dad," but Ave, who clearly operated on a more commanding level than anybody else, was the father I wanted. Until my father's reappearance in my life after the war, Ave seemed to encourage this relationship. Indeed, more than once over the years, his two daughters, Mary and Kathleen, told me they'd always felt that I was the son "he wished he'd had." If so, Ave was happy to keep it from becoming a reality. As I would later understand, making me something beyond a fantasy son would have entailed a more emotionally complicated relationship than he was capable of. It's significant that his two daughters never called him anything but Ave or Averell—never Dad or Father.

As long as I was doing something with Ave, I felt comfortable. He didn't like me just hanging around; he really didn't like anyone just hanging around. The only spontaneous moment of intimacy with him I can recall occurred one day when I was still in short pants. Walking past the open door to his bathroom, I saw Ave leaning over the sink and looking at himself in the mirror. I ventured in. I had never seen him like this before. He had white cream all over his face, and he was stroking his cheeks with a strange, shiny tool.

I tried to make myself invisible.

"Hello, Petey," he said, not smiling. "What are you doing here?"

"Hi, Ave."

Silence. Stroke, stroke. I knew I was in a place where I shouldn't be, but I was too frightened and too fascinated to run. Suddenly, Ave crouched down and put his face with the white stuff on it close to mine.

"What's that?" I asked, pointing to his face.

"It's called shaving cream, Petey."

"What's it for?"

"It's for shaving," he said. "Shaving is what men do when they grow hair on their faces. When they get older."

"Can I try?"

He thought about it. Then he picked up a tube and squirted some of the white stuff into his hand. "Here," he said, kneeling down and slathering it on my face. Slowly, he stroked the razor down my cheek. "There," he said. "That's how you shave. Someday you'll do it yourself."

Then it was over. Abruptly, he rose to his full height, resumed his position in front of the mirror, and said, "Run along now, Petey."

Never had I felt closer to Ave.

=

I've always thought Ave really preferred animals to people. He loved to command, and the animals loved to obey. "Heel!" he'd say to a dog. When the dog did, a smile would spread across Ave's face. There were always dogs around. Ma had her wirehaired dachshunds and, later, Jack Russell terriers. Ave had his Labs. Once, down in Hobe Sound, he saw one of his aides throwing a stick on the beach for a favorite Lab named Brum. "Goddammit!" I heard him mutter. "No one should ever play with another man's dog!"

This same aide was later fired because he had the temerity to underscore things he thought Ave should take note of in the newspapers. "How the hell would he know what I should read," I'd hear Ave growl when he picked up his morning *Times* and found it underlined in red crayon.

I've never been more terrified in my life than the morning Ave lost his temper over a dog. I was five or six, and I'd headed over to his cottage because he'd promised to take me out on the lake. While Ave was immersed in his paper, I sat there, whittling a stick. One of his Labs came over and started growling, and I poked him on the head several times.

Suddenly Ave was out of his chair. Grabbing the stick, he whacked me on the behind, then on the back of my legs. "Don't ever strike an animal like that!" he said in a voice I'd never heard before.

I burst into tears and ran to the other cottage, where Frances was baking bread. Zellie heard my screaming and came in.

"Ave hit me!" I wailed.

"But that's not possible!" Zellie said. "What did you do?"

"I hit Scotch."

"That is very bad!"

I let out a louder wail.

Ave walked in and put a hand on my shoulder. "Petey," he said, "I hope you learned your lesson."

I nodded.

"Do you still want to go to the lake?"

"Buggy ride."

"Get ready."

Zellie suggested I write Ave and tell him how sorry I was that I'd hit the dog. She helped me write the note, which I signed, "I love you, Ave—Peter." Together we took it to his bedroom and placed it on his pillow. The next morning, I ran over to Ave's, took my usual place at his breakfast table, and waited for him to say something about the note. He didn't. For days I waited, biting my tongue to keep from asking if he'd read my note. If he did, he never said a word about it. He had moved on to his next agenda.

Ave was the most determined man I've ever known. In his memoir *In Search of History,* Theodore H. White observed that "once Harriman was wound up and pointed in the direction his government told him he must go, he was like a tank crushing all opposition." His doggedness may have come from the fact that, for all his wealth and privileged upbringing, he had had a lot to overcome: a childhood stammer, sickliness, and, most of all, an overbearing and demanding father. When he was at Groton, young Averell had to send home weekly reports on his progress. His father also made him contribute a big chunk of his allowance to put a less fortunate boy through school.

Ave had to be the best at whatever he did, whether it was making money; playing polo, croquet, or bridge; shooting birds; being an ambassador; or advising presidents. He had to win. The last time he and I went duck hunting was down in Hobe Sound. Ave had just turned seventy-five, and he probably hadn't held a firearm in twenty years. But he shot like a man fifty years younger. With every flight of ducks, he'd calmly raise his gun, take aim, and hit the target. Occasionally, in a breach of duck-shooting etiquette, he'd bring down a bird that was clearly on my side of the blind. "Damn," he'd say, "I guess that was yours. Sorry." Then he'd do the same thing again.

From the beginning, I sensed Ave's competence: how, with the slightest tug or tap of his whip, he could direct a horse to speed up or slow down, turn or stop. Later I learned that he had once driven his own trotters at the famous track in Goshen, New York. He was a wonderful teacher. When I turned eight, I graduated from my little pony to a full-size horse. Ave would mount one of his two huge horses, Fact and Boston, that had been given to him by Stalin, and stand in the field for an hour or more, appraising my figure eights and my posting, raising his voice a little when I repeated a mistake: "Petey, once again! Relax the reins! Give him a kick with the outside foot!"

When I got a little older, he took me out on the polo field at Arden, handed me a small mallet and ball, and showed me how the two should connect. Every time I hit a good one, he let out a whoop of joy. Later, when I graduated to croquet, the sport that aroused his competitive instincts the most, I realized how much winning meant to him—and how it didn't mean that much to me. Ave's favorite way to win at croquet was with one great shot at the end. Triumphant, he'd murmur, "Not bad," and walk away from the group. If he lost he'd say nothing. But for the rest of the day, you'd know about it.

It says a lot about Ave that while his croquet buddies maintained impeccably manicured English courses, his courses at Sands Point and Hobe Sound were of his own eccentric and diabolical design. Their terrains were rutted and thick with crabgrass. They had no boundaries. In Hobe Sound, the most treacherous side of the course was a jungle. In Sands Point it was Long Island Sound. Nothing gave Ave more pleasure than to hit another player's ball so that the opponent would take two turns to get back in play. Most of his croquet friends hated playing on the Harriman courses, which pleased him enormously—and gave him a distinct psychological advantage. Not until the British prime minister Anthony Eden came to visit in Hobe Sound did Averell have the course properly rolled. Ma, who was breakfasting by the pool when the

Ave and me at Arden. He was a somewhat remote figure
of absolute authority for me. He and I didn't go out in the
buggy very often. In the photograph above we're probably
on our way to church in the Arden chapel.

steamroller arrived, hooted with laughter at Ave's putting on the dog for "those damn Brits."

Ave had an aristocrat's sense of service. He never actually sat me down for moral instruction, but in offhand remarks he let me know the importance—if you were to be regarded as a "gentleman"—of "giving back" as much as you "took." How many times I heard him say: "He's a sweet man, but he doesn't do a damn thing." Or "I've known that fellow for a long time. He's a Republican who does nothing but eat and drink. He should have learned that he could have had a helluva lot more fun as a Democrat. As I have."

It was antiquated fastidiousness, not snobbery, that prompted Ave to say things like "Never have a meal with your lawyer, Petey. You don't want to get too close to him. Keep it on a business level." It wasn't that he looked down on people who earned their livings as lawyers. It was simply that anyone he paid to perform a service for him—lawyer, doctor, tailor, barber—he regarded as a "tradesman." There was no hierarchy among them. In Ave's eyes, Bill Kitchen was as important as the personal financial adviser I only heard him refer to as Cook. He treated them all with equal courtesy, but he would never dream of setting foot in their domains. If they had business with Ave, they came to him.

You never saw Ave ever actually deal with the physical fact of money—a subject he hated. He never carried cash, and if you went with him to a restaurant where he wasn't known, you'd end up with the check—to be reimbursed later only if you remembered to notify Cook of the amount.

Four times a year, Cook would arrive to give his update on the Harriman finances, a topic so sizable that the documents relating to the family's fiscal transactions were said to occupy the better part of a floor at Brown Brothers Harriman, the family banking house in lower Manhattan. Ave was utterly bored by these meetings and would enter and leave them in a cloud of irritability.

One of his old friends, the publisher Harold Guinzburg, who founded Viking Press, once remarked to his son Tom and me that he'd never understood what having real wealth meant until one day when he was breakfasting with Ave. "We were both reading the papers," Harold recalled, "and I was looking at the stock quotes on the business page. I happened to own a thousand shares of Union Pacific and to my great delight saw that it had jumped two points— a gain of two thousand dollars. Averell, of course, owned at least a million shares, which meant a gain of at least two million dollars. 'Jesus, Averell,' I said. 'Union Pacific is up two points.' Without taking his eyes off the newspaper, he replied, 'That's nice.' "

Unlike most rich men today, Ave had no interest in displays of wealth. From time to time, he bought a great painting or great piece of furniture. And of course he always had his town clothes made by the tailor who came to the house. But he was more comfortable in his Brooks Brothers country rags, which he wore till they were in shreds. And he was most at home in modest surroundings. As a diplomat, he had a legendary ability to live out of a suitcase.

The house where I spent virtually all of my childhood summers—Ave and Ma's place in Sands Point, Long Island—was sandwiched between the huge Swope mansion and the Guggenheim mansions (one of which is now an IBM corporate country club). Compared with its neighbors, Ave's place was a shack: a one-floor, rambling beach house. It had been built as a place simply to change clothes in when he was on Long Island to play polo at the Meadowbrook Club. Slowly he had enlarged the house, adding a pool, a croquet course, a tennis court, and a dock.

In the 1930s, when he was working on Wall Street, Ave would leave the house in his dressing gown and walk across the lawn to the dock, where he would board his motor yacht, *Spindrift*. By the time his valet had shaved and dressed him and served him breakfast, the boat would be pulling into the pier near his offices.

Sands Point was modestly staffed. The only permanent help was Mr. Phillips, the Scottish caretaker, who lived on the property with his wife. In June, Ma and Ave would arrive with Vicky, Ma's maid; Jeanne, the French cook; and a couple of maids from New York. Mr. Phillips was a wonderful gardener, a jack-of-all-trades with a deeply lined, leathery complexion. One of my scariest moments as a child was seeing him struck by lightning when he was out on the lawn one day during a thunderstorm. It illuminated him like a creature from Mars and knocked him to the ground. I rushed out, but he had gotten up and was angrily looking around for his pipe. He wasn't hurt, but his pipe was destroyed.

Mr. Phillips's passion was fishing. When Harry Whitney and I were lucky enough to go out with him, he'd row us back and forth in the quiet of the evening, pipe clenched between his teeth, filling our heads with the lore of Scottish history, Scottish clans, Scottish wars. We'd troll long sandworms, dug up that afternoon on the beach, or cast top-water plugs. Striped bass were plentiful then, and it was not unusual to pull in a couple of twenty-pounders.

My record was a forty-three pounder, which took me—at the age of ten—more than an hour to land with the help of Harry, Mr. Phillips, and his Irish setter. After the grueling fight, we carried the monster from the rowboat up to the lawn behind the porch, where Ma and Ave were playing bridge with their neighbors George and Evie Backer. Hearing our yells, they rushed out. Mr. Phillips shone his flashlight on the great fish, which was nearly as big as I was. Everyone gasped. My face was as hot as a poker. My bare toes clutched the grass.

The topper was when Ave came over, gave me a big kiss on the cheek, and said, "Petey, this is the greatest fish I've ever seen! How grand that you caught it! Tell us about it!" Mr. Phillips and Harry beamed like proud fathers, the Irish setter circled the fish, and Ma announced that we'd have a dinner party the next day in the fish's honor. I wept with pleasure.

I loved Jeanne, the cook, as much as Mr. Phillips. She was a strong French woman, always dressed in a white uniform, except on her days off, when she'd put on a very severe suit and a hat with a huge pheasant feather. I loved sitting around the kitchen, watching her work. After breakfast, when the tide was dead low, she'd take me down the beach to the flats in front of the Swope house, pitchfork in hand. There we'd dig up buckets of steamers, to be eaten at lunch. Jeanne would wade out along the dock and pull bunches of fresh blue mussels from the pylons to make one of her fabulous *marinières* or *poulettes*.

=

Ma and Ave had still another house, the Harriman cottage in Sun Valley. It was a plain concrete structure with six bedrooms, all modestly furnished and functional. When I was eight, we went to Sun Valley for Christmas.

Ave appeared at dinner in Austrian lederhosen. I thought it the strangest costume I'd ever seen. But, on reflection, this Alpine getup was characteristic of Ave's custom of wearing a different "uniform" for each of his environments: pinstripes for Wall Street and Washington; old khakis and riding clothes for Arden; baggy shorts and polo shirts for Hobe Sound and Sands Point. Over dinner, he told me how my mother had been a "great help" to him in decorating Sun Valley's lodge and many of its rooms. It might have

Ma and Ave in Sun Valley in 1937, the year I was born.

been the first time he had ever brought up the subject of my mother to me. I felt a little uneasy and eager to hear more.

"After dinner," Ave said, "I'm going to show you the room I named after her."

I couldn't understand what he was talking about. A room named after my mother? It turned out to be the bar—a long, rectangular room, rustically furnished, with pictures of celebrity skiers on the walls. Over the front door was a plaque that read THE DUCHIN ROOM.

From that evening on, while the others were floating around the huge heated pool after a day of skiing, I'd sneak into the Duchin Room to gaze at the plaque. The day before we left, I said to a couple of buddies, "I want to show you something." When I pointed at the plaque, one of them said, sounding not terribly impressed, "Oh, my parents come in here all the time. They call it the Dooh-Dah Room. They say it's named for your father."

"No it's not!" I shot back. "It's named for my *mother*!"

=

Ave was the cheapest man I've ever known. One of Ma's favorite stories was about a Sunday after the war when she and Ave were in Paris. Early in the afternoon, Ave thought he'd stop by the Orangerie to look at one of the Cézannes he and Ma had lent to the gallery. He took along his briefcase, filled with Marshall Plan papers. At the museum, he wandered over to the Cézanne and was standing there, gazing at it, when an attendant came up and said, "Excuse me, sir, the entrance fee is two hundred francs." Ave reached into his pocket and came up empty-handed. "I'm very sorry," he said and walked out.

It was a beautiful day, so he told his driver to take him to the Bois de Boulogne. Spotting a vacant bench, he sat down and spread out his papers. After a minute, an old crone appeared and said, "That will be twenty centimes [about two cents] for the bench." Ave again searched through his pockets. Again he came up empty.

"I'm very sorry," he said. Putting away the Marshall Plan, he got up and told the driver to take him home.

"Back so soon, Averell?" Ma said.

"Yes," Ave replied. "Paris has become so damned expensive these days!"

Ave had no gift for small talk. I can't remember him ever making a casual remark, not even about the weather. But he did make a point of answering whatever anyone asked him, especially if it had to do with a historic event in which he had played an important part. He didn't embellish his stories with much human detail, but when he did, the detail stuck. I once asked him what Stalin had been like at the Yalta Peace Conference. "While Roosevelt and Stalin were talking," Ave said, "I couldn't help notice that Stalin was doodling. I looked over and saw that he was drawing a wolf."

He was immensely self-involved. One night, my first wife, Cheray, and I were in our bedroom at Hobe Sound when Ave burst in without knocking. He was waving what looked like an old magazine. "Look at this!" he roared, oblivious of the fact that we were undressed and groping for our bathrobes. "It's the first nice thing I've ever read about my father!"

"Gee, that's great, Ave," I said.

He handed me an ancient monograph about a steamship trip to Alaska that E. H. Harriman had organized for his family and thirty leading scientists in 1899. Not surprisingly, the writer, John Muir, had produced a highly flattering piece about his host. Ave was so thrilled he had 500 copies printed up and sent to friends.

Such emotional displays were rare. In fact, I can recall only two occasions when Ave really lost his cool. The first was at a dinner

Ma and Ave during his successful campaign for governor of
New York in 1954. I think he didn't really appreciate Ma until
he saw how great a campaigner she was.

party Cheray and I gave in 1966. We had just moved into our house on East Seventy-first Street, and we had gone to a lot of trouble to make things right. Besides Ma and Ave, the guests included their Sands Point neighbors Ed and Marian Goodman, and George Ball, who would soon resign as undersecretary of state over his opposition to America's involvement in Vietnam. Toward the end of dinner, Marian, who was seated next to Ave, casually remarked, "I certainly sympathize with those boys who don't want to go to Vietnam. Who would want to give up his life for a cause that doesn't make any sense?"

Ave turned white. "You're a traitor!" he nearly yelled. "You're a traitor to your country to talk that way!"

There was a terrible silence. To smooth things over, I said, "For God's sake, Marian, don't take it seriously."

Fortunately, it was time for the men and women to separate, as they always did after dinner in those days. Marian went home without saying good-bye to Ave. The next day he sent her some flowers and a note:

> Please forgive the misunderstanding. I've always been for the eighteen-year-old vote.

"It was completely baffling," Marian recalled. "It wasn't a real apology, and of course it had absolutely nothing to do with what we'd been talking about."

A year later, after Ave had belatedly switched positions on the war, he and Ma were throwing a dinner party in Sands Point. Among their guests were the publisher Bennett Cerf and his wife, Phyllis. After dinner, Phyllis, Ave, and a few others went out to the porch, where the conversation turned to Vietnam. Phyllis, who was never shy with an opinion, began needling Ave about why it had taken him so long to become a dove. Patiently, Ave answered that if he had broken too soon with the Johnson administration, he would have lost influence in the inner circle. That wasn't good enough for Phyllis, who persisted until she was all but calling him a war criminal.

Suddenly there was a sharp sound. Ave had slapped Phyllis across the face. This was followed by a dreadful silence, with Ave staring at his hand as though it were someone else's. Bennett just sat there looking sheepish.

The battle was over, and Ave and Phyllis fell all over each other with apologies. But nobody who was there ever forgot that slap.

Ave remained a father figure for me all his life. He was the man who would give me the news that Dad had died. He would attend my graduations from Eaglebrook, Hotchkiss, and Yale. He was always ready with advice, emphasizing that it was wise to get as broad an education as possible, to study ancient history, philosophy, and art as well as the modern stuff. Usually, he ended such conversations with "Don't waste your time playing bridge, which is what I did too damn much of at Yale."

When Skull and Bones, Ave's secret society, made overtures to me (no doubt instigated by him), I said I didn't believe in the elitism of such organizations. Ave was so furious he refused to speak to me for a month. It was as close as we ever came to a real falling-out—rivaled only by the rage I sent him into when I told him, some years later, that I was supporting George McGovern for president. Ave called the idealistic senator from South Dakota "a wet smack," whatever that meant.

Except when Ave was angry, he was emotionally remote. But on the rare occasion when he managed to let you know that he did care about you, your self-esteem jumped a notch. In Ave's hands, the world seemed shapable. He looked at things in a big way. He acted in a big way. And I wanted to measure up.

Dad as a naval officer. He chose combat over
entertaining the troops.

8

STORMY WEATHER

My father had been one of 136,000 Allied soldiers and sailors at Normandy, an officer on a destroyer escort in charge of monitoring the sonar devices used to detect enemy submarines. It was a job he'd been given because of his perfect pitch. He could have spent the war entertaining the troops. In fact, before he enlisted he was about to film a movie about the life of George Gershwin, playing the title role. But early in 1942, while he was playing at the Palmer House in Chicago, his friend Brose Chambers talked him into enlisting in Naval Officers' School.

After training at various submarine chaser schools, he sailed off on a destroyer escort, the USS *Bates*, first into the Atlantic war zone, then into the Pacific, where he took part in the invasions of

Okinawa and Iwo Jima. After the Pacific invasions, he was ordered to Pearl Harbor for commanding officers' school. Five days later, his ship was kamikazied and sunk, losing most of his old crewmates. He became operations officer for a squadron of destroyers and ended the war as a lieutenant commander.

It's only recently that I learned about my father's war record. He gave an interview in the late forties in which he claimed to have chosen combat because, he said, "I have a son. And when he grows up and asks what his daddy did during the war, I don't want to have to tell him that all I did was play the piano." Oddly, he never volunteered to talk to me about this, but over the years, many of his old fans and friends have become fans and friends of mine, and I've received dozens of letters from men he served with on his destroyer.

In one of my scrapbooks are two letters Dad wrote to me in the fall of 1943, when he was making the first of his many Atlantic crossings. They are sweet, cheerful communications describing his efforts to grow a mustache and his concern for all of us at home. The small white upright piano that was installed in a corner off the living room in the cottage arrived almost simultaneously with these letters.

"What's that?" I asked Zellie.

"That's a piano. Your father wants you to take lessons so you can play with him when the war is over. I'll show you."

Zellie bent over the keyboard and depressed a cluster of notes. Out came a strange but pleasurable sound. It made the room seem like a whole different place. She did it again. I must have smiled.

Even now when I sit down at the keyboard, I remember that first sensuous feeling as I stared at those keys. I wanted to stroke them—to *feel* them. I still do.

"Now you try it," Zellie said.

I sat down and started banging. I liked the noise and banged louder. Zellie gently lifted my hands from the keyboard. "That's wonderful, Peter," she said. "Next week a teacher's coming."

I remember nothing about my earliest piano lessons other than the fact that my teacher was a woman who came weekly to Arden for the next couple of years and that I hated to practice. All I could think of as I sat there playing those stupid scales and "Jolly Peasants" was how much I'd rather be outside fishing with Bill Kitchen or exercising the horses with Alan Crawford. And how much I hated everyone, from Zellie to Ma, for telling me how much fun I'd have playing duets with my father when he came home from the war. It never happened, not even after I finally went to live with him and his new wife.

In 1945, when Dad was released from active duty, he was mainly interested in getting his career back together and pursuing Irene Selznick, ex-wife of the producer David O. Selznick and daughter of the movie mogul Louis B. Mayer. One weekend in 1946, Dad took me out to Irene's country house in Stamford, Connecticut, hoping that I'd become friends with her children, Danny and Jeffrey. We got along fine, and over the years I've stayed friendly with Danny. Recently, I called him up to ask what he remembered about his mother's affair with my father.

"Only that he was more interested in marrying her than she was in marrying him," Danny said. "She once told me she found your father incredibly charming but that he wasn't intelligent enough for her. Sorry, Peter."

I bristled. "You mean maybe he wasn't intellectual enough."

"I think she also said that he wasn't *neurotic* enough for her either." Danny laughed.

From newspaper accounts, I know that Irene Selznick seems to have cared enough about my father to help decorate the "party of the decade" he threw with Cary Grant, Jimmy Stewart, and John McClain in 1946. Whenever I ran into Cary over the years, he would refer to that night as "the best party I've ever given." Knowing how tight Cary was with a buck, I imagine it might have been the *only* party he'd ever given. According to one account, my father—also famously tight with a buck—had initially suggested serving hot dogs and baked beans. Thanks to the restaurateur Mike Romanoff, who offered to cater the affair, the menu improved considerably.

On March 24, 1946, a telegram flew around the country: WE FIGURE IT'S ABOUT TIME WE THREW A PARTY, SO WILL YOU COME TO THE OLD CLOVER CLUB, 8477 SUNSET BOULEVARD, 8 PM, NEXT SATURDAY, MARCH 30TH. SORRY ABOUT THE SHORT NOTICE BUT WE'VE ONLY JUST BEEN ABLE TO HIRE THE JOINT. PLEASE ANSWER EARLY. WE ARE NERVOUS. BLACK TIE, LOW CUT DRESSES. ARDMORE 8-6056. EDDY DUCHIN, CARY GRANT, JOHN MCCLAIN AND JIMMY STEWART.

The guest list conjures up a whole era: the Fred Astaires, the Vincent Astors, Lew Ayres, the Richard Barthelmesses, Constance Bennett, the Jack Bennys, the Edgar Bergens, the Frederick Brissons (Rosalind Russell), the Humphrey Bogarts, the Frank Capras, Lady Adele Cavendish (Adele Astaire), the Charles Chaplins, the Gary Coopers, Joan Crawford, the Bing Crosbys, George Cukor, Olivia de Havilland, the Douglas Fairbanks, Jrs., Geraldine Fitzgerald, the Henry Fondas, Joan Fontaine, Kay Francis, Clark Gable, Lillian Gish, the Samuel Goldwyns, the Averell Harrimans, the Rex Harrisons, the Howard Hawkses, the Leland Haywards, Rita Hayworth, William Randolph Hearst, Mark Hellinger, Sonja Henie, the Alfred Hitchcocks, the Bob Hopes, Hedda Hopper, John Houseman, Howard Hughes, John Huston, Barbara Hutton, Van Johnson, the Danny Kayes, Sir Alexander Korda, the Mervyn LeRoys,

Anita Loos, Ida Lupino, the Fred MacMurrays, the Herman J. Mankiewiczes, the Joseph L. Mankiewiczes, the Harpo Marxes, the Zeppo Marxes, Elsa Maxwell, Louis B. Mayer, the Ray Millands, the Robert Montgomerys, the George Murphys, David Niven, the Gregory Pecks, Cole Porter, the Tyrone Powers, Otto Preminger, the Basil Rathbones, the Hal Roaches, the Edward G. Robinsons, Cesar Romero, the Randolph Scotts, David O. Selznick, Irene Mayer Selznick, Ann Sheridan, Toots Shor, the Frank Sinatras, Sam Spiegel, the Spencer Tracys, Lana Turner, the Walter Wangers, the Jack Warners, the Lew Wassermans, Clifton Webb, the John Hay Whitneys, the Keenan Wynns, the Darryl Zanucks.

The four hosts, all dressed in tails, formed a receiving line. Mike Romanoff's food ranged from green turtle soup to oysters, crab, shrimp, trout, chicken, stuffed turkey, roast ribs of beef, ham, coq au vin, boned squab, vegetables and salads, and numerous desserts. At five in the morning, 250 guests were still there, sitting on the floor and listening to Bing Crosby sing every song he ever knew, to the accompaniment of Hoagy Carmichael.

=

I had my first memorable outing with Dad after the war when I was eight or nine. I can see him arriving at the Harriman house in the city (then on East Sixty-eighth Street), looking very impressive in his black and gold-braided lieutenant commander's uniform. I remember holding his hand as we walked down the street. Before we reached the corner, we were stopped by two girls.

One said, "Wow! Eddy Duchin! Can we get your autograph?"

I watched as my father scribbled his name in their books.

"What's an autograph?"

"Some people like to collect signatures of people they like."

"How did they know who you were?"

He laughed, sounding embarrassed. "They probably heard me play the piano on the radio. Or they saw me playing the piano in a hotel. Maybe they have my records."

I was fascinated by the whole ritual: not just by the adulation of the two girls, but by Dad's obvious pleasure in having been recognized. I became something of an autograph hound myself, collecting the signatures of baseball players and, later, Hollywood stars, most of which were procured by Dad.

This was the first time I'd looked at my father through the eyes of others. For the next twenty blocks, the words rang in my ears: "Wow! Eddy Duchin!"

Shortly after the autograph episode, I got another view of my father in the world when we visited Toots Shor's restaurant on Fifty-first Street. My first impression was of a cavernous, smoky room full of men, most of them bigger than Dad, who himself was over six feet tall but slender. Everyone knew him. "Hey, Eddy!" they called out. "How ya doin', Eddy?"

Then the biggest of them of all came up. Everything about Toots Shor was huge. Stomach. Feet. Hands. Lips. His face was like a big slab of steak, red and mottled and rubbery. His black hair was slicked back and parted straight down the middle. His bellow filled the room as he wrapped Dad in a hug and said, "Eddy! Where ya been?"

"Here's Peter, Toots," Dad said. "Peter, this is Mr. Shor . . . Toots Shor."

I was hoisted aloft. "Pete, kid! How are ya?" He set me down. "Let's go in and eat something, for Chrissake."

Dad put an arm around me, and we followed the giant into a sea of red leather and white linen.

Toots bellowed, "Hey, Joe, look who I got! An old buddy!"

Two men were sitting at a round table in the corner. Between them was a very small, pretty, blonde woman, wearing a little hat with a half veil. One of the men stood up and embraced my father. I almost died. It was Joe DiMaggio.

The blonde got up. She was no taller than I was. "This Eddy's kid?" she said, giving me a wink. "You come over here. Sit next to me. I've heard so much aboutcha."

"Meet Husky, my wife," Toots said.

She flashed her dimples and nudged me in the ribs. "He calls me Husky. You can call me Baby."

Dad said, "Peter, I'd like you to meet Joe DiMaggio."

The greatest man in the world held out his hand.

"Hey, kid, nice to meet you. Say hi to my brother, Dom."

He gestured toward the other man at the table. I recognized him from my baseball cards as Dominic DiMaggio, center fielder for the Red Sox.

"Come on, you bums," Toots said. "Let's eat."

So I became a member of the most exclusive club I've ever joined. From the day we met, Toots was the most generous man in my life. Along with Ma and Ave; my guardian, Donald Stralem, and his wife, Jean; and my stepmother, Chiquita, Toots and Baby came to my graduation at Yale. It was an awfully odd-looking group, but it was family—the only one I had. Afterward we all had lunch at the Old Heidelburg. Leaving the restaurant, Toots nudged me and said, "You see, Pete, all those millionaires and look who gets stuck with the check."

A few years later, he was bankrupt.

=

My stepmother, Chiquita, made a hell of an effort with me. After Dad died in 1951, she kept the door open wherever she lived,

Me with Dad and Chiquita at their wedding in 1947. The
reception was held in the New York house of Ma and Ave, who
was then secretary of commerce. I was a spoiled kid and gave
Chiquita a hard time, but she coped gracefully.

whether it was at her apartment at the Hotel Carlyle in New York or later at her farm in Frederick, Maryland. I wasn't exactly a bargain. I was a spoiled and headstrong teenager, and she was stuck with me. Chiq had never had a child of her own, which must have made it even harder, but I never heard her complain. Still, in the few years I spent with her, I came to think of her, perhaps unfairly, as a tough authority figure. She was half Spanish and half English, and she had an old-fashioned, European sense of discipline that I didn't appreciate in the least.

A few years ago, Chiq and I met in London for drinks at Claridge's Hotel. As always with our reunions, we began where we'd left off. At times we'd been close; at times, prickly. But I was fond of her, and I think she was of me. After all, she was the only living link to whatever blood family I'd ever had.

Now in her late seventies, she was still a damn good-looking woman in a crisp, dark suit and good jewelry, carrying a certain look I associate with the forties: the sort of "smart" woman who always wore gloves when she went out.

Oddly, we had never talked about my father. Nor had Chiq and I ever talked about *them*: how they'd met in the first place, how they'd decided to get married, how it had gone with me. Now, many years later, Chiq didn't need much prompting:

"It started in Honolulu, during the war. Eddy was on shore leave, and I was staying at Margaret Emerson's [a socialite who had been married to one of the Vanderbilts]. I was in the middle of a tennis game when Eddy came over and stood there watching. Eddy asked Alfred Vanderbilt [Margaret's son] who I was, and Alfred said, 'Never mind, don't get near her. She won't have anything to do with you.' Eddy just laughed. A week later I saw him the night before he was leaving for Okinawa. He came over to Margaret's for supper. After coffee, he got hold of me and said, 'I want to see you again.' Of course, I was a married woman [Chiq's husband, four-teen years older, was a lawyer named Montgomery Wynn]. So I just said, 'Well, naturally, since we're both great friends of Margaret, you *will* see me again.' He said, 'No, I'm *really* going to see you again.'

"That was the last I heard of him until after the war. In April 1947 I was on my way back to England to my mother's, and I stopped in New York. Through the grapevine, Eddy heard I was in town, and he called me up. 'Hello,' he said. 'How are you? How's Monty?' I told him that Monty had just died. There was a great cheer on the other end. Then he said, 'Oh, goody! How about dinner tomorrow night?' "

"Nice, Dad," I murmured.

"He was very sweet. We went to '21' for dinner and then to the Plaza for a nightcap. That's when he said, 'Why don't we just get married?' I said, 'What will the Harrimans think? That you just picked up some girl! Besides, I'm Catholic.' Well, it was daylight when he brought me back to my hotel. Pigeons were flying."

"So he swept you off your feet."

"You could say that again."

"Did Marie resent you?"

Chiq made a face. "Well, she and Ave *did* give the wedding reception at their house on Sixty-eighth Street. Marie was all for Eddy getting married to me. But, yes, she did resent me. I supposed she felt I had taken Eddy and you away from her."

"How did I fit in?"

"You were very cute. We weren't married yet when Eddy took me out to Arden for a weekend. Marie was there, and so were Ginny and Brose Chambers. All we talked about was you—your fishing, your riding, your piano, your love of baseball. The whole time was focused on *you*. On the way back to New York, Eddy said he was dying to get you out of that atmosphere because you were getting too spoiled. But you didn't act spoiled at all. You seemed perfectly happy and normal."

So happy and normal that, curiously, I can't remember a single thing about leaving Arden and going to live with my father on Long Island. Nor do I remember what I initially felt about my step-mother—only that she was beautiful and pleasant, though not quite as welcoming as Ma. A winter Sunday at a football game in Giants Stadium jumps out. The three of us—Dad, Chiq, and I—were there as guests of Toots and Baby. It was freezing cold, and the game went down to the wire—a "two-pint game," in Toots's vernacular, meaning that he had every reason to double his usual intake of brandy. Chiq was wearing a mink coat, and I wanted so badly to bury myself in its deep, soft fur that I could hardly con-centrate on the game.

More curious is the fact that I can't remember anyone actually sitting me down to tell me that Dad and Chiq were getting mar-ried. Of course, their marriage was heavily covered in the columns, the gist being "Eddy Duchin, bandleader, war hero, and brave sur-vivor of tragedy, at last finds happiness." News photos indicate that I was present at the wedding in St. Patrick's Cathedral on Novem-ber 2, 1947, and later at the reception thrown by Ma and Ave. But I don't have a single memory of the day itself.

My actual leave-taking from Arden is another black hole. Un-doubtedly, the job of packing me up was done by servants—all those beloved hands. But how did I say good-bye to Zellie? Bill Kitchen? Alan Crawford? My little Arden pal, Lionel Bond? There must have been hugs and handshakes and the sense that I wasn't leaving for good but only going off to another Harriman house somewhere. And in fact, once I'd moved into the big, comfortable white house with the two pianos in the living room on Shelter

Rock Road in Manhasset, they all did their best to make my life as continuous as possible.

Since I was already off at boarding school—a fifth-grader at the Eaglebrook School in western Massachusetts—I saw my father and stepmother mostly during Christmas, spring, and summer vacations. We'd climb into Dad's big Buick, me in the backseat, and head for Florida or Idaho. Waiting for us at the other end would be Ma and Ave and rooms I had known all my life.

Dad and Chiq were warm and easy with each other, and if I wasn't as used to their company as I was to Ma and Ave's, I did enjoy the looks from total strangers who recognized my father and took the three of us in with the curiosity of fans.

On our first Christmas together, we took the train out to Sun Valley. It had long been a favorite place for the movie crowd—the Aspen of its day. Ann Sothern, Gary and Rocky Cooper, Norma Shearer, Darryl Zanuck, and other Hollywood types were there, and they all made a big fuss over me when Dad made the introductions.

Ernest Hemingway had a house there, too. People were endlessly saying they'd spotted him on Baldy Mountain or at the Pioneer Bar in Ketchum or fishing for steelhead in Stanley. His imminent arrival for dinner in the lodge was always expected, but it rarely happened. In my imagination, he became almost as big as Joe DiMaggio. But on the couple of occasions when I did spot him, I couldn't see what everyone was talking about. He was just a round, bearded man with a gruff manner who dressed pretty much like the other men, only a little more so. I was introduced to him, and a few years later we fished and shot dove together with his buddies Joe Burgy and "Beartracks" Taylor, an old trapper. He liked being with an awestruck kid to whom he could tell stories about the Spanish Revolution and deep-sea fishing off Cuba.

After Dad and Chiquita were married, I went to live with them
in Manhasset, Long Island. Since I was already at boarding
school—Eaglebrook—I was home mostly just for vacations. Our
first Christmas together we went to Sun Valley (below), where
Dad played the piano at a party one night.

I had skied Sun Valley many times, and I felt terribly important as I showed Dad and Chiq around the little Tyrolean village and helped them down the bunny hill. Dad was hopeless, but Chiq—a terrific athlete—got the hang of it right away. On New Year's Eve, we climbed into a horse-drawn sleigh, burrowed under fur blankets, and were taken to the cabin in Trail Creek. There, a big party was in progress, with all the stars. Over in the corner sat a trio of musicians, dressed in lederhosen.

After a bit, Dad walked over to the piano, and the room got quiet. He rippled through his big hits—"Night and Day," "Stormy Weather," "Too Marvelous for Words"—and people started swaying and dancing and singing along.

"Come on over here, Peter," he called out.

Gingerly I stepped forward. Dad put a hand on my shoulder and pulled me over. "I guess I do this better than ski," he said.

Everyone laughed, and I glowed, happy to see him doing what he did better than anyone else in the world. Since then, I've often wondered why Dad got up that night and played. Was it because he felt it was expected of him? Because he loved it? Or because of me?

Long after midnight, Chiq, Dad, and I returned to the lodge. Heading back to our rooms, we walked through the Duchin Room, which was now silent and closed for the night. Was Dad, I wondered, thinking of the woman for whom it was named?

≡

That spring vacation, we drove to Hobe Sound. On the way, we stopped off for several nights at Arcadia, the antebellum plantation owned by George Vanderbilt near Columbia, South Carolina. George was a lovely man with an even lovelier daughter my age, named Lulu. She awakened my first romantic stirrings as she showed me around the plantation, every tree dripping with Spanish moss.

I was particularly entranced by "the village," a settlement of picturesque houses built for the servants a hundred years ago. There, I was introduced to the oldest man I've ever met, a tiny, gaunt black man with the soft, brown eyes of a deer. He was 107 years old, and he sat on a rickety porch in a gilded, Louis XVI chair that was undoubtedly a hand-me-down from some great Vanderbilt ballroom. When he heard I'd come from New York, he shook his head in wonder. In all his life, he said, he'd never been more than twenty miles from Arcadia.

I asked why.

"Because everything's so wonderful where I am," he answered.

There were wild boar on the place, and one had been shot and killed for a pig roast. The servants had dug two enormous trenches, one for the boar on a slowly revolving spit, the other for clams, smothered in seaweed and steamed on coals. Between my lust for Lulu and my hunger for the clams and the boar, I was exhausted after dinner. While the grown-ups played cards, I went off to bed.

My room looked out onto a colonnaded veranda. Just before falling asleep, I felt hot and got up to open the door. In the darkness, which was illuminated by gas lanterns, I saw a figure out on the lawn, sitting in a rocking chair. It was an old woman, with her white hair tied in a bun and her face covered by a thin veil. There was nothing threatening about her, so I stepped outside. When I got to within about ten feet of her, she looked at me and smiled. Then she levitated right off the chair and disappeared into thin air. I went up and touched the chair. It was real.

I ran into the house, shouting that I'd just seen a ghost.

The grown-ups put down their cards.

Dad said, "It's OK, Peter, it was just a bad dream."

George Vanderbilt got up, sat me down on the couch, and opened a big leather book. "Now," he said, "I want you to describe what you saw."

I did: the old woman's hair, her veil, her dress, her smile, her levitation, her disappearance. Then George read from the book: a half dozen descriptions of the old woman by guests that had been written as far back as the Civil War. Every account matched mine.

George closed the book. "She's been around for years," he said matter-of-factly. "She was a member of the family who owned Arcadia before the Civil War. I call her Carrie." Patting me on the shoulder, he added, "Don't worry. She's completely harmless."

Dad and Chiq were speechless. I felt immensely privileged and oddly peaceful as I crawled back into bed, far too excited to sleep.

Lulu, by the way, still lives in Arcadia, and she and her children take the ghost's presence for granted. "She's very thoughtful," Lulu tells me. "Often, when it's raining, she will have gone into the children's room and closed all the windows."

=

Most of the time, Dad, Chiq, and I got along fine. But I must have been harboring a good deal of anger, the only explanation I can give for the summer afternoon when I decapitated all of my stepmother's prized daylilies. Bored on a hot, listless day, I'd been examining the Japanese sword Dad had brought back from the war. Then, imagining myself a warrior, I walked into the garden and with many furious swipes beheaded every lily in sight. That evening I caught hell from Chiq. It consisted of a brief, icy speech: "Go to your room and don't come out." All the while, Dad just stood there, silent and furious.

The moment I closed the door to my room, I burst into tears. Nobody ever asked me why I'd cut off the heads of those daylilies. And if they had, I'm sure I couldn't have told them.

My father and I were perfectly friendly, but there was always a gulf between us. I never spoke to him about my mother, and he never volunteered anything about her. Having a son who was more than a snapshot in his wallet was as new an experience for him as having a real father was for me. He insisted I take piano lessons, and I did, hating every second of them. I found it harder and harder to sit inside and practice when I'd so much rather be bouncing a tennis ball against the back of the house, or running down the road to throw a football with the Paley kid, Jeffrey, or exploring in the gardens of the Phipps estate in Old Westbury with Nonie Phipps.

During his first year of marriage to Chiq, Dad and his band seldom traveled outside New York City, so that he could come home after the last set. I rarely heard him play one of the two pianos in the living room. Nor did he ever come over to the piano while I was doing my detested practicing. My progress was still at the "Skaters' Waltz" level, and the way I played it, nobody would have waltzed. The closest we got to playing duets was one rainy afternoon when he showed me the bass part to "Heart and Soul"—the eight-bar vamp of which he used to open his sets.

He was more interested in talking with me about sports, especially baseball. One of our few real discussions of any sort was a long-running argument over who was the greater player, Joe DiMaggio or Ted Williams. Dad, coming from Boston, was a rabid Red Sox fan. I lived for the Yankees.

Whenever there was a Red Sox–Yankees game in New York and Dad was free, he'd take me to Yankee Stadium, where we'd sit with Toots in his box at field level, right on the third-base line. Those were wonderful days. Everyone else in Toots's box, except Dad, was a Yankee fan: Earl Warren, the governor of California, or Jim Farley, the postmaster general, or John Daly, the host of the TV show *What's My Line?*, or Bob Considine, the Hearst columnist. They all treated me like one of them and seemed very impressed by my knowledge of baseball statistics. I felt a little superior to Dad, because he couldn't cheer as loudly for his team as I could for mine. But he didn't seem to mind, and I loved seeing him so relaxed and happy.

Dad had the last say in the Williams-DiMaggio argument when I came home one afternoon after a baseball game at the Sands Point Club. "There's someone out back," he said. "He wants to say hello."

Sitting under the umbrella by the pool was Joe DiMaggio. I stopped dead in my tracks. To have him right in our own backyard! When he got up and said, "Nice to see you again, kid," I couldn't say a word. I was never more impressed with Dad in my life.

=

We had one terrible fight. There was an old playhouse on the edge of the property, and one afternoon I lured two neighborhood girls into it to play doctor. The three of us were scared and excited as hell as we stripped and began poking around. I examined them. They took turns examining me. That evening, one of the girls ratted to her mother.

I was sorting through baseball cards in my bedroom when Dad grabbed hold of me and hauled me into the living room. He sat me down in a chair and placed himself in another, facing me. What had I *done* with those girls? Did I know what a *terrible* thing it was?

I didn't say a word. Not since Ave had yelled at me for hitting the dog had an adult spoken to me like this. And when it was over, I knew that Dad wasn't going to pat me on the shoulder and take me on a buggy ride.

"Answer me, Peter!" he shouted. "*Answer* me!"

But I wouldn't.

Finally he gave up and walked out. It was Chiquita's turn. She came in glaring. Then her European sophistication got the better of her. "Look," she said. "Never mind. Your father is very angry, but it will pass." It did.

=

My school, Eaglebrook, was set high in the western Massachusetts hills and seemed like an extension of Arden, with the plus that I had friends my own age for the first time. Eaglebrook catered to kids who needed a structure they couldn't get at home, because of divorce or family problems. (Harry Whitney had preceded me, which I guess is why I'd been sent there.) Our days were as tightly organized and regimented as the Marine Corps. You got up, scrubbed your face, assembled at the flagpole, said the Pledge of Allegiance, and marched off to breakfast—everyone in the same uniform: black blazer with red piping, button-down white or blue shirt, blue-and-red-striped tie, gray flannels, brown shoes. You got the whole outfit, from top to bottom, by going into the boys' department at Lord & Taylor, which had a complete inventory of the uniforms for every prep and pre-prep school in the East.

The facilities were spartan. Our rooms were jerry-built "cubies," each containing a tiny desk, a bureau, and a bed, and separated from one another by the thinnest of partitions. It was an arrangement that invited staying awake long after lights-out, giggling, whispering, and jerking off *ensemble*.

Thurston Chase, Eaglebrook's headmaster, was a big, burly, gentle Quaker with salt-and-pepper hair who believed that a real education must include instruction in life's basic skills. Like Bill Kitchen, he had great faith in the moral benefits of working with your hands, especially with wood. Under the tutelage of Orvo, the patient, hulking Norwegian shop master, I discovered carpentry. Orvo, who could have crafted an entire Viking ship with his huge, gnarled hands, tried to inspire us to make objects of higher beauty. A duck? A tree? We worked on the lathe, endlessly sanding and shaping wooden bowls to be taken home and relegated to the back shelf of the pantry. I didn't give a damn about making bowls, ducks, or trees. I was obsessed with making the world's fastest snow boat, a six-to-nine-inch vehicle we used to race down specially designed icy courses.

All my mental energies the fall and winter of 1951, my fifth year at the school, went into the shaping of wooden pieces in an aerodynamic fashion, balancing them with lead weights, then applying lacquer and a thick coat of wax. Finally, when the first snow had fallen, I bolted into the cold with my buddies, all with our new, untried snow boats in our mittened hands. We raced to the hill and began building the complex courses down which our missiles would fly like greased lightning.

On the morning of February 9, I had awakened with one thought in mind: to get through classes and down that hill faster than ever. The bell went off at seven, and we trooped outside to the flagpole. The snow was perfect—six new inches. The classes were the usual: chemistry (at which I was terrible), math (equally terrible), Latin (not so good), history (pretty good), English (very good). Lunch was the usual sodden macaroni and cheese. I gobbled it down and raced out to the slopes. I'd made one run and was trudging back up the hill when a friend came over and said, "Hey, Pete, the head wants you in his office. On the double."

Mr. Chase's face would go into the most wonderful smile when he was about to say the most serious thing. He came to the door, beaming that crinkly smile. He put his arm around my shoulder and in his kindliest voice said, "Peter, your dad's taken a turn for the worse. We think it best that you go down to New York."

I nodded, my mind still out on the slopes. He added, "Oh, by the way, Reverend Houghton will be going down with you."

I hadn't taken in the fact that my father was actually dying of cancer. A year earlier, he and Chiquita had been planning a trip to Europe when he'd noticed a persistent sore on his left heel. They'd gone to a doctor, and the trip had been postponed. Since then, Dad had been in and out of New York Hospital. But I'd never heard anyone say the word *leukemia*—not that I'd have known what it meant. Nor had anybody said he might *die*. I only knew that he was sick—and sick people got better.

We had had one memorable conversation in the hospital just before he came home for what turned out to be his last Christmas with Chiq and me and our Manhasset neighbors, Jock and Betsey Whitney, Bill and Babe Paley, and Donald and Jean Stralem. I had made up my mind that I didn't want to play the piano anymore. I had tried it for *his* sake, and it just didn't interest me.

Dad took the news well: "That's perfectly all right," he said. "We'll agree, and the three of us—you, Chiquita, and I—will sign a piece of paper and instruct Eaglebrook not to teach you any more piano."

That was that. A letter was written, which the three of us signed. With immense relief, I delivered it to the music teacher at Eaglebrook. He seemed relieved as well.

That Christmas, Dad had looked great—up and around with his pals, carrying on like the healthiest man in the world. He'd put a new pair of Northland skis for me under the tree in the den, and while I was unwrapping them, he'd said, "I'm going to lick this disease, Peter. And when I do, we're all going to take a big trip somewhere."

"Absolutely," Chiq had said. "Let's go to Spain!"

As I stood with my suitcase and Reverend Houghton on the snowy platform, waiting for the afternoon train, I couldn't imagine why I was being sent to New York. We took window seats, facing each other. Reverend Houghton had always seemed perfectly nice in a rather formal, distant way, but now he seemed uncomfortably agitated, crossing and recrossing his legs, clearing his throat a lot, and trying too hard to make conversation: Was I *enjoying* myself at Eaglebrook that year? He'd heard that I had a "musical interest." How *splendid*! He was *awfully* glad I'd taken an interest in "the Edey boy"—nothing like a *good* friend. Then he went into his Reverend mode, launching into an Episcopalian litany about my "privileged upbringing," but "don't take that for granted . . . give back more than you receive . . ." et cetera, et cetera.

All the while, I mumbled answers and stared out the window as the Grandma Moses scenery flew by.

A faint alarm went off when we pulled into Grand Central Station. To my surprise, there was Ave, standing on the platform in his dark blue overcoat and gray felt hat, with a rolled-up *Times* under his arm.

"It was wonderful riding with you, Peter, you're a good boy," Reverend Houghton said. He patted me on the head and walked off.

"Hi, Pete," Ave said. He bent down to kiss me. I responded as I always did, kissing him on the cheek.

"Hi, Ave."

"Well, we're going back to our house."

I nodded, wondering what this was all about. Ave reached down to take hold of my suitcase.

"That's OK," I said, picking it up myself.

It was cold, and we set off at a brisk pace. We were passing a newsstand when I said, "How's Dad?"

Ave stopped, slowly turned, and looked me right in the eye. Ave's face had never given away much. Now it showed a real sadness. Gruffly he said, "Your father died this morning, Pete."

The suitcase left my grip and toppled over on its side. My eyes blurred, and I had a watery vision of the week's magazine covers: *Time, Newsweek, Collier's,* the *Saturday Evening Post.*

"I don't believe it."

"One doesn't kid about things like that, Pete."

Ave put his arm around me and held me tight. "Your father died with no pain. He died a hero. Just before he died, he was given a citation by the secretary of the Navy for the things he did in the war."

I managed to get the suitcase right side up. Holding me tight, Ave led me outside.

"Walter," he said, pointing toward the black Zephyr, "is over there."

The house on East Eighty-first Street to which Ma and Ave had recently moved was filled with mourners. Chiq ran down the red-carpeted stairs into the marble foyer and hugged me hard under the Walt Kuhn painting of a circus clown. She was sobbing. "Everything will be OK," she said. When we entered the big room upstairs, everyone stopped talking.

Ma came over. Behind her dark glasses, she was crying. She pulled me into her.

I felt a hand on my shoulder. It was Toots. He bent down and whispered, "I've just sat in one of Marie's chairs, and the goddamn thing collapsed on me. Come help me pick it up."

With his ex-bouncer's skill, he steered me out of the room. "There it is," he said, pointing to the broken chair in the corner. "You gotta help me, Pete."

Which I did.

=

More than forty years later, sitting with my stepmother in the lobby at Claridge's, I heard how my father died.

"Did he know he had leukemia?"

"Not from me," Chiq replied. "I certainly didn't want to *face* it. I knew what he had, but I didn't want to tell him. The funny thing is, all the time he was sick, I sort of forgot about it. Finally, when the doctor pulled me aside and said, 'We can give Mr. Duchin an extra day or week or we can let him go, but we need your permission one way or the other,' I told him to forget it, just let him go. That was the moment I knew."

"Could Dad talk?"

"Yes, but the last couple of days he was under an oxygen tent."

"So he ended in the place I began . . ."

She smiled. "Funny, I never thought of that before."

"How was it when he died?"

"It was quite a scene. We were drinking champagne, and your Aunt Lillian came in. I can see her face now: she was absolutely horrified. 'What?' she said. 'Drinking champagne?' Her eyes went to Eddy's right hand. He was clutching a Catholic relic of St. Jude, the saint of lost causes. I'd got it from a church near the hospital. Poor Lil nearly passed out. I guess she thought I'd made him a Catholic! A few hours later, he died."

With Chiquita at Dad's funeral in 1951.

"You still miss him."

Chiq looked at me. "I'll tell you right now, Peter. Eddy was the only person I was ever absolutely in love with."

"I knew that."

≡

My father was cremated, and his ashes were scattered over the Atlantic from a Navy combat plane. Years later, Aunt Lil told me that my grandmother Duchin had been very hurt by this, because cremation is a violation of the Jewish faith. However, one day when she was visiting her daughter in Florida, she and Aunt Lil went for a swim in the ocean. Standing chest-deep in the water, my grandmother, a woman of eighty, took off her bathing cap and loosened her long black and gray hair so that it floated around her like seaweed.

According to Aunt Lil, she said, "Now I know why Eddy didn't want to be buried. I can feel him all around me."

9

"WHO'S PLAYING CLARINET?"

The first really close friend I made of my own age was a kid named Maitland Edey, who arrived at Eaglebrook in the eighth grade. Right away I spotted him as a maverick. Even though he was a fairly big guy with good coordination, he didn't go out for football like everybody else. Instead he signed up for soccer, which in those days was for weenies. Mait had a round face and a cowlick a mile long. He wore glasses and had an unpredictable, contagious laugh. There was an interesting look in his eyes, slightly amused and far-away. This guy's a little different, I thought. Like me.

Mait was assigned the room next to mine, and I got to know him better. I liked his honesty, his plain, worn clothes. I liked it that he was so articulate. Before long, we got to talking about things I'd never discussed with anyone my own age before. We were both fascinated by *The Nature of the Universe* by Fred Hoyle, and we'd sit outside on the hillside and ponder the stars, planets, and constellations, wondering how they all came to be there and whether such a thing as infinity really exists.

We talked a lot about religion. We read aloud from the Greek myths. Our favorite was the story of Ulysses, which we loved for its adventures of survival against the odds and its image of Penelope, the wife of infinite loyalty—our ideal woman. Mait compared his dalmatian, Ace, with Ulysses' dog, Argus, who had been the only one to recognize the wanderer when he finally returned home. I yearned for a dog.

Mait didn't give a damn about making an impression, and he seemed so much more in touch with important things than I was that I felt like an idiot. But after a while, I opened up.

One day he said, "I suppose I'm an atheist."

I was shocked. "I'm more a pantheist, I think," I said. "I mean, I feel that if there is God, He is in nature and He's a part of all things in nature."

"Well," Mait said with a wry smile, "which came first, God or Nature? Or was it Man who created God to explain the mysteries around him?"

I don't remember my answer, but I remember that our adolescent probing into philosophical issues continued—along with our discussions of the mystery of girls. Most of all, we talked about music, especially jazz.

Even though I hated to practice the piano, I had a good ear—a gift inherited from my father, perhaps. I've never been terribly good at reading music. I would hear one of the hit songs on the radio—"Ain't Misbehavin'," "The Naughty Lady of Shady Lane," "Walkin' My Baby Back Home"—and I'd go to the piano in the

My best friend at Eaglebrook and then Hotchkiss was Maitland Edey.
We listened to jazz records endlessly, talked about girls, and took
motorbike trips through Europe in the summer. I even moved in with
his family for a while. In this photograph we're at Eddie Condon's
jazz club in New York, listening to Dixieland.

lodge and pick through the melody, trying to add the appropriate harmony.

One day that semester, a classmate, Fred Waring, Jr., the son and namesake of another famous bandleader, heard me fiddling around and asked if I'd like to join a Dixieland group he was organizing. I shrugged it off, thinking I wasn't good enough. Fred said that one of the masters had told him that putting a band together would get us invited to girls' schools. That did it. I joined my first band.

There were six of us: besides Fred, who was a damn good trombonist, there were a trumpet player, a drummer, a clarinetist, a bass player, and me. We got our material from the wife of the school band director, Archibald Swift, who lent us sheet music of popular tunes from which we'd improvise our primitive Dixieland arrangements. Mait, still a new boy at school, would sometimes linger in the lodge to listen to us practice.

One afternoon, back in my room, I got a knock on the door. It was Mait. "You want to hear something great?" he said.

I followed him into his room. There, neatly stacked on a shelf, was the biggest collection of records I'd ever seen: two dozen long-playing albums featuring Louis Armstrong and the Hot Fives and Sevens, the New Orleans Rhythm Kings, the Original Dixieland Jazz Band, Jelly Roll Morton, Bix Beiderbecke, and on and on.

"Listen to this."

He pulled down an Armstrong album, lifted the lid of his record player, and lowered the disk onto the spindle. He lay back on the bed.

While I perched at the foot of it, "Lonesome Blues" filled the room. I'd been an Armstrong fan for years, but listening to him with someone else was a whole new experience.

Mait asked, "Guess who's playing clarinet?"

My first band. Me, Mait Edey, Dave Ross, and
Roswell Rudd at Hotchkiss.

I had no idea.

"Johnny Dodds."

I nodded.

"Who's the drummer?"

"Beats me."

"Baby Dodds. That's Johnny's brother. Ask me who's on piano."

"Who's on piano?"

"Lil Hardin Armstrong. That's Louis's wife—she also wrote the tune. Banjo?"

I shook my head.

"Look at the album."

I read the name out loud: "Johnny St. Cyr."

"Right!"

So began a game that continued throughout our friendship— two years at Eaglebrook, three years at Hotchkiss, vacations from college. As our record collections grew larger, the hours got longer as we'd sit glued to the phonograph, quizzing each other about who was playing what instrument. Our taste expanded from Armstrong and Bix to Teddy Wilson, Billie Holiday, and Benny Goodman, and eventually to Thelonious Monk, Charlie Parker, Dizzy Gillespie, and Miles Davis.

Years later, when Mait and I were touring the south of France on Lambrettas, we were circling through the town of Juan-les-Pins one evening, looking for girls, when we squealed to a stop. "Sidney Bechet!" we both exclaimed. There in an open tent in the town square was the great Bechet, one of our real favorites, soaring on his soprano sax. It was beautiful beyond anything we'd ever experienced.

Mait loved the outdoors as much as I. We'd go on long walks in the woods around Eaglebrook and just talk—about girls, about things we'd read. Most of all, we'd talk about who was the better pianist: Jelly Roll Morton or James P. Johnson? Earl Hines or Fats Waller? "The Boss," of course, was Art Tatum.

We had the same sense of mischief. We'd sneak into the school kitchen and steal big cans of tuna fish rather than eat the usual glop. We had our own names for each other and our own language. He was Ede. I was Duch. People who didn't appreciate music and poetry were "apes." We called creative writing "waxing." If one of us suggested a walk in the woods, it was "Let's go dig!" One afternoon we hollowed out some corncobs, filled them with the corn silk, inserted a little wooden tube in each cob, and struck a match. Then we inhaled. Then we got sick.

≡

The Easter vacation after Dad died, I went down to Hobe Sound to stay with Ma and Ave. There I fell in love for the first time. Her name was Paula Denckla. She was a wild-looking girl, four or five years older than I was, with an enormous mane of black hair. For days I watched her from afar, casting long glances and getting nowhere. Finally, I made my move.

One night, during a dance at the beach club, I got myself included in a group of older kids who were leaving for a party at Paula's. Someone suggested a midnight swim. I charged into the ocean with the others, splashed around, and climbed out looking for Paula—only to discover that she and her friends had vanished into her mother's house, without a nod at me. I sat down on the sand. I was thinking I'd better go home when I heard a voice next to me.

Her name was Holly, and she was a year or two older than her friend Paula. She was blonde, athletic-looking, and very tanned. When she asked what I was studying in school, I said, "My studies are over."

She looked doubtful. "What? You're not in school?"

I was off and running. "Well, I go to Yale in the fall."

"That's wonderful. What do you plan to major in?"

"Music."

"Oh, that's right. Your dad was Eddy—" She stopped.

I'd heard this a hundred times before. "That's OK."

Her eyes sparkled in the moonlight. I reached out and touched a bare leg . . . a soft hand.

"You must feel so awful. . . . Paula told me . . ."

"Yes . . ."

I kissed her. She kissed me back. Then she pulled away.

"No. Not here. I have to get back."

I saw Holly several times again that vacation, but never alone. Back at Eaglebrook, I wrote her passionate, ridiculous letters. Mait and I would lie around, leafing through poetry books, lifting things from Millay, Byron, and Shelley. I got one breezy reply from Holly. She said she'd be starting a job in New York City in June. In other words, I was free to call.

=

The fact of my father's death didn't really sink in until my graduation from Eaglebrook that spring. Chiq, along with Ma and Ave and the Stralems, came up to see me get my diploma, and they were all immensely supportive. But what I felt most was my father's absence. All my classmates were surrounded by real fathers and real mothers—people who had the same last name when they were introduced. The presence of my weird little "family" was gratifying, but it was still weird.

I thought of the time before Dad had gotten sick when he'd come up to Eaglebrook and given a concert. When he sat down to play, he made me cringe with embarrassment. "Peter asked me to

knock out a few tunes for you kids," he said, "and I didn't want to
get in Dutch with him, so here goes!" I remembered wishing his
piano style weren't so frilly. Why didn't he punch the keys like
Count Basie? Why didn't he *swing*? But he made a huge hit, and
afterward my buddies came over and clapped me on the shoulder
and said, "Your dad's really great!"

Thirty-five years later, when my younger son, Colin, was at Eaglebrook, I played in the same hall for the entire school. I made a
point of *not* mentioning my son's name, but afterward he said he'd
felt exactly as I had—proud and embarrassed.

Now, as I stepped forward to receive my diploma from Mr.
Chase, I thought of Dad's triumph. How I wished he could have
been there to hear the applause—this time for me.

=

At Chiq's insistence, I'd gotten myself a summer job in Sun Valley
as a member of the resort crew, building ski trails and cleaning up
Baldy Mountain for the coming ski season. Between leaving Eagle-
brook and flying out to Idaho, I had a week in the city, staying with
Ma and Ave at Eighty-first Street. The first thing I did was call up
Holly.

"How about *An American in Paris* at the Music Hall?"

"I'd love to."

After the lights went up, we danced out of the Music Hall and
straight down Fifty-first Street to Toots Shor's. Toots threw me a
sharp look when I introduced him to Holly. There was no problem
ordering a beer. After dinner, no check. The only bumpy moment
came when Toots sat down and Holly said, "Isn't it great that
Peter's going to Yale next year?"

Toots's eyes bulged at me. Then he bellowed, "Sure is!"

Holly's place was in Greenwich Village, a walk-up on Sheridan Square. As we climbed the stoop, she took my hand.

"Would you like to come up for a drink?"

"I'd love to."

She turned the key. "I'm going to do you a big favor," she whispered.

It was easy, exciting, and over in a flash. Afterward, I examined myself in the bathroom mirror to see if I looked bigger. When I came out, Holly had on her bathrobe.

"It was wonderful," she said, "but maybe you'd better go."

I hesitated at the door.

"Have a great year at Hotchkiss," she whispered as she kissed me good night.

≡

Hotchkiss, in the northwest corner of Connecticut's Litchfield County, is a magnificent place: acres of white-trimmed brick in the foothills of the Berkshires, with Alpine views of lakes and farms and valleys. Although it's miles from the nearest town of any size, it didn't feel isolated. The school's atmosphere of learning was as open as the vistas. Everything was available to us: the forest trails, the library, the rolling golf course; most of all, teachers who loved to teach. For me, the brightest lights were Albert Sly, the school organist; Malcolm Willis, the music teacher who lured me back to the piano; and Dick Gurney, the English teacher, fly fisherman, and baseball coach, who gave me permission to write my English exams in verse. Fortunately, they've not been saved.

Before Hotchkiss, I'd learned about the world by being physical with it. At Hotchkiss I discovered another way: *listening*. My first serious musical education began at the morning chapel services, with the organ music of Bach and Schütz played by Al Sly. A shy, reserved, balding man with black-rimmed glasses and unnaturally white skin that reddened when he got excited, Al would invite me, Mait, and other music lovers into his rooms to listen to recordings of Bach's St. John and St. Matthew passions and the B-minor mass, which he thought was the greatest piece of music ever written. I thought so, too, and I still do. Al's rooms were simply furnished, but the world they opened up to me was indescribably rich. Listening to Bach, I felt a great ordering of things. Everything I had been straining to understand about music suddenly fit together: the harmonies, the bass lines, the rhythms—all the confusions were resolved.

At Hotchkiss I started practicing piano seriously, progressing from the dreaded "Spinning Song" to the Mozart sonatas. I joined a Dixieland band called The Syncopators. There were a half dozen of us, including Dave Ross, who later became a fine poet, on trumpet, and Roswell Rudd, who became a first-class trombonist. Mait dabbled at the piano (more boogie-woogie than anything else), and he'd come around and kibitz. We spent hours playing with blues changes. ("Blues in F" was our favorite number.) We'd try duplicating the solos on records by Armstrong and Bix. Since there was no leader, we'd just sit down and play.

I loved the uncompetitive nature of those sessions. To me, they were far more satisfying than being on the baseball and ski teams. Not that I didn't love those sports, but winning didn't mean that much to me—just as it's never bothered me when a fish slips off my line.

The Syncopators provided the music at the rare school dance. On those occasions I discovered something else: I loved playing for people. It wasn't that I liked being listened to. It just felt great to be giving everybody a good time.

I signed up for the Glee Club, which was directed by Al Sly. Like my father, I wasn't any good at singing, but the Glee Club was the best ticket to girls. We were allowed only one weekend a semester away from school, and we were desperate for them—or at least the next best thing, which was getting hold of a girl's picture. Returning with this trophy from Miss Hall's, Miss Porter's, or Ethel Walker, you'd Scotch-tape it to your dresser mirror. It meant you had "soul." Since smoking was forbidden, many of us smoked like chimneys, Luckies and Camels being the coolest brands. We did our lighting up in the woods. One afternoon after a few smokes in a cave by the lake, Mait and I solemnly made small incisions in our right wrists with our penknives. Then we crossed our wrists together and bound them with a handkerchief while the blood flowed. We were brothers for life.

From Al Sly and Malcolm Willis, my piano teacher, I learned that music has meaning, that it isn't just a bunch of notes put down at random but something *made* out of thoughts, feelings, and imagination. Mr. Willis, a fine classical pianist (and Sanskrit scholar) with a little goatee, taught by example and analysis. He'd play a sonata by Beethoven and explain that there was a reason why the phrase had to be played just so if it was to connect with the material that had come before and the material that followed.

Hotchkiss awakened a love of classical music that has been one of the deepest constants in my life. Even then, I knew I'd never be a concert pianist—I just didn't have the chops for it. My fingers are stubby and peasantlike, gardener's fingers. There was no way I could get through Chopin's "Revolutionary Étude" at top speed. In fact, playing the piano has never come naturally to me. It's what I do because I've done it for so long.

At Hotchkiss there was no anti-intellectual bias. It was as cool to be in music as it was to be a jock. It was even cooler to be obsessed

In my room at Hotchkiss. Since smoking was forbidden,
we smoked like stoves.

with a weird poet or an obscure mathematician. Dick Gurney made the poetry of Byron, Shelley, Keats, and Coleridge so real— so personal—that we all wanted to read it. Another English teacher, Charlie Garside, once got so carried away with explaining a particularly beautiful line of Milton's that he leapt out the second-story window to make his point. It was at Hotchkiss that one of my best pals, Ned Bradley, discovered the beauties of Horace and Lucretius, which led him to become a classics professor at Dartmouth. It was cool to read—to be seen immersed in Hermann Hesse's *Steppenwolf* or the writings of C. S. Lewis or *Arrowsmith* by the other Lewis.

Another teacher who meant a great deal to me was Robert Hawkins, who taught grammar. "The Hawk" was a friend of Lakeville's most illustrious resident, the legendary Bach harpsichordist Wanda Landowska. One day I found myself, along with three or four other musical types, invited to tea at Madame Landowska's. She lived on a shady knoll in a big, dark frame house that might have been transplanted from her native Poland. Following the Hawk into her cavernous, wood-paneled living room, I had a feeling not unlike the one I had when I'd first encountered Joe DiMaggio.

Madame Landowska was a tiny woman with enormous black eyes and an enormous nose. She was dressed all in black: a fearsome crow. We nibbled hard cookies on a worn old sofa in a room filled with pianos and harpsichords of strange shapes, the walls lined with photographs of the lady with bearded eminences from what seemed to be another century. After we were settled and hushed, she seated herself at one of the instruments and tore into a Bach prelude and fugue with electrifying intensity.

I've often wondered what accounts for the power you feel around great artists. It's a feeling I would later experience with

Fred Astaire, Arthur Rubinstein, and Lester Young—maybe a couple of others. At Hotchkiss, I became a terrible snob about artists. Mait and I agreed that they were at the top of humanity's pecking order. All others were "apes."

≡ ·

In the postwar fifties, it was assumed that adventure, freedom, romance, the *world,* were all there on the other side of the Atlantic. Spending a summer in England, France, or Italy before college was mandatory. I had my first European adventure between my junior and senior years at Hotchkiss, when I signed on for a bike tour in France.

There were about a dozen of us, all under the wing of a master and his wife from St. Mark's School. Both of them, as I think back on it, were remarkably cool. One day, somewhere in the south of France, four of us decided to split off from the group. The only thing our leader said was "Fine, but you'd better be in Paris on such and such a day."

One of the renegades was a kid named Johnny Loudon, who looked so much like me that we were often taken for twins. After we'd been on the road a couple of days, Johnny and I got sick of cycling and decided to peel off from the other two. We hopped a train and ended up in Saint-Tropez. In those days, before it was discovered by Brigitte Bardot, Saint Trop was the prettiest fishing village in France. Black American jazz musicians had just begun to come there. It was cheap and beautiful, and they were respected and admired by the French. "There is no color line here," one of them told us. "These cats are really cool." From there, a train took us to Nice, then to Geneva, so we could see whether the castle of Chillon lived up to Byron's description of it. It did.

I wanted to check out the music school in Lausanne, so we cycled there. We were coming into town just after dark when we spotted a beautiful stretch of grass and a sign we thought was French for "Camping." We peed in the bushes. We unrolled our sleeping bags and stretched out on the grass. We went blissfully to sleep. In the morning, we were awakened by a sound I'd never heard before—the twittering of thirty nuns. We had just spent the night on the front lawn of their convent.

They took us in, clothed us, fed us, and washed our clothes. One of the sisters was extremely cute, and though she wouldn't let me near her, the memory of her lasted well into my senior year—a siren whose image I could conjure up whenever I felt the call of Europe.

=

A few months after my father died, Chiq had sold our house on Shelter Rock Road to Leland Hayward, the agent and theatrical producer (and father of my second wife, Brooke). For the next couple of years, my home had been the two-bedroom apartment Chiq had taken in the Hotel Carlyle on Madison Avenue. Not that I was often there. Whenever I showed up, Chiq seemed delighted to see me. But our bond was tenuous. She was rebuilding her own life, and apart from the several summers we spent together in Sun Valley, we began seeing less and less of each other.

It was in Sun Valley that she met her new husband, a nice, quiet outdoorsman named Morgan Heap, who worked for the Sun Valley Corporation. Morgan knew horses extremely well, and they seemed to respond instinctively to him. It wasn't like being with Ave, skilled as he was with horses. Ave's horses had always seemed nervous around him, as though they knew he was about to discipline them or push them to their fullest on the polo field. Around Morgan, horses were calm. They behaved as if he were one of them.

Morgan was also a great shot. Later that summer, we rode out into the high sagebrush, where he taught me how to shoot dove. He walked with the slight stiffness of someone who has been in the saddle much of his life, and I never saw him miss a bird. When we said good-bye, he gave me a magnificent pair of cowboy boots. I wore them at Hotchkiss that fall and got hooted at. At Hotchkiss, moccasins or white bucks with their hideous pink soles were the shoes of social acceptability. The boots went into the closet, never to be worn except when I was on my own.

The following summer, Chiq and I had gone out to Sun Valley again. I was very glad to see Morgan, and so was Chiq. Morgan blushed whenever I caught them together, and I wasn't surprised when they announced they were getting married. I'd hoped Chiq would move to Sun Valley so I could come out to ride and shoot with Morgan and ski for free on the mountain. But Chiq had insisted on living back East. They bought a beautiful historic farm in Frederick, Maryland—Chiq thinking, I suppose, that it would be rural enough for Morgan and close enough to New York for her. But Morgan didn't much take to the Kool-Aid-colored linen pants and blue blazers at the local club. And he didn't know what to do with himself in New York. For exercise he'd walk around the entire circumference of Manhattan, every day. I had a feeling their marriage wouldn't last very long, and it didn't.

$$=$$

Though Chiq's doors were open to me, I preferred spending weekends and vacations with Harry Whitney and his wife, Axie, at their crazy old house in Chestnut Hill, Philadelphia. Axie was an earthy woman, a sculptress, with spectacular, Cleopatra-like, wide-apart eyes. She had an unlimited ability to put up with Harry's shenanigans, which were more pronounced than ever: his insane car racing, his tearing off on archaeological digs to the Middle East or a remote Pacific island, his solitary excursions into the Adirondacks to stalk deer, his passion for opera, his motorcycles. She even followed him around on her own motorcycle, which I thought was extremely cool. Ma adored her but thought she was a bit nuts to put up with Harry the way she did.

Everything was a bit nuts around Harry. The neighborhood was classy, but what you were likely to see as you approached the Whitney house was a motorcycle in a hundred pieces on the front lawn, or the eggplant-colored Allard getting a touch-up in the driveway, or a couple of Harry's buddies working on their Formula Two racing cars out by the garage. Inside, Harry might be having a discussion in the living room about the possibilities of Bucky Fuller's geodesic dome for low-income housing with his friend the visionary landscape architect Ian McHarg, while *The Magic Flute* blasted at full volume through the hi-fi. I was intoxicated.

In the meantime, I'd found another home—the Edeys' estate in Brookville, Long Island. During our junior year at Hotchkiss, Mait asked his mother if she and Mr. Edey could adopt me. A formal adoption wasn't in the cards. But Mrs. Edey went to my guardians, Donald Stralem and Chiquita, and asked if it would be all right for me to regard the Edey household as my "home away from school." They agreed. And so I moved in with the Edeys—into the big room above the garage where Mait and I could fantasize all night about girls, the poetry of Edna St. Vincent Millay, and jazz.

Maitland Edey, Sr., was a top editor at *Life* magazine, a good-looking man, charming and outgoing, one of those adults who makes an effort with kids. He was a fine athlete and competitor, terrific at tennis and bridge, and an avid sailor. When I once asked if I could fish from his boat, he looked at me in mock horror and said, "Peter, the only fish that will ever touch my deck will be an errant flying fish."

I thought Mait even luckier with his mother. Helen Edey was a civilized, hyper-intelligent woman who had become a psychiatrist after giving birth to four children. She was the first adult I'd ever met who seemed genuinely curious about who I was and how I would turn out. One evening I got brave enough to say I was worried that my birth might have caused my mother's death. Helen stopped what she was doing and looked me straight in the eye. "Why do you think so?" she asked.

I told her that in the scrapbooks from my childhood, my nurses had obliterated all references to my mother's death. This brought out the shrink in Helen: "Have you ever talked to anyone about this?"

I hadn't.

"Well," she suggested, "it might not be a bad idea sometime. In the meantime, remember that many people use past events like this as excuses for their eccentric behavior. You don't seem to be consciously bothered by it, but the more you try to be honest about your deepest feelings about your mother's death and the more you come to grips with them, the saner and healthier you'll be."

Nobody had ever talked this way to me before. The kind people who had raised me had been determined to put a bright face on anything that might disturb me, or pretend it hadn't happened at all. It was as though I were to be kept in a state of permanent innocence, forever in that oxygen tent. Helen Edey made me realize that although *I* wasn't to blame for my mother's death, I was responsible for the feelings it stirred up in me, and they were better faced than hidden.

What I respected about her most was her sense of standards. She had thought carefully about right and wrong and had passed those thoughts along to Mait. Until now, I had seen anger in adults as a reaction, a sudden, mysterious reflex. When Helen disapproved of something, you felt her reaction as the expression of a deep morality, one she'd been cultivating for years.

Helen didn't give a damn about style. Unlike Ma or Chiq, who cared enormously about what things—and they—looked like, Helen had no interest in decor or fashion. To her, what mattered were things of the mind and the emotions. I was used to adults gushing over me because of who my father was. But Helen didn't seem the least bit impressed by Eddy Duchin, and I liked her all the more for it.

What I liked best about staying at the Edeys' was the feeling of being part of a "normal" family—one that was bound together by nature. Now I see that things were a little more complicated.

After Mait, the eldest Edey, came his brother, Kelly, one and a half years younger, a sensitive, deeply self-involved, perhaps lonely child. Early on, he showed a great interest in clocks, and today his collection of antique timepieces is one of the finest in the world and his horological opinions are sought out by museums. Their sister, Beatrice, seemed to us to be a conventional girl who had her heart set on doing good. Marion, the youngest, marched to her own, different drummer. She spoke of "hearing voices" and grew up to become a well-known environmentalist.

I liked all of them for their individuality and the freedom with which they spoke up at the dinner table. I had never been in a family where what had happened during the day was subject for discussion in the evening. Mait and I had read that Edna St. Vincent Millay had called her parents Mumbles and Daddles, and we conferred those names on his parents.

=

As inseparable as Mait and I were, there were pronounced differences between us. One Thanksgiving, Kate Roosevelt Whitney, a close friend from Manhasset, invited us down to Greenwood, her stepfather John Hay Whitney's plantation in Thomasville, Georgia. It was a huge, wonderful place that seemed to be used strictly for shooting quail, dove, and wild turkey. One of the other guests was John "Shipwreck" Kelly, the famous all-American football player and a great crony of Jock's.

A towering, stormy figure, he suddenly interrupted everyone at dinner to ask if Mait and I were joining the quail shoot the next morning.

"You bet!" I said. "Can't wait!"

Shipwreck cast his gimlet gaze on Mait, who was looking down at his plate. "How about it, kid? You a good wing shot?"

"Well, sir," Mait replied, "I don't think I'm going to go out and shoot because I don't believe in it. I think it's wrong."

There was dead silence. The eyes of the servants, standing with the silver trays, went heavenward.

"What are you?" Shipwreck bellowed. "Some kind of goddamn *nature* boy?"

Mait stared at him.

A woman jumped in. "I think he's *very* courageous—"

She was drowned out by Shipwreck. "Well, that's what I'm going to call you . . . *Nature Boy!*"

Jock Whitney, the nicest of men, threw a disapproving look at his buddy. Turning to Mait, he said, "Don't let it bother you, son. You certainly don't have to shoot with us. But do come and ride."

Mait smiled. The moment passed. But from then on, whenever I ran into Shipwreck, he'd greet me with "How's your friend, *Nature Boy?*"

"Just fine," I'd say, thinking about what guts my friend Mait had.

10

YOUTHFUL
IMPROVISATIONS

Mait and I went on from Hotchkiss to different colleges—he to Princeton because it was his father's alma mater, I to Yale because of its music school, where the curriculum had been set up by Paul Hindemith.

I was anything but a mainstream Yalie, which in those days meant belonging to a group: fraternity, athletic team, political club, campus publication, singing ensemble. I went out for no teams except the most inept one of all—the ski team, which finished dead last in the Dartmouth Winter Carnival. I turned down all offers to pledge a fraternity, though I occasionally got hired to play at fraternity parties. I wasn't a joiner, and I put down those who were. My only fraternity was the effete Elizabethan Club, which I joined more for its croquet course than for the discussions of Shakespeare and Marlowe over skinless cucumber sandwiches and weak tea.

Quite a few of my buddies from Hotchkiss were also in New Haven, and we formed something of a clique, united by our disdain for the Yale traditions, our love of the arts, and our freshman adviser, Rick Haynes. Rick, a terrifically smart, handsome, black law student who later became the U.S. ambassador to Algeria, would invite us over to his rooms, where we'd sit around discussing Plato and a civil rights leader named Martin Luther King, Jr. We'd all read Ralph Ellison's *Invisible Man,* and we white boys were fascinated by what it was like being a Negro in America. Once Rick and his girlfriend, Anna, a fellow law-school student, realized that our interest was genuine, they opened up. In those days Rick was one of very few black students at Yale. Looking back on those all-night bull sessions, I am moved by how fervently all of us, white and black, believed in the absolute necessity of integration.

In my sophomore year, I became close to another slightly older man, Mike Forrestal. Mike, whose father, James Forrestal, committed suicide when he was secretary of defense in the Truman administration, had been taken in by the Harrimans and included as part of the family. With his brilliant legal mind and interest in foreign affairs, he had become a protégé of Ave, accompanying him to Moscow several times. He would later run the Vietnam desk as an assistant to John Kennedy's national security adviser, McGeorge Bundy.

I'd always thought of Mike as a rather distant older brother, but since he wasn't interested in athletics or the outdoors, he hadn't become a real pal like Harry Whitney. I had once taken great pleasure in stealing a girl from him in Sun Valley. Mike always joked rather acidly about the incident, since at the time I'd been nineteen, the girl had been twenty-six, and he'd been thirty.

Tall, a little chubby, with very white skin and black-rimmed glasses, Mike had become the youngest partner in the ultra-Wasp New York law firm of Shearman and Sterling. Noticing that I was developing artistic interests, he decided to take me under his wing. His great passion was opera. (He would later become treasurer of the Met in New York.) Every so often when he was in New Haven interviewing prospects for his firm, he'd camp out in my rooms. I once suggested he interview Rick, who was about to graduate from the law school.

"What position is he in his class?" asked Mike.

I had no idea, but I replied that he had to be in the top third.

"I generally only interview the top *five*," Mike said rather snottily.

"Well, he's a wonderful guy," I said. "Also, he's a Negro."

"Negro?" replied Mike in mock horror. "We don't even have a *Jew*."

Such was 1955.

Mike always brought along the latest recordings of Mozart, Verdi, and Donizetti operas, which we'd play until all hours of the night. Behind his high, rather hysterical laugh, he was immensely attentive, very professorial. He insisted I read the librettos while the music was playing, pointing out moments of particular dramatic and musical interest. Thanks to Mike, I developed a liking for opera. Still, it never reached his and Harry Whitney's level of obsession—which I've always thought must have been an outlet for the inner turmoil they both lived with.

At Yale I made the serious decision to become a musician. I signed up for basic courses in harmony and counterpoint. I joined a jazz group of piano, sax, and bass, and on weekends we played in a seedy bar on Chapel Street. My new idol was the bebop stylist Bud Powell, whom I emulated by breaking up rhythms and reducing the melody to one-note stabs, embellished by darting, unexpected runs. I wasn't just playing the music, I was beginning to hear it. It's a funny thing about jazz: You can't really know it unless you play it. Spontaneity is so much its essence that it can't be codified like other music. A bunch of guys sit down together to play, and for no reason at all—or for a whole lot of reasons—one day it works, the next day it doesn't.

I wanted music to be my life, but I wasn't sure what sort of life that might be. Maybe a jazz pianist. Maybe a symphony conductor. Maybe, even, a serious composer. One day I got up the courage to sit in on a conducting class at the music school. The dozen or so other students were all aspiring music professionals, and as they got up, one by one, to conduct a small ensemble, I was overwhelmed by their air of self-assurance. The ruthless criticism of the teacher seemed water off their backs. I didn't expect to be called, but I was terrified, slouching in my seat and trying to make myself as small as possible. I decided to put off being a conductor for a while.

During the summer between my freshman and sophomore years, I was "discovered"—abortively. Mait and I had had the perfect bumming-around holiday. We'd sailed to Europe on a student cruise ship, bought ourselves Lambrettas in Le Havre, then tooled around France and the Italian Riviera. We ended the trip in grand style in Paris at the house of my godmother Ginny Chambers. The writer Francine du Plessix Gray, who was one of the brighter, livelier young women around then, remembers the first time we met. "You were eighteen going on forty-three," she reminisced recently. "You came in and didn't sit on the sofa, but sort of lay on it like an enormous, drowsy lion. You had this air of great sexual precocity. I thought, Here's someone who would be as capable of taking on Marella Agnelli as Marilyn Monroe. And you were perfectly filthy. I don't know when you'd last bathed. I got you into a tub and scrubbed you all over, and the water turned completely black. Afterward you sat down at the piano and played Bach."

One afternoon I was improvising on Ginny's piano. After a few minutes, I felt someone listening. Standing in the doorway was a woman I recognized but couldn't place.

"That's nice," she said. "Do you know 'My Heart Belongs to Daddy'?"

I did.

"Your dad sure didn't play it like that," she said, coming over to the piano. "He stuck more to the melody."

"Well, I've always been more into jazz than he was," I said a little defensively.

"You've got nothing to apologize for, young man," she said. "By the way, I made my first record singing that song with your father. I'm Mary Martin."

I almost fell off the piano bench. In 1949 I'd been taken to the opening night of *South Pacific* by Jock and Betsey Whitney as a companion for Betsey's daughter Kate. Like everyone else, I'd fallen in love with Mary Martin's Nurse Nellie Forbush.

I zipped into the opening bars of "I'm Gonna Wash That Man Right Outa My Hair."

She smiled. "Not bad."

Over tea, Mary told me she was preparing a television special that fall in which she planned to sing "My Heart Belongs to Daddy." Would I like to accompany her?

Would I!

"Well, I'm staying at Main's [the fashion designer Mainbocher]," she said. "Why don't you come over and play for us some evening?"

A few nights later, I had my first audition—in Mainbocher's splendid drawing room, where he and Mary Martin and a half dozen of their friends were standing around. After the introductions, she led me gently to the piano. "Just do something nicely in the background," she murmured.

Without music, I sat down and played some show tunes with what I considered a jazz feeling. When I finally had the courage to look up from the keyboard, I saw Mary and her friends smiling. I picked up the tempo.

"You were terrific," Mary said when the party broke up. "You'll be wonderful on television."

Ginny, when I told her, said, "How wonderful, darling. But don't forget, you're only eighteen and your studies come first." She said she'd write to Marie and my stepmother and see what they "thought about it."

Obviously they didn't think much of my making my professional debut accompanying Mary Martin on national television at the age of eighteen, because the matter was never brought up again. I was too timid to pursue it, and only years later, after Ginny died and I was sent some letters she'd kept, did I learn something of the truth:

In October 1955 Mary Martin had written my godmother about my audition in Mainbocher's living room:

> You could instantly see and feel the reaction—yes, a fresh talent saying something a little different and new. . . . The very good news is that [Peter] came through with flying colors—marks of 100. You would have been happy—very happy and proud, too. . . . Therefore it was sad to get a message that Peter would not be allowed to be a part of the program. I am sure there must be much we don't know that made such a decision necessary. We were told that the Harrimans and his guardians thought Peter too young. Undoubtedly it must have had something to do with his schoolwork.

Undoubtedly it did.

≡

Like the rest of my Hotchkiss clique at Yale, I considered myself a cultural snob—above such lowbrow tastes as popular and Broadway music. I was ambivalent about the new craze of rock and roll, hating the white stuff (The Crew-Cuts, Bill Haley and the Comets, et al.) but digging the black stuff (Fats Domino, Little Richard, Chuck Berry). I thought Elvis Presley was a terrific singer, but otherwise—what a fruitcake. I loved "art" films and spoke profoundly about the merits of Jean Renoir's *La Règle du Jeu* versus Luis Buñuel's *Un Chien Andalou*. I even recall spending one all-nighter holding forth about the Christ symbolism in *On the Waterfront*.

One day Chiquita called to tell me that Hollywood was making a film about my father's life. What's more, we'd both get some dough out of it. There went my cultural snobbery.

Making *The Eddy Duchin Story* was a labor of friendship for the people at Columbia Pictures who had known my father—Leo Jaffe and Abe Schneider, the guys who ran the New York office, and Donald Stralem, who was on Columbia's board of directors. Their first choice to write the screenplay was another friend of Dad's, Moss Hart. But Moss was too busy. When he dropped out, the job went to Samuel Taylor, a Broadway master of the bittersweet.

Three of Dad's best Hollywood friends—Cary Grant, Van Johnson, Tyrone Power—had wanted to play the title role. The choice of Power, with his dark looks and boyish charm, seemed perfect. Kim Novak as my mother seemed a classic case of miscasting. How could a Hollywood bimbo with midwestern, working-class roots play Marjorie Oelrichs of Newport and New York society? But I had just seen Kim Novak as the small-town beauty in *Picnic*. As she did for every other horny American adolescent male of the fifties, this soft, sphinxlike blonde with the flat, husky voice had become the girl of my wet dreams.

Hearing that she was filming in Central Park one weekend, I asked a couple of Yale buddies if they'd like to meet her. If I'd wanted to, I could have gotten the whole university on that train to Grand Central.

They were shooting just inside the park off Fifth Avenue. Once I told the guard who I was, we were waved onto the set. We spotted her immediately. Dressed in a white silk robe, Kim Novak was sitting in a folding chair while an army of makeup people fussed over her cheekbones. I crept up behind her, kissed her lightly on the ear, and said, "Hi, Mom."

She let out a little shriek. Then she turned and threw me a catlike smile. "You're not little Peter, are you?" she said in a low, thrilling voice.

I grinned.

That night, Kim took us all out to dinner. Afterward, we took her to Jimmy Ryan's club on Fifty-second Street. Every head turned when we walked in. But Kim was still the little Polish girl from Chicago whom Harry Cohn, the boss of Columbia Pictures, had discovered when she was touring the country as Miss Deepfreeze. Along with the glamorous aura was a very real woman: unpretentious, down-to-earth, oozing with sensuality. Though she'd been messed over by some of the biggest shits in Hollywood, she had stayed completely nice.

Kim wanted to hear everything I could tell her about my parents, which wasn't very much. She gave me her phone number, and a couple of weekends later I called and offered to introduce her to Marie Harriman.

I was staying at Eighty-first Street, and after helping Kim out of her mink, I took her upstairs.

Kim's eyes got big at the sight of the fabulous paintings and the figure of Ma, regal behind her dark glasses, doing her crossword puzzle under the huge Derain portrait of herself.

Ma had met too many movie stars in her time to be impressed. She shook Kim's awkwardly outstretched hand. "So nice to meet you, Mrs. Harriman," said the great star.

Soon they were chatting away. Ma trotted out her favorite stories about her best friend. Kim took it in eagerly. I sat there, all ears.

In her gentle purr, Kim asked whether my mother had been as beautiful as she appeared in the Beaton photographs.

"Oh, she was even more beautiful!" replied Ma. Glancing at Kim, whose skirt was above the knees, showing off two of her best assets, Ma added, "Except for the legs, which she always kept covered. She was one of the first women to wear slacks."

"Did she have any strange mannerisms?" asked Kim.

"Nothing you can play on the screen. But for a big girl, she had tremendous energy. She was always *moving*."

"Was she nervous?"

"No. She was *alive*. When she walked in, the room lit up. She was interested in *everything*. You couldn't keep up with her. And you must remember that she wasn't really this rich socialite. She had to *work*."

Kim nodded happily. That was a side of my mother she understood.

Kim had invited me to a Broadway play, the name of which I have forgotten. When we got up to say good-bye, she put out her hand. "Oh, Mrs. Harriman," she said, "it's been so nice visiting with you. I hope we can visit again sometime."

Ma threw me a look over her dark glasses.

I remember nothing about the play, but I remember the rest of the night, during which I got as close to Oedipal ecstasy as I'll ever

Tyrone Power and Kim Novak as my mom and dad in
The Eddy Duchin Story, 1956.

During the shooting of *The Eddy Duchin Story* I met Kim
Novak and spent a wonderful evening with her.

know. When I stumbled back to Eighty-first Street at six in the morning, I discovered a note on my pillow. It was from Ma, and it said: "Hope you had a real nice visit, honey."

≡

Despite being at different colleges, Mait and I had stayed the closest of friends. When I told him I was spending my junior year abroad in Paris, he decided to leave Princeton and join me. It was there that our friendship broke up. Not because of any falling-out, but our lives were heading in different directions—Mait's into marriage with a beautiful Swedish girl, mine into having a ball in Paris. We simply drifted apart.

I hadn't seen Mait in more than thirty years when I called him recently at his house on Martha's Vineyard. I said I was writing a book about myself and suggested the two of us get together. All I knew was that he had holed up on the Vineyard and raised a family. Apparently his life had been as private and grounded as mine had been public and on the move, and I set off excited but a little nervous about seeing him.

When I landed at the Vineyard airport, I was astonished to see Helen Edey heading toward the terminal. By coincidence, we'd both been on the same plane from New York. Mait's mother was in her eighties, but she looked a lot less changed to me than I—now forty or fifty pounds heavier—must have looked to her.

Mait, who was building a new house, had said he was temporarily homeless, so we met in the borrowed house of a friend. Grayer, only slightly thicker in the middle, he otherwise looked his old self as he climbed out of a gray pickup, blinking behind his glasses, unshaven and barefoot, in cutoff shorts and a faded polo shirt. He still had his open, quizzical smile.

We began by asking about each other's kids. Once that was over with, we opened some beers and headed out to a deck with a spectacular view of Vineyard Sound.

Mait, who was articulate as ever, seemed to have remembered everything about our school days, now nearly forty years in the past:

"You know, I was a pretty shy kid when I arrived at Eaglebrook. Before you, Duch, I'd had other close friends—one was a kid in third grade who suddenly died—but you quickly became my very best friend. I spotted you right away as a very popular guy. You were funny and original, and you had this great sense of mischief. Remember the night you and another kid got caught out on the roof when you should have been in the dorm?"

Until now, I hadn't.

"When the master asked what you were doing out there, you gave this wonderfully disarming answer: 'Just stargazing, sir.' The guy was speechless."

"You liked looking at the stars, too, as I recall."

"Still do."

I wondered how he had perceived my relationship with my father.

Mait replied: "I remember visiting the house in Manhasset and feeling a kind of vacuum there. Your father was this glamorous, remote character. I had the feeling you admired him because of how he'd climbed out of his immigrant background and become a star. You were proud of him, but from afar."

That sounded right. But had I seemed changed—different— after my father's death?

"Not to me. The morning after you left school for his funeral, one of the masters got up in assembly and announced that your father had died. He told us all to tell you how sorry we were when you got back, but not to make a big deal out of it."

"Good little Wasps."

"Right. You came back, and we all made courteously long faces until we realized you were still the same kid. If you were troubled or sad, you never showed it."

"I guess it took a long time to sink in."

"I'm sure it did. Of course, in those days none of us talked much about our parents. They were creatures on another planet. They weren't a *subject*, the way they are today. But I always thought that if Eddy had played jazz, you'd probably have talked more about him. I had the feeling you didn't really dig him as a musician."

That was right, too. I'd liked the effect my father had on people—and I still love it when people come up to me and tell me how much they enjoyed him. But he wasn't Tatum, Wilson, or "Fatha" Hines.

"Not that you put him down," continued Mait. "But you didn't seem to have much to do with him. In fact, it wasn't until we were in Paris that I realized how comfortable you were in his world. It was a world that had no interest for me. Maybe that's why we parted."

This was news to me. Mait had seemed perfectly comfortable in Ginny's living room. Or perhaps I just hadn't noticed.

Mait and I became nostalgic as we recalled the night we'd both fallen in love with a Swedish girl in a Montmartre jazz joint—Anne, the girl who had become Mait's first wife.

With his astonishing memory for detail, Mait recalled the week we'd spent sleeping at a funky Italian beach club near Genoa: "Remember the bandannas we wore around our necks because we couldn't do any laundry? After a while, all the little boys in the village were wearing bandannas around their necks. And remember the guy who kept asking us about American movie stars? He'd say, 'Bub Bub,' meaning 'Bob Hope.' "

What I remembered was the sheer freedom of it—as well as the feeling that all Europe was there with open arms for us, simply because we were Americans.

Later, at dinner in a loud, smoky restaurant, Mait and I relaxed. As we said good night, we promised that our next reunion wouldn't take thirty years.

The next morning we drove over to his mother's place. Helen Edey lived in serene seclusion at the end of a dirt road in a spacious house overlooking the sound. When I asked what she remembered of the time I came to live with her family in Brookville, her response was vintage Mumbles:

"My impression was that you were this neglected rich boy who had been given wonderful things, but that nobody had paid much attention to you. Mait said you needed a home, and I said, 'Well, he'll have to become domesticated. He'll have to tell me when he's coming and going and he'll have to want to be part of the family.' "

"Did I get domesticated?"

Helen laughed. "No! You were a wild animal. You weren't used to people telling you what to do. You did like to practice the piano a lot. One day I asked what you were going to do with yourself. You said, 'One thing I know, I'm never going to be a bandleader like my father.' At the time, I assumed it was because you didn't want an itinerant life. I thought you wanted a home."

"I did."

Mait smiled. "My sense of Peter was that the homeless life suited him just fine."

"I think you wanted both—the home and no responsibility," his mother said acutely. "May I remind you of the last summer you stayed with us? You were nineteen and between your sophomore and junior years at Yale—we asked you to come with us to Edgartown for the summer. You said you'd rather stay in Brookville and practice the piano. That sounded a little fishy to me, but I said OK, only no wild parties! We didn't hear one word from you. When we got back in September you were gone, without a note. You left the place in a mess. You'd left all your possessions—your clothes, your records, even your watch. I was furious. Remember that letter I sent you?"

How could I not? When I had turned down Helen's invitation to join the Edeys in Edgartown for the summer, I wasn't totally lying about wanting to stay in Brookville and practice piano. But as soon as I was alone, I realized I was *free*. I had a big, beautiful house all to myself, with nobody around to see whether or not I'd made the bed, washed the dishes, stayed out too late, or didn't come home at all. I had my little Ford, which I was paying off monthly with the allowance I was getting from the small trust fund left by my father. I had a book full of girls' phone numbers. For the next six weeks, I had the time of my life.

Arrangements had been made for me to spend the following year in Paris, and a few days before I was to leave, I woke up in a fit of guilt. But it occurred to me that if I simply vanished, everything I'd done wrong would also vanish. There was one problem: I'd forgotten about Stella, the cleaning woman.

I'd been in Paris a couple of weeks when I received the most scorching letter of my life. Helen Edey took no prisoners. She began her letter began by explaining why she'd taken me in: "We hoped that the feeling of being wanted here and having people so interested in you would arouse in you a feeling of affection and loyalty and interest, and that emotion might be the start of a character change which is sorely needed."

Then she twisted the knife: "Apparently, we are just a pleasant convenience."

Worse, I had been a slob. This, according to Helen, is what Stella walked into after I disappeared: "The grease on and in the stove was thick enough to be removed with a shovel, the icebox stank to high heaven."

Stella the double agent had also taken notes on my nocturnal habits—my "psychopathic little love affairs," as Helen put it.

The letter ended with this parting shot: "How *could* you have gone off to Europe without letting your stepmother know?" I hadn't even called Chiquita to say good-bye.

Now, Helen laughed. "I hope I wasn't too furious."

"I deserved it."

"You sure did," said Helen, fixing me with her psychiatrist's stare. "Why *do* you think you ran away?"

"Paris, I guess," I said inadequately.

In 1956–57, I spent my "junior year abroad" in Paris. I was
completely free for the first time in my life.

11

PARIS

Number 13 Rue Monsieur is an eighteenth-century apartment complex, a *hôtel particulier,* on a quiet residential street on the Left Bank. To get to Ginny and Brose Chambers' house, you first had to go through a set of massive, studded wooden doors, then past the concierge's apartment, then across a cobblestone courtyard big enough for several coach-and-fours. Then you opened another set of ancient doors to discover an entire house in the Norman style, with a surrounding garden. Paradise.

Ginny had bought the place from Cole Porter just after the war, when Brose was in Paris working with Ave as a lawyer on the Marshall Plan. Cole had transformed an eighteenth-century house into a country manor, adding timbers and stucco to the façade and planting an astonishing "secret garden" of flowering shrubs and trees around the sizable lawn in the back. Once you arrived in the inner sanctum, the only reminder that you were in a city was the occasional two-note police siren.

Ginny had furnished the former ballroom on the ground floor with her collection of modern paintings. Some of them were hung; others stood on easels; others were strewn about the floor. She called it "the studio" even though nobody ever painted in it. It was reserved for the works of artists who were her friends. Upstairs, she'd kept the eighteenth-century parquet floors and *boiserie* and furnished the procession of sitting rooms, bedrooms, and dining room with an eclectic assortment of thoroughly lived-in antiques. Ginny and Brose had two giant, precocious poodles, who were given full rein of the house. They were so attuned to their mistress's comings and goings that the moment they heard her car turning into the Rue Monsieur, they dashed upstairs and sat in the window, whimpering with excitement as she made her entrance in the courtyard below.

Everybody who came to Ginny's for one of her lunches or dinners wanted to move in forever, especially into one of the bedrooms at the top of a spiral staircase in the tower overlooking the garden. Ginny's kitchen, supervised by Leon, the butler, turned out some of the best food in Paris. Her wine cellar was superb. Her Bösendorfer grand piano in the library was concert quality. Ginny was what the French call a *maîtresse de maison*. She ran a house better than anybody.

Like her best friend, Marie Harriman, Ginny was an anomaly in a mostly Wasp world. She came from a cultivated family of Sephardic Jews in Virginia, the Fargeons, the British branch of which was prominent in the arts. Her English cousin Herbert Fargeon was a famous theatrical producer; his daughter, Eleanor, a well-known popular novelist. Ginny's father had been an insurance executive who specialized in protecting many of the great American art collections, which explained her considerable knowledge of paintings.

Ginny could never have been a beauty. She was slightly hunchbacked and had gray, thinning hair. In old age she wore a wig. Her husband affectionately called her Monk, a diminutive of "little monkey," in reference to her funny, animated face. Ginny's voice was even huskier than Ma's from years of booze and cigarettes. Like Ma, too, she suffered from progressively failing eyesight. A dozen years later, after she sold the Paris house and moved to New York, she went virtually blind. But this didn't prevent her from charging out of her apartment in the Mayfair Hotel and running into the street to hail a cab.

She was the epitome of understated chic, even when she appeared in the morning in her pink quilted dressing gown, nursing a hangover. There was nothing veiled about Ginny, who had the sweetest smile in the world. She was the most inviting woman I've ever met.

Her tragedy was that, despite her great maternal instincts, she never had a child of her own. To fill the void, her Paris house became a way station for the children of her American friends, whom she Auntie Mamed through their adolescent rawness and first love affairs. Ginny had offered to bring me up after my mother died, and it was only natural that the project of civilizing me became a top priority when I arrived at Rue Monsieur in August 1956. I had stayed there before but never for more than a week or ten days. This time, Ginny had an entire school year to work on me. She approved of my desire to study music and French history, but she warned me that the daybed in her studio would be available only

The Smart Set
by Cholly Knickerbocker

Mon., Jan. 22, 1945—8

Ginny and Brose Chambers at the Stork Club during the war.
They bought Cole Porter's place in Paris when Brose was
working with Ave on the Marshall Plan, and it was always
filled with the most interesting people in town. Ginny was my
godmother, and I was welcome there anytime.

for a couple of weeks. It was important, she explained, that I develop "self-reliance." I nodded dimly.

The Communists had splashed "U.S. Go Home" all over Paris. But to most Parisians, Americans were more than welcome. The older French respected us as "liberators," although it didn't take long for us to realize that while they boasted about their role in *la Résistance,* most of them had been totally supine under the Nazi boot. The younger French were crazy about American movies, American jazz, American writers—especially Faulkner, Hemingway, and Fitzgerald. What everyone liked best about us was our money, of which we seemed to have a great deal more than they. For Americans in the fifties, Paris was the way it had been for Hemingway and Fitzgerald in the twenties—a movable feast.

Now I was really free. Until then, I'd moved in a world governed, monitored, and manipulated by adults who expected me to measure up to some set of standards that were always implied but never exactly spelled out. I'd been eager to fit in, to be liked, not to displease. My only rebellions had been minor transgressions of the adult code. When I'd been caught, the usual reaction had been, "You've disappointed us." From the moment I arrived in Paris, I felt responsible to nobody but myself.

Paris was the first city I claimed as my own. Thanks to Zellie, I spoke the language fluently, which immediately made me accepted by the French. For weeks, I walked the streets as if in a dream. I loved the way everything had its place in the grand scheme of things: the bird market, the flower market, the fish market, the whore market.

Paris sounded wonderful. It might be a dog barking, or someone practicing Chopin behind an open window, or people calling out to one another, or just a howl of wind. Each sound had its own identity, the way a Miles Davis riff suddenly breaks out, then stops, only to haunt the silence. Very soon I was able to distinguish among the variety of French accents: the aristocratic, the working-class, the provincial, the colonial.

One destination became an obsession: the Musée de Cluny in the Latin Quarter. There, in the ground-floor gallery, I would sit gazing at the six millefleur unicorn tapestries from the Middle Ages, each depicting one of the senses (the sixth being freedom of choice). I had been enchanted by unicorns since I was about seven or eight and found a big art book in Ma and Ave's cottage. Nancy Whitney had come in and told me that the strange animal in the pictures, standing alone in a leafy bower, was "not a real animal— it's *mythological.*" The sound of that word *mythological* made the creature even more magical, and for a long time I'd refused to believe that unicorns weren't real. I was sure I'd spot one in the woods at Arden and, even later, in the woods around Eaglebrook.

At the Cluny I was drawn particularly to two of the tapestries, the ones depicting touch and sight. In the former, a beautiful princess gently grasps the creature's horn. It was an act I found unbearably erotic. In the second tapestry, she holds a mirror in which the animal can look at himself. I was haunted by the princess's vulnerability and bravery. What I liked about her animal/lover was its innocence and trust.

From the museum I would wander over to the Luxembourg Gardens to see "the Birdman." He was a *clochard,* one of the raggedy old men of the Paris streets, and he'd be sitting on a bench, covered with live birds. One day I bought a bag of corn, seated myself on a bench opposite, and sprinkled the kernels over my hair and lap. In a flash, the birds were all over me, gobbling up the corn. Once it was gone, they zoomed back to their perches on the Birdman, from where they eyed me suspiciously.

≡

At 13 Rue Monsieur, you might see Simone de Beauvoir schmoozing with Audrey Hepburn, James and Gloria Jones with Raymond Aron, Jacques Barzun with John J. McCloy, Anita Loos with Pauline de Rothschild. Ginny made no distinctions between young and old, rich and poor, famous and unknown. All she expected of me was that I show up reasonably clean, sound reasonably intelligent (in French), and help Leon with the drinks.

Occasionally she'd fix me up with attractive daughters of Brose's French business friends. Shortly after I arrived, I was introduced to Claudine, a gorgeous eighteen-year-old blonde, who invited me to a debutante party in the Bois de Boulogne. Lacking a tuxedo, I tried on Brose's evening clothes. They fit fine, but our feet were different sizes, and I didn't have a pair of black shoes. Ginny came up with the idea of blackening my brown oxfords with shoe polish. After several coats had been thickly applied, I left to pick up Claudine in my Deux-Chevaux.

She looked fantastic in a white, strapless ball gown as we walked into a million twinkling lights, masses of flowers, a battalion of waiters bearing Dom Pérignon, and a spread of food, all sculpted and glacéed, as only the French can do it. We danced and danced, and though I received many scornful glances from her snooty French friends, I was sure she only had eyes for me.

Toward the end of the evening, I was cut in on by a dark young man who looked like Louis Jourdan. As I reluctantly retreated, I glanced back to give Claudine a debonair wink. To my horror, I saw a wide black band encircling the hem of her gown. Her partner followed my downward gaze.

"*Qu'est-ce que c'est ça?*"

Claudine looked down. "*Je ne sais pas!*"

Her hand went down to the black, then up to her nose. Her eyes found mine. I pointed to my shoes and did my best Fernandel imitation. She threw back her head and laughed.

=

Mait was staying nearby, and almost every night we'd hit the clubs. There was a wonderful array of them on the Left Bank, where you could hear jazz in every style, played by top American musicians and a lot of terrific French players. Among the Americans were Sidney Bechet, Lester Young, Bud Powell, Chet Baker, David Amram, Allen Eager, Billy Byears, Kenny Clarke, and Don Byas. The French stars included Martial Solal, Stéphane Grappelli, and Claude Luter. One day Miles Davis blew into Le Vieux Colombier off the Boulevard Saint-Michel, and Mait and I were there for every set, five nights running.

Our evenings would end around four in the morning with long "existential" walks along the Seine. One night we met a French student who invited us to his pad. There we had our first hit of marijuana. It felt great, but later, as we made our way home on rubbery legs, we were sure we'd taken the first step to heroin. Hard drugs were cheap and plentiful in those days, and others in our crowd were already making the most of them.

I ran into an old friend from New York, Harry Phipps, whose father was Ogden Phipps of the immense steel fortune. Despite his blond, perfect-preppy good looks, Harry had always been the sweetest, kindest, yet most mysterious member of the group of Long Island friends who were a few years older than I. In the hard-playing, athletic North Shore crowd, Harry had stood out because of his artistic inclinations, which included a great interest in jazz. One night after Harry and I closed the clubs, I found myself back in his apartment, below the Tour d'Argent restaurant. While I made myself a drink, he took out a little envelope, poured some white powder on the table, and snorted it up his nose with a drinking straw.

"What's that?"

"Heroin. Want some?"

"No thanks."

While I watched, he shrugged and snorted some more. Then he put his head back against a pillow and went quietly to sleep, peaceful as a baby.

I split, pursued by demons.

From then on, I saw a great deal of Harry and his heroin addiction, even joining him in London for a wedding where we were introduced to an attractive couple from Washington, Sen. John F. Kennedy and his beautiful wife, Jackie.

Harry was the first person whose survival I'd ever really worried about and whom I thought I could save. On the occasions when he was clearheaded, I'd tell him that heroin was ruining him. His response was always the same: Of course he was going to stop—it was just something he was "doing for now." The next time I saw him, he'd look as though he were about to fall asleep standing up. He was still on the junk.

I had grown fond of marijuana, but I never tried heroin. I knew I'd like it. It's the same thing that has kept me from ever snorting cocaine—something my children refuse to believe.

Six or seven years later, back in New York, Harry came to the end of the road—one that had undoubtedly begun when his self-absorbed parents were divorced and he was left, like so many privileged Wasp kids, to be raised largely by society. I had been at lunch with Harry's wife, Diana, a brilliant, Czech-born woman who shared his artistic interests but not his drive to self-destruct. As I dropped her off at her apartment on Central Park West, the doorman took me aside. "Mr. Duchin," he said, "Mr. Phipps has been found dead."

Diana came over and said, "What's wrong?"

When I told her that Harry had died, she let out the most awful shriek and fell to the sidewalk. I caught her and half-carried her to the elevator. Upstairs, we learned that Harry, age thirty-one, had OD'd that morning in a Times Square hotel room.

$$=$$

I thought I had just about charmed Ginny into letting me stay the whole year on the Rue Monsieur when I went too far. Kate Roosevelt, Betsey Whitney's daughter by her first marriage, to James Roosevelt, the president's oldest son, had been a close friend since my days at Arden. In Manhasset, we had often played together just down the road on the Whitney estate, Greentree, which was so big that we both regularly got lost. I was delighted when Kate arrived at Ginny's to stay for several weeks in one of the tower bedrooms, and every night—or early morning—I would go up to her room and tell her about my nocturnal adventures. One night when I was perched at the foot of Kate's bed wearing nothing but my bathrobe and holding a cigar and a tumbler of Scotch, Ginny walked in. "Good God!" she said. "I think you've been here long enough, young man!"

$$=$$

I found the barge through a newspaper ad. Built in the nineteenth century to haul grain up and down the Thames, it still had its original deck and a mast with rotting tanbark sails. At some point, it had been converted to a houseboat. Somebody had sailed it across the English Channel and down the Seine, where it was now docked on the Right Bank, between the Pont de l'Alma and the Pont des Invalides.

I ran over to see it and fell in love. For light, it had a good supply of Coleman lanterns; for heat, a potbellied woodstove. The barge's plumbing consisted of hoses that drained into the Seine. Running water came from a hose attached to a spigot on the quai. In what was formerly the hold were three bedrooms, a small galley, and a pine-paneled living area with cheap furniture, including an old upright piano. George Plimpton later described the main cabin as "dark and finely odiferous." I thought it was the most romantic place in the world.

The asking price was $6,000. I got it for $5,400. Since I didn't have the money myself, I got Mait to pony up two-thirds. I persuaded another friend, Mark Rudkin, whose family owned Pepperidge Farm bakery products, to put in the other third until I could weasel the money out of Donald Stralem and Chiquita, the administrators of my modest trust fund. Ginny came over for a look and pronounced it "very amusing."

Then, unexpectedly, the barge was mine. Mark left to study landscape design outside Paris. Mait, who had been pining for the Swedish girl, left Paris to court her in Göteborg. I needed a roommate to help with the expenses.

It was George Plimpton, editor of *The Paris Review*, who suggested I meet Robert Silvers, the magazine's new Paris editor. I went around to where Bob was staying on the Île Saint-Louis and was bowled over. At twenty-six, he looked a bit like the young Orson Welles, and he was clearly another wunderkind.

Bob, who has been editor of *The New York Review of Books* since helping to found it in the mid-sixties, had grown up on a chicken farm in Long Island—something you'd never suspect from his immensely cultivated manner. At age fifteen, he'd gone to the University of Chicago. At seventeen, he'd been accepted into Yale Law School. He'd dropped out to be a reporter and at nineteen had become press secretary to Chester Bowles, the governor of Connecticut. He was studying at Columbia when he was drafted into the Army. After serving in SHAPE, the Allied command headquarters in Paris, he had attended the Sorbonne and the École des Sciences Politiques on the GI Bill.

He'd joined *The Paris Review* as an editor in 1954, and when George Plimpton went back to America in 1955 to run the magazine from New York, he'd asked Bob to take over the Paris office. Bob's main concern at the *Review* was to find European writers to publish in translation, as well as artists who would contribute portfolios of drawings. He came around to look at the barge and liked what he saw. And I suddenly found myself at the center of one of the most interesting scenes in Paris.

The Paris Review was already three years old. The brainchild of two American expatriates, Peter Matthiessen, the novelist and naturalist, and the eccentric publisher and novelist Harold L. (Doc) Humes, the magazine had become a mecca for well-connected young Americans, mostly fresh out of Harvard, who were eager to make their literary marks. One of their gurus was the novelist Irwin Shaw, who knew everybody who was anybody in a Europe that was bordered on the east by Klosters, on the north by Deauville, on the west by Pamplona, and on the south by Saint-Tropez. I met Shaw at one of Ginny's more memorable dinner parties. I had just read his war novel, *The Young Lions,* and when I heard who the tough-looking, animated guy with the permanent five-o'clock shadow was, I stood there tongue-tied. He was a geyser of names, all glamorous, famous, or wealthy: the Duke of Windsor, Hemingway, James Jones, Darryl Zanuck, Gary Cooper, Aly Khan. Listening to him with great interest was a good-looking, very fit man, the screenwriter Peter Viertel, who had walked in with another astonishing figure—his wife, Deborah Kerr. It was hard to

the PARIS REVIEW

18

ERNEST
HEMINGWAY
an interview

JACK COPE

drawings by
GIACOMETTI

and

VALI

W. S. MERWIN

SHORT STORIES

POETRY

SPRING 1958
*Fifth Anniversary
Issue*

$1.00   3/6 in U.K.

250 frs

HOMMES   DAMES

My roommate on a barge in Paris was Bob Silvers,
who edited *The Paris Review,* then in its third year. Thus
I was surrounded by well-connected young American
writers having a great time being bohemians.

believe that the prim lady sitting quietly in the corner was the same woman I'd last seen in *From Here to Eternity*, rolling around the sands of Waikiki with Burt Lancaster.

I was fascinated by two Mutt and Jeff characters who were also orbiting Shaw. Both wore business suits and had identical round, black-rimmed glasses. The Mutt figure was a strange-looking little man with a shiny pink head as bald as a cue ball and batlike ears. He was introduced to me as Irving Lazar, though everyone called him Swifty. He seemed to be some sort of agent. The Jeff figure was Harry Kurnitz, a playwright and novelist.

In time, I developed a passing friendship with Shaw, who would sometimes drop in on the barge to chat with Bob. He was always curious about and supportive of what the *Review* was publishing, and for the magazine's twenty-fifth anniversary issue he wrote an assessment of how my generation of would-be Hemingways differed from his. The latter, who were products of the Depression, had been

ferociously competitive, honest in their opinions of their friends' work to the point of snarling hostility, fanatically and openly ambitious, poor, and out of grim necessity ready to do any kind of writing that promised to support them and their families. . . .

In contrast, the literary hopefuls of the [*Paris Review*] contingent spoke in the casual tones of the good schools and could be found, surrounded by flocks of pretty and nobly acquiescent girls, in chic places like Lipp's on the Boulevard St. Germain or on the roads to Deauville or Biarritz for month-long holidays. They were mild-mannered, beautifully polite, recoiled from the appearance of seeming ambitious and were ready at all times to drop whatever they were almost secretly composing to play tennis (usually very well), drive down to Spain for a bullfight, fly to Rome for a wedding or sit around most of the night drinking. As far as I could see, none of them had a job and although they all lived frugally in cheap rooms they gave the impression that they were going through a period of Gallic slumming for the fun of it. One guessed that there were wealthy and benevolent parents on the other side of the Atlantic.

All true. We weren't really living the Bohemian life—we were playing it. George Plimpton has remarked that "we were all very good at leading two lives—the life of the incredibly inexpensive hotel room, where you could live for fifteen dollars a week, and the lavish drawing room. As long as you had a dinner jacket in the armoire, you'd be invited to the most fabulous houses of unbelievable wealth."

I should add that when George dropped over to Paris, he'd spend a few nights with Bob and me on the barge, sleeping on an army cot with his feet sticking out. In the morning, he'd amble up the street to the Plaza-Athénée, where he'd write letters home on the hotel's embossed stationery.

No one could accuse Bob Silvers of being anything other than serious, however. He seemed to know more about more subjects than anybody I'd ever met, yet he was the least intimidating of intellectuals, never too busy to share what he knew, even with a lout like me. You could ask him about anything—the difference between the philosophies of Wittgenstein and Whitehead or the complexities of French politics in 1925—and he'd come back with a concise answer. Sharing the barge with Bob was like living with a cozy encyclopedia.

Another mentor was Eddie Morgan, whom I had known since his marriage to Nancy Whitney. They were now divorced, and Eddie had started a car sales and rental business in Paris, dealing mostly with GI's who were finishing up their military service and wanted a foreign car to take back home. In his mid-thirties, Eddie was an intellectual and stylistic Pied Piper for us all, even for Bob Silvers. He had fought in the war in the Marines, which gave him gravitas. He knew Paris inside out. His mind was amazingly well stocked, particularly in arcane matters of history and politics. Big, dark-haired, aristocratic-looking, and dressed in fashionably threadbare suits, he had the vaguely tragic aura of a man destined for great things and doomed never to realize them.

Eddie was a night owl. The later it got and the more beer he drank, the more eloquently he would discourse on the virtues and shortcomings of Alexander the Great compared with those of Charles de Gaulle. Or the story of the Morgan family, which the way he told it became a mini-history of American business and privileged society since the Civil War. Eddie would hold his tongue until the rest of us were exhausted. As one of my friends, Teddy Van Zuylen, once remarked, "Eddie never really opened his mouth until 3:00 A.M."

One of the reasons I found Eddie so compelling was that he seemed in the grip of some immense inner turmoil. He would wring his hands so fiercely that they developed calluses on the palms. Eddie projected density. He was a constant reminder that I'd better stop frittering my time away on the pursuit of pleasure.

Because of Bob and Eddie, I was admitted into an impressive group of brains, beauty, and connections. One of Bob's assistants was Gill Goldsmith, the witty wife of Teddy Goldsmith, the eccentric brother of the financier James Goldsmith, who is now the owner of Ginny's house on the Rue Monsieur. Teddy, whose parents owned various grand hotels, claimed to be writing the "history of the world." He once rushed to Gill and exclaimed, "I've just finished chapter fourteen!" "Darling, how wonderful!" she said. "You've written fourteen chapters?"

"No, idiot!" he screamed. "I've *started* with chapter fourteen."

Another assistant at the magazine was Elizabeth de Cuevas, daughter of Margaret Rockefeller and the Marquis de Cuevas, who had his own ballet company. Bessie, as everyone called her, was a rather shy beauty, married to an elegant Parisian businessman, Hubert Faure. There was Gaby Van Zuylen, a poetic Radcliffe girl, whose husband, Teddy Van Zuylen, was an enormously rich, half-Belgian, half-Egyptian count who owned a fabulous castle, Le Haar, in Nijmegen, Holland. One of Bob's first acts as Paris editor had been to move the printing operation to a plant in Holland. Later, when Gaby joined the *Review,* we were invited to use Teddy's place for long weekends of visits to the newly built van Gogh museum, strolls in the private forest, and gambling all night.

Closer to Paris was another favorite weekend haunt. Bob, Eddie, and I would fold our bulky American bodies into my tiny, second-hand Citroën Deux-Chevaux for the drive to the château of Lionel and Nolwen Armand de l'Isle in Dreux, near Chartres. This many-turreted edifice was divided into the Light Side and the Dark Side. In the former lived Lionel and Nolwen and their beautiful young daughter and son. There, the routine was completely casual. A bit down at the heels, it was a place where dogs, children, and adults tumbled all over one another. In the Dark Side lived Lionel's parents. This was a hushed, dim procession of stuffy, cold rooms into which we ventured only for formal holiday dinners. Presiding dourly was Lionel's father, a once celebrated doctor whose research with rabbits some years earlier had unleashed a plague of mixemetosis that had nearly wiped out Europe's rabbit population. Boris Karloff would have been perfect casting as Dr. Armand de l'Isle. His wife, Madame de l'Isle, seemed to spend all her time outdoors, wearing a huge shawl and carrying a basket on her arm, slowly picking her way through the mist, searching for nuts or mushrooms.

≡

Adding to the charms of the barge was the proximity of the Crazy Horse Saloon, just up the street. The most popular of the postwar nightclubs, the Crazy Horse featured floor shows that weren't as extravagant as those at the Folies-Bergère or the Lido, but its girls were considered the most stunning in Paris. To avoid paying the cover charge, I'd park myself at the bar just as the last show was ending. Soon the girls would arrive, some in costume, some not— a United Nations of pulchritude. I played the wide-eyed American student and would-be jazz musician to the hilt. Eventually the girls who hadn't succeeded in landing bigger fish would settle at my table. They needed a friend as much as I did, with no strings. I felt a great tenderness for them, especially the ones who thought they had to barter their charms for extra cash or a rich husband. All I had to give them was my youth and raging libido. Invariably I'd end the night with one of them, often on the barge, where I'd sit at the piano and doodle at something beautiful and hip by Thelonious Monk or Bud Powell while the girl arranged herself in a pose by Degas.

Another prime hunting ground for girls was the Latin Quarter, which teemed with bright, young, beautiful people of all nationalities, most of whom were tasting freedom for the first time. The pill hadn't yet arrived, but these were not girls from Miss Porter's. These girls went all the way.

One night I met an exotic beauty named Nina Dyer. Recently divorced from the German industrialist and art collector Heinrich von Thyssen, she was said to spend a good deal of her settlement on the care and feeding of a black panther, which she kept at her country house in a cage. When she wasn't throwing the beast large haunches of bloody meat, she liked to parade him around on a chain. We hit it off when I told her how my great-aunt Blanche had kept an ocelot that she would take out for walks on the streets of New York.

"You must meet my panther," murmured Nina.

I walked her home and went up for a drink. After the butler left us, I joined her on the couch. I was making the first move when I heard the rapid approach of not so tiny feet. Suddenly a large, toothy mouth was inserting itself between our faces and preparing to take half of mine in its jaws.

"*Arrêtes*, Pushkin!" screamed Nina.

Pushkin, an extremely elegant borzoi, sat down and licked his chops. It wasn't serious, but his teeth had drawn blood. Nina ran for a towel. While she dabbed at me, Pushkin and I eyed each other.

A week later at Neuilly, I was introduced to Nina's panther. This time I kept my distance. But as things progressed between Nina and me, the panther grew fond of me. At least he didn't seem to care when Nina and I got close.

Another encounter with a girl and her pet did not end so well. It began at a dinner given by Bessie de Cuevas, where I was seated next to a fetching young woman, a Rothschild of some sort whom I'll call Celestine. Over the sorbet we looked deep into each other's eyes. Later, she agreed to let me walk her home to the Rue du Bac. There we exchanged more deep looks, and she invited me up. "But first," she added, "we have to take Loulou for a walk. Would you mind?"

Not at all.

Celestine ran upstairs and returned with Loulou, a yapping Yorkshire terrier with a pink ribbon around a topknot. The three of us set off, Loulou in the lead, Celestine and I arm in arm. We hadn't gone far when Loulou spied another dog and jerked out of her mistress's grasp. Gallantly I raced after her. With one leap, I landed my left foot on her trailing leash. She stopped, but my right foot didn't. There was a sickening crunch of tiny backbone. I scooped up Loulou, deposited her in a dustbin, kept running, and didn't look back.

The next morning I sent Celestine two dozen sunflowers with a note saying I didn't know how I could feel worse. She didn't write back, and for weeks I avoided the *quartier* around the Rue du Bac. As luck would have it, I never saw Celestine again.

=

I had enrolled in the School of Life but had somehow not found the time to enroll at the Sorbonne. Several weeks past the deadline for registration, I received a rocket from Chiquita, who had gotten a letter from the director of the Junior Year Abroad program—one Monsieur Rideout—which she had enclosed. M. Rideout began: "To say that Peter has been a disappointment to me is making an understatement."

From there, M. Rideout proceeded to charge me with "acting independently" and an "inability to set [my] sights on a single goal."

Moreover, M. Rideout was "very much concerned" that I might "continue to be a lone wolf and perhaps a waster of time." He conceded that I seemed "a young man of considerable intelligence and native ability." What was wrong was my "frame of mind." Apparently I was, he wrote, in "rebellion against Yale and everything else that attempts to dictate his life to him."

All true.

A few days later, I got another rocket, this one from my guardian Donald Stralem in New York. Donald was furious that I had bought the barge without his permission, and he was not happy about sending me the money to pay back my friends. "As far as I can make out," he wrote, "all you have succeeded in doing is being an utterly foolish juvenile."

Not quite all true.

===

There were two musical grandes dames in Paris to whom aspiring American composers beat a path in those days: Mlle. Nadia Boulanger and Mme. Andrée Honegger, widow of the distinguished French composer Arthur Honegger. Madame Boulanger, whose finishing school had accommodated Aaron Copland and Virgil Thomson, was too advanced for me. Madame Honegger taught composition "for beginners" at the École Normale de Musique. Having squeezed myself into a couple of courses in French history and literature, I signed up for an audition.

The woman who answered my timid knock was small, gray haired, and severe. She was impressed that I'd been at Yale, the domain of Paul Hindemith, but she cautioned that *her* approach emphasized dictation—that is, the taking down of complex scores while she played them on the piano.

I nodded with false confidence.

"*Ça va,*" she said.

Madame Honegger's class, which met twice a week, was—to put it mildly—daunting. There were a dozen other students, all far more advanced than I, and I worried constantly about making a fool of myself in their grim, driven eyes. Madame Honegger's method was to concentrate on a different French composer each year. Mine was the year of Gabriel Fauré.

My previous musical education had pretty much stopped with Mozart and Beethoven. Fauré, whose career spanned nineteenth-century French romanticism and early-twentieth-century modernism, was a total exotic. His sonorities were utterly foreign to me. Nor could I discern any logic behind his perfumy harmonies and sinuous melodies. Madame Honegger understood every nuance of Fauré's music, which she explained lucidly and patiently.

Back on the barge, I would sit at the upright and pick my way through Fauré's barcarolles, nocturnes, and preludes, hoping that this weird music was getting into my pores. Aided by the rocking of the barge and the romance of the setting, it did. In his album notes, written for my first recording of dance music, George Plimpton recalled the barge piano's "sharp sad tone, catarrhic from the river mists." To this day, I hear Fauré's intoxicating music in the tubercular timbre of that mildewed upright.

＝

Since the barge was without a telephone, anybody who wanted to drop by for a chat or to see Bob on editorial matters showed up without warning. There was always something delicious to eat on the stove—a pot-au-feu, coq au vin, boeuf bourguignon—left by our nautical maid, Josette, who did housekeeping on the other boats along the quai. If she hadn't prepared something herself, Josette would have brought us a leftover from the restaurant in the Eiffel Tower where her husband worked as the two-star chef.

Late at night, while Bob pored over manuscripts, I'd often be at the piano, jamming with guys I'd gotten to know through the saxophone player Allen Eager. I had first met Allen going into the Café Bonaparte on the Boulevard Saint-Germain to play pinball. You couldn't miss him: a razor-thin figure in dark glasses with slicked-down black hair and deathly white skin, blowing on his horn at a sidewalk table while a couple of chicks looked on. I sat down to listen.

When he stopped, I offered to buy him a drink, and he accepted. There was something menacing about Allen—he'd been through it all—but I liked his cynical sense of humor. When I told him I was an aspiring musician who lived on a barge down the street, he offered to come over and "show me a few things." Pretty soon I was learning bebop riffs from the man whom jazz critics were calling "the next Charlie Parker." One night, Allen said, "Why don't you come over to the club? The Prez is in town."

Sooner or later, most of the top American jazz musicians would show up at the dingy, cavelike Club Saint-Germain, much of which was under a sidewalk. Generally, the place was jammed to capacity. But when Lester Young—The Prez—arrived, there wasn't enough elbowroom to light your Gauloise.

I got there early and was seated up front with a glass of *vin ordinaire*. Out came five musicians, including Allen and Lester Young. Allen may have been the next Yardbird, but there was only one Lester Young—the most lyrical tenor sax man who has ever lived. Nearing the end of his life, he played with immense reserve, the notes leaking out of him as though he were barely breathing. He was in Paris for a month, and I heard him every night. On the fourth or fifth evening, I arrived early and ran into Allen.

"Hey, man," he said. "René's out for the evening. Can you sit in?"

This was what I'd been waiting for. René Urtreger, the French pianist, had gotten sick, and they needed a replacement. Allen introduced me to the guys, including Lester, who nodded indifferently under his porkpie hat. The moment we started, the butterflies left me. I'd never played with musicians anywhere near this level. They were so immersed in what they were doing that everything else completely vanished, replaced by a huge, complex universe of mysterious glances, gestures, and musical instincts.

Socially, most jazz musicians seem shy to the point of muteness. But it's only because words are not generally their medium. Jazz, with its peculiar song lines, rhythms, and improvisatory quality, is their conversation. Unlike classical or popular players, jazzmen aren't performing someone else's music, they're making up their own as they go along. They like to talk about what they do as getting inside each other's heads. That night, I learned what they meant.

Afterward, Allen said, "You did OK, kid." The Prez nodded before disappearing into a halo of smoke and a tumbler of Scotch. Arriving home around four in the morning, I couldn't sleep. I sat outside on the deck under the stars and relived the whole night—the melodies, the rhythms, the riffs, the whole fantastic business of getting inside each other's heads.

I sat in with Lester and Allen on a few more occasions and decided that the jazz life was for me. Not that I contemplated deserting Madame Honegger, but one day I did ask Allen whether he thought studying classical music was useful for jazz.

"Sure, man," he said. "Good music is good music. Those cats like Bach and Beethoven wrote some incredible stuff. I dig that as much as anything else. Learn it. *Use* it."

$$\equiv$$

Ginny had said that once a week I could drop off my sheets, towels, pillowcases, and underwear in her laundry room. I'd arrive at Number 13 around noon, sack slung over my shoulder, hoping she'd invite me to join her lunch party. If she didn't, I'd sneak into the kitchen, where Leon would feed me leftovers. Ginny's most sensational dish was a kind of cheese soufflé. As tall as a chef's *toque-blanche,* the soufflé contained poached eggs that were suspended at different levels like Christmas ornaments.

Ginny was determined to expand my cultural horizons. Besides modern paintings, her great love was classical music. Since the war, she'd spent every August at the festival in Salzburg, after which she, Anita Loos, and an English pal, Lady (Foxy) Sefton, would rid themselves of their excesses in the Tuscan baths at Montecatini. Brose wasn't much of a music lover, and Ginny made it a point to invite me to the important concerts in Paris. One day she invited me to a recital of German lieder by Elisabeth Schwarzkopf. I didn't know who Schwarzkopf was, and the idea of sitting through an evening of musty romantic German art songs was not at the top of my list. But I said I'd go and had one of the most extraordinary musical experiences of my life.

Le tout Paris was waiting for the first appearance since the war of the soprano who had been one of Hitler's favorite songbirds. They were prepared to slaughter her. There was much advance speculation about what program Schwarzkopf would sing, and when she announced it would be all German, the knives were sharpened. The Salle Pleyel was packed, everybody dressed to the nines. She kept them waiting. Then she glided out: a blonde ice goddess in a blinding white and gold dress. She was greeted by a smattering of applause and a few catcalls. With scarcely a glance at the audience, she stepped into the crook of the piano and began.

The response to her first group of songs—Schubert, I think—was tepid. With the next group, the temperature rose. And rose. By the time Schwarzkopf reached the intermission, the French were screaming in ecstasy. At one point, Ginny's hand clutched mine. "You'll never hear anything like this again, darling," she whispered.

I was lost in the beauty of the voice, the euphoria of the audience, and the indomitable presence and beauty of Schwarzkopf. Perhaps only the French could have been so quick to forgive the past, prompted by the power of art. Even Schwarzkopf's encores were in German. The French loved them.

I was living in a dreamworld. In a letter to Harry and Axie Whitney about a weekend I'd spent at Gill and Teddy Goldsmith's country house, I rhapsodized:

I'm sitting at a very good friend's house in Saint-Germain-en-Laye, looking out the window at a long valley punctuated by spotty red French roofs of presumably peasant houses. Occasionally a spire reaches up, amidst green trees and housing developments, as if recalling an older slower world: Beethoven's "Les Adieux" piano sonata, with its octave jump in the melody. Never has an octave jumped to such perfection. The room is gray with the day, as light spats of rain sputter on the window. Several stuffed birds curiously sit on their stands, inanimate, yet swaying in the breeze which comes through the open window. It is spring, and so smells the breeze . . . it smells of pick-axed gardens, rotting stones, a flower smell, a cooking-pork-with-garlic smell, and the busy smells of life in the Saint-Germain valley.

Beethoven, if anyone, makes me write badly. I feel him so intensely that I can really say nothing but small banalities compared to my true feelings of him. A sip of whisky and soda. . . .

It wasn't all Beethoven and stuffed birds. Bob and I had a battered old radio, and we listened to Radio Free Europe. That was the winter of the revolution in Budapest, which had been swiftly crushed by the Soviet Army. For days we talked about taking off for the Austrian border to help out at the Red Cross stations where the Hungarian refugees were pouring in. Instead, they came to us. One morning, we found dozens of Hungarians asleep on the quai. The next morning, some of them made it onto our deck. For several weeks, we ran a soup kitchen, dishing out nourishment prepared on our stove by Tom Keogh, *The Paris Review*'s house artist.

≡

Perhaps the first portent that my idyll was coming to an end was the great flood that seized the Seine in the spring of 1957 after a

Bob Silvers (below left) and me at a party in New York in the sixties (photograph by Jill Krementz). He and I both abandoned Paris around the same time, giving up the barge on the Seine (above), which was anchored just down the street from the Crazy Horse Saloon.

week of torrential rains. The waters rose to the elbows of the stone Zouave soldiers on the Pont de l'Alma. Old-timers said it was the worst flooding since 1910, when rowboats had been out on the Place de la Concorde and the Zouaves had been up to their necks in water.

The current was swift and angry. Thanks to the advice of a neighbor, we anchored the barge midstream so that it wouldn't land on top of the quai when the water receded. From there, we stretched a line to a tree so we could pull ourselves ashore in the dinghy. The line also acted as a conveyor belt over which friends would pull baskets of supplies. Teddy and Gaby Van Zuylen sent particularly splendid pâtés, wild game, and wines.

As the waters raged, we were terrified that the old vessel wouldn't survive. If the rusty anchor came loose, our next stop would be the very solid stone of the next bridge. Leaving the boat was as scary as staying onboard, since to get ashore we had to lower ourselves into the leaky dinghy and go hand over hand along the line to the quai.

One morning when Bob was setting forth on an errand, the dinghy slipped out from under him, leaving him dangling above the Seine in my Hotchkiss sweater. Bob was hardly cut out to play Harold Lloyd, but he managed to get himself ashore, to great cheering from me.

For a week we lived in this biblical state, fascinated by the debris that floated past: all kinds of furniture, thousands of wine bottles, and one dead cow.

≡

Mait had written to say that he and his Swedish bride, Anne, would be arriving in early summer. He thought it only right that they take over the barge. Bob left to stay at Ginny's. I daydreamed that Mait,

Anne, and I would share a life together. When I mentioned this to Ginny, she said, "I hardly think that's what they have in mind."

The end came one day in the first week of June, at about eleven in the morning. I'd been up most of the night with a beautiful young woman who was now lying next to me. Both of us were naked and asleep when a rap on the hatch jolted me awake. I jumped out of bed and slid back the cover.

The first thing I saw was a pair of black wing-tip shoes; the next thing, a pair of pin-striped, blue trouser legs. Finally, the face of Ave in his gray fedora, squinting down at me in my nakedness.

"How are you, Petey?"

"Ave!" I said, grabbing a towel. "What are you doing here?"

"I'm here for some meetings. Thought I'd stop by to see when you're planning to go back to Yale."

For a moment I blinked. Then Ave reached into his pocket and said, "I've got a prepaid ticket for you, right here."

12

ADVANCED
HARMONY AND
COUNTERPOINT

Back in New York, Ma took me aside. "Peter," she said, "you've got to get a summer job. You can't just sit around and do nothing. Why don't you call up Sonny Werblin? I'm sure he'll find something for you at MCA."

It was either Ma or Chiq who called up the man who had been my father's agent and best friend and who now ran the New York office of the Music Corporation of America, the biggest talent agency in the world. My father had been an early MCA client, and, as Ma had predicted, Sonny came through with the proverbial job—in the mail room. "It pays peanuts," he said, "but that's how you learn the business."

Sorting and delivering mail nine to five at MCA's offices on West Fifty-seventh Street wasn't my idea of summer bliss. But I had a room on Eighty-first Street, Sands Point on the weekends, and a stack of deb party invitations. I figured I'd survive.

Delivering mail, you meet everybody in the company. Right away I got friendly with Bobby Brenner, a short, peppery guy with terrific energy and an idea a minute. Bobby made the recording deals for every MCA client from Harry Belafonte to Dinah Shore to Jackie Gleason. One of his ideas was that the piano-playing son of Eddy Duchin might have the potential for a career of his own. I'd been at MCA for about a week when Bobby suggested I get out of the mail room and work for him.

That sounded like a step up, and soon I was poring over recording contracts, while Bobby explained the complexities of protecting "talent." It was an education that paid off a few years later, when Bobby engineered my break into the band business.

≡

I'd waited until the last minute to apply for a room in one of the Yale residential colleges, hoping they'd all be spoken for so that I could live off campus. It worked. That September I rented a functional one-bedroom apartment on Chapel Street. It wasn't the Pont de l'Alma, but it gave me the freedom to come and go as I pleased, eat when I wanted to eat, and share my bed with girls—whose presence was still forbidden in undergraduate rooms after dark. I grew my hair to a Byronic length and stalked the campus in a green loden cape I'd acquired in Paris. It had been given me by Hugh Latham, a flamboyant friend and night owl, on a cold December morning when the two of us were reeling through Les Halles, ending a long night with cognac and onion soup. Hugh had noticed my shivering and had thrown off his cape and draped it around my shoulders, exclaiming, *"Voilà, un berger honnête!"* In New Haven, though, it wasn't the honest shepherd pose I affected but the aloofness of Rodin's *Balzac*.

I signed up for the sort of "Renaissance man" curriculum favored by Yale's medievalist president, A. Whitney Griswold. In addition to courses in advanced harmony and counterpoint, I studied Eastern philosophy, Western tragedy, classical art and architecture (taught by the spellbinding Vincent Scully), and French literature (taught by the equally spellbinding Henri Peyre). My third-floor walk-up became an off-campus refuge for my old pals, who would drop in at all hours for food, drink, music, and talk. I bought *Joy of Cooking* and mastered beef stroganoff and chicken paprika. I also bought a small, hyperactive canary I called Bird. It flew freely around the apartment, shitting everywhere.

Much of the time I was thinking about a beautiful girl at Vassar whom I'll call Sally. Tall, blonde, with aristocratic bones, she was as fey as Emily Dickinson and, at first, as unattainable as Grace Kelly. We'd met as the result of one of my ploys. One weekend I arrived at Vassar in my cape, glided into one of the common rooms, sat down at a piano, and began playing. It never failed. This time, I was stunned by the girl who wandered over.

"I love your cape," she said.

So it started.

Our courtship began with many rambling poetic discussions on the phone. We discovered we loved the same books (Hermann Hesse's *Steppenwolf*, Robert Lowell's *Life Studies*). We loved the same music (Renaissance, Bach, and jazz). Before long, I was feeling brand-new feelings. I wanted to shelter Sally, to protect her. She was looking for self-discovery, and so was I. I wanted to go off with her, just the two of us, forever.

I wasn't shocked when a Yale friend implied that he'd slept with her. The news that Sally was a woman of the world made her all the more irresistible. I was delighted to think that she wasn't like all the other girls who were saving their virginity for marriage. (So we were supposed to believe.) Sally was gutsy. A free spirit.

Gingerly, we toyed with the idea of sleeping together. One weekend in Poughkeepsie, we took the plunge. When we arrived at the neon-lit motel, my knees started to buckle. Sally gave me one of her smiles and put her arm around me. Somehow we got through the door. Pulling out the inevitable six-pack, I cracked a few beers and said something inane.

"Shhh—enough of that," said Sally.

Sally wasn't a woman of the world after all. I was nonplussed to discover that she was a virgin. This development, much to my surprise, made me feel closer to her than I had ever felt to a girl, as well as more protective and possessive of her than ever.

Through my graduation the following June and into the summer, we were seldom apart. In July, she came to my twenty-first birthday bash in Sands Point. After everyone had gone home, Sally and I strolled out onto the pier and sat there, our toes dangling in the water as we listened to the foghorn on Execution Rock. Behind me was a house I'd grown up in, Ma and Ave, servants I'd known forever. Out there was water I'd fished in, the wonderful smell of seaweed. Next to me was Sally. The picture was complete.

But in a few days I would be leaving for Greece. After that, it was two years in the U.S. Army.

"Will you wait for me?" I asked.

Sally was more honest than I was: "I hope so," she replied.

As things turned out, she didn't.

===

The next morning, Ma got up around noon, and Sally and I sat with her while she had her usual runny soft-boiled egg and toast, washed down with coffee and hot milk. "Pete," she said, "I'm really proud of you. I had my doubts that you'd ever graduate. But I must say, I'd rather you were going on to something besides the Army. What a goddamn waste of time."

I had opted for the Army to put off having to decide on a career. I had no interest in graduate school. Military service was inescapable for unmarried nonstudents, so I'd asked to be drafted in order to get it over with, on my schedule, such as it was. Two years in the Army was a dreary—even terrifying—prospect, but I couldn't see any way around it. I'd received papers ordering me to report for basic training in October. That gave me the summer for one last blowout.

In August I flew to London to meet a fellow with whom I'd become friendly that summer on the deb party circuit in the Hamptons. George Livanos was the son of one of the biggest Greek ship owners and the brother-in-law of Stavros Niarchos and Aristotle Onassis, his father's two biggest rivals. He'd said he'd love to show me around Greece for a month. I'd said yes on the spot.

We did the first leg of the journey, London to Paris, in George's Aston Martin, tearing through Normandy with the top down. George had promised a couple of nights in Monte Carlo onboard the *Christina*, Aristotle Onassis's huge yacht. Arriving in Monaco, we discovered that our places onboard had been preempted by Winston Churchill. As consolation, Onassis had arranged for us to be put up in the Presidential Suite in one of his properties, the Hôtel de Paris. The digs occupied an entire floor, and waiting for us were buckets of champagne, pounds of caviar, and two beautiful girls. "From Ari," George said nonchalantly.

The next day we were ferried out to the *Christina* for lunch. Onassis reminded me of a compact, very wily goat. You knew you were around a guy who had done damn near everything to satisfy his huge appetite and didn't care who stood in his way. The force of his magnetic field was overwhelming.

Churchill sat immobile in a wheelchair under a rug. When I mentioned that I had been raised by Averell and Marie Harriman, he came to life. "A wonderful man," he said. "I believe he was the one most responsible for getting the Americans to support us during the war."

His face, as soft and pink as a baby's, crinkled into a smile. "Did Averell ever tell you about the time I instructed him in the art of martini making, using Madeira?"

"No."

"It was during the war, and he'd come over to Chartwell for the weekend. We'd had a beastly day, and we both needed a good, stiff drink. Averell suggested a martini, but we couldn't find a drop of vermouth. Then I came up with it. Madeira! An old British field trick. Wonderful stuff."

We moved on to Rome, where we met a young Italian count, Giovanni Volpi, who challenged us to a "grand prix" down the Via Veneto at dawn. Nose to nose with Giovanni's Ferrari, we somehow made it out of Rome alive.

In Athens I met George's friends, who were all rich and bored and totally uninterested in looking at ruins. They thought I was crazy when I suggested spending a night in the Parthenon.

I went on my own. At closing time I hid from the guards, and while the sun was going down I found myself completely alone. Sitting against a column, I watched the moon rise and the stars come out and thought of Ulysses and Penelope. The air smelled of sage, and somewhere a dog was barking. I spent the sleepless night in a trance, feeling close to the gods.

With D. S. Robertson's *Handbook of Greek and Roman Architecture* under my arm, I tramped through the ruins at Olympia and Delphi with George and a couple of bored Greek society girls. Now I was able actually to see the truth of Vincent Scully's distinction between Roman and Greek sculpture. The Roman images merely described faces, limbs, and drapery. The Greek marbles had soul.

George and I taverna-hopped, and wherever there was a piano, I'd sit down and improvise while the Greeks clapped along. One night, a party of us climbed into an assortment of the world's fanciest sports cars for an evening outside Athens. Several bazouki musicians were blowing in the funky little taverna where we ended up. I joined them at the old, beat-up piano in the corner. Pretty soon we were cooking, and the ouzo was flowing. First, the glasses were smashed against the stucco. Then the bottles. Then the plates, tables, and chairs. After one of George's friends drove his Porsche through a wall, the cops arrived. They herded all the men into a Greek paddy wagon. As we were taken away, we could see the girls through the rear window, lending moral support in the sports cars.

Just as the sun was coming up, a voice came over the police radio. The driver slammed on the brakes, and all the cops got out. While we watched, they lined up on the highway and performed their morning routine of push-ups, knee bends, and jumping jacks.

At the police station, we were herded upstairs and presented with a bill for damages close to $50,000. I never heard so many Greek expressions for "No way!" During the shouting, George pulled me aside. "It'll only get worse if they find out you're American," he whispered. "Climb out that window over there and get your ass back to the hotel."

I was no Errol Flynn. But the vines were strong, and one of the girls was waiting below in George's Aston Martin with the engine running.

While I was stationed in Panama in 1959, I won an army
talent contest that got me onto *The Ed Sullivan Show.*
It was my TV debut.

13

A GLOCKENSPIELIST
IN PANAMA

Hell is Fort Jackson, South Carolina. Out in the middle of no-where, in a sandy, swampy terrain of scrubby pines, were mile after mile of grim barracks and a colony of sadists. It was amazing to think that just thirty miles away was Arcadia, home of the Vander-bilts' ghost.

The best piece of advice I've ever been given came from Bob Sil-vers, who had been in the Army and who knew. Taking me aside at my twenty-first birthday party, he said, "When you get to basic training, you're going to be totally disoriented and petrified. If you're smart, you're going to realize you're in a situation you can't get out of. You're fucked. At some point, some sergeant is going to yell, 'Is there any asshole out there who's had military training?' Raise your hand. They'll make you a squad leader."

I raised my hand.

Being squad leader to a dozen scared, poor blacks, illiterate red-necks, and a few ex-jailbirds made my life relatively tolerable if only because I got yelled at less than they did. But none of my up-bringing at Arden, Eaglebrook, Hotchkiss, Yale, and Ginny Chambers's had prepared me for being awakened at dawn by a blinding light and a screaming sergeant and having to scramble outside to be screamed at for the rest of the day. Paradise was the few hours we got off each weekend, when I could hit one of the seamy bars in Columbia, sit down at a piano, and play some jazz. I got a girl-friend, who called herself Butch. I was so desperate I got myself a job as rehearsal pianist for a local production of *Brigadoon*—a mu-sical I still loathe.

At some point, I entered an Army talent contest, did well, and got a two-day pass to appear on *The Ed Sullivan Show* in New York. Once in the studio before the live audience, I wanted to run straight back to Fort Jackson. Sullivan introduced me as "Peter Dooshin" and spent most of the time talking about my father. Somehow, I got through two songs: "Summertime" and my father's theme song, "To Love Again," based on Chopin's Nocturne in E-flat. The other day I looked at an old tape of the show and couldn't believe I was once that scrawny, frozen-faced soldier with the geek haircut. But my playing, backed by the 8,000 strings of Ray Bloch's orchestra, zipped along passably, stumbling only once for a wrong note in the nocturne. The next day, the *Times* gener-ously summed up my television debut as "brief but enjoyable."

≡

Not even a perfect score on the French language exam and Ave's pull were enough to get me assigned to SHAPE headquarters in Paris. With typical military logic, I was ordered to report to Fort

Clayton in the American Canal Zone in Panama. My duties? Chief glockenspielist in the 79th U.S. Army Band.

Before flying down to Panama City, I had a week off. Chiquita came up from Maryland to say good-bye, and over dinner at "21," I wailed about how I'd been screwed by some little bastard in Washington. Chiq nodded sympathetically, doubtless thinking that the best thing that could happen to me was to have to face up to a few realities for a change. Bob Kriendler, one of "21"'s owners, stopped by to say hello. When he heard where I was going, he said, "Don't worry, Pete. I have a good friend down there. Fellow named McGrath. Knows everybody."

I had hardly unpacked my duffel bag when Roberto McGrath, a wealthy businessman in Panama City, had me over for a dinner party and introduced me to the cream of Panamanian society, including a disproportionate number of beautiful women. Panama was looking up.

Other invitations followed. One evening I met the American general who commanded the Canal Zone. He knew all about my background and had heard that I was stationed in his command. After a couple of drinks, he offered me a deal: If I played at the Officers' Club on weekends, he'd let me live off base in Panama City. I'd have to pay for the apartment myself, show up on time for reveille, and not shirk any of my duties on the glockenspiel.

He had one more condition: "I'd like you to keep your ears open for any information of a political nature and pass it along to me."

"You bet, sir," I said happily.

"Particularly," he added, "stuff from the Cubans, who are all over the place. We want to know everything we can about what that Castro fellow is up to."

"I'll do what I can, sir."

"By the way, private," he added, "do you like to fish?"

"Sure do, sir."

Something came up to keep the general from making it onto his forty-five-foot Bertram the following Saturday, so I brought along a couple of buddies. The boat we climbed onto would have been perfectly at home on any dock in Palm Beach.

Six of us, including the captain and a crew of Panamanians, set off around noon. We fished our way out to the Perlis Islands, catching bonito to use as bait for marlins the next day. At sunset we anchored in the lee of one of the islands. The Panamanians were bottom fishing, and we were throwing back the rum when a shout brought us to our feet. One of the Panamanians had pulled up a huge, dog-toothed snapper. As we were laying the fillets on a hibachi grill, we noticed a small dugout canoe approaching.

At first it looked as though there were two people in the boat— one paddling, the other squatting in the middle. But as the canoe got closer, we saw that the paddler was an ancient Panamanian and his passenger, a large, leafy plant. From what we could gather, he was interested in trading two cans of sardines for the plant.

The captain explained: "Well, if you guys want some of the greatest grass you'll ever have, I've got the sardines."

Panama was really looking up.

=

One of the most singularly unpleasant things you can do on a hangover is march up and down a parade field in 120-degree heat at nine in the morning, playing a glockenspiel. The sound of the glockenspiel in your ear is like an ice pick plunging into your brain. I wore my Army-issue glockenspiel strapped tightly around my middle. It weighed twenty pounds and felt like a hundred.

Fortunately, I had a few other duties, which included playing piano at band concerts and helping to copy and write new arrangements. I really couldn't complain. At the end of the day, I'd jump into a battered old Plymouth I'd bought for 400 bucks and hit the town.

Just as the general had predicted, I was soon running into Cubans, all of whom were sympathetic to Fidel Castro. Many were from good families—serious, deeply committed people who had given up their property for the revolution. They believed that Castro was the savior of Cuba, the George Washington of a new Latin America. They didn't think he was really a Communist but simply a man like them who, fed up with the corrupt Batista regime, had had the courage to act.

My command of Spanish was pretty basic, but with the help of a little French, I was able to talk revolutionary politics far into the night. It also helped that I appeared to be nothing more than a glockenspielist who happened to be stoned much of the time.

In fact, I was beginning to feel rather revolutionary myself. The Zone was a ten-mile strip spanning both sides of the Canal, inhabited entirely by military personnel assigned to the Army and Air Force bases, and the engineers and other people who ran the Canal. Except for the exotic flora and fauna, including the occasional three-toed sloth, it could have been a suburb of Kalamazoo: row after row of tidy, air-conditioned ranch houses with basketball hoops in the driveways, set behind perfectly manicured lawns. At the numerous PXs, the American residents, as well as the Panamanians who worked there, could buy whatever they wanted at prices five times less than they could in town. Most of the Americans had never bothered to learn a word of Spanish except to speak to their servants. Many of them took pride in saying they had yet to set foot in Panama City.

Just beyond the fence was another world: a world of color, rhythm, old Hispanic buildings, gleaming new banks, and fabulous residential areas, cheek by jowl with slums of tin-roofed squatters' shacks and lots of mud. This was where the Panamanians lived. If they resented the gringos, who could blame them?

My heart was with the Panamanians, but I owed the general. One evening I told him that an anti-American demonstration was brewing. It seemed that the Panamanians wanted their own flag flown in the Canal Zone. Anti-American demonstrations didn't play well in Washington, said the general. He'd do what he could about it. Whatever he did didn't work. A week later, on the Fourth of July, the Panamanians had their demonstration.

It was the closest I got to combat. As the protesters began multiplying outside the fence and lobbing rocks in our direction, the Army band members were issued rifles without ammo and ordered to stay out of the way. After dodging the rocks for a while, we were marched up to another section of the line—the farthest point from the action. There we all sat down and rolled joints to enjoy the rest of the day.

Around two o'clock, three very tough looking protesters showed up outside the fence. What they yelled was pretty bad, and most of us knew enough Spanish to understand it. Then, one of them broke into English: "Who was first on the moon, you motherfuckers?" he yelled.

Private Carbo jumped to his feet. "The Panamanians?" he yelled back.

It was a diplomatic stroke worthy of Ave. The toughs cracked up, threw us high fives, and moved on down the line.

≡

Along with some of the better players in the Army and Air Force bands, I formed a jazz orchestra. What began as jam sessions strictly for the fun of it grew into gigs all over Panama City. We

Private Duchin and The Stablemates represented the
Caribbean Command at the 1960 All-Army Entertainment
Contest in Fort Belvoir, Virginia.

soon had quite a following. One of our biggest fans was a tall, cool-looking dude with a mustache who showed up everywhere. He'd help us set up the bandstand and bring us drinks during the breaks. Everybody knew him—Flacco (or Slim), they called him.

Slim was a great jazz buff, and he and I hit it off. One day, he asked if I needed a driver and jack-of-all-trades. I was having a hard time getting from my apartment in town to reveille at Fort Clayton, which was five miles away. Here was the man to wake me up and get me there. Before long, Slim was also cleaning my apartment and living in a room behind my kitchen.

Slim is now living in New York. I brought him here when I left Panama and helped get him a job spinning records at New York's first discotheque, Le Club. Since then, he's become the most successful club deejay in the city, has put two children through college and graduate school, and has remained one of my closest buddies.

With Slim's help, we rounded up the best Panamanian musicians to give us a fuel injection of Latin rhythm. The legendary Cuban pianist and bandleader Perruchin came to town and sat in with us. From Perruchin, I learned how to make the piano into a purely rhythmic instrument—the engine that sends the temperature up. Soon we were joined by the local percussionists, who came flying out of doorways with their pots and pans and anything else that made a racket.

I've always been envious of musicians who can really make a piano sing—people like Walter Gieseking, Arthur Rubinstein, Sviatoslav Richter, Art Tatum, Oscar Peterson, Bill Evans. I think the closest I ever got to that level was when we played at the local mental hospital. I've never had a better audience. Sousa marches, classical overtures, Charlie Parker, Cole Porter—they dug it all. They sang along to everything, never mind the tune. They danced about in great primal leaps. They wandered among us, peering at their reflections in the shiny brass instruments. Whenever I'd take a solo, they'd drape themselves over the piano, vying for the best spot. With the crazy ladies' arms around me, I thought my heart would burst.

Six of us formed a jazz combo we called The Stablemates. In June 1960, we were flown up to Fort Belvoir, Virginia, to play in an Army talent show. Afterward, I went to the Pentagon for a meeting arranged by Ave. I'd come up with a great goodwill idea: Why not send our combined Army, Air Force, and Panamanian band on a tour of Latin America? It sounded great, but then the Army and Air Force brass got to squabbling over which branch of the U.S. Armed Services we would be representing. That was the end of that.

=

I was nearing the completion of active duty when Chiquita called. She had divorced her rancher husband Morgan and recently married Bob Everitt, an American businessman in Mexico City. She offered to fly me there. I was sorry she hadn't married an American businessman in Paris, but the Panamanian monsoons were in full force, and Mexico City was high and dry.

We met at a restaurant where Chiq introduced me to my date for the evening, a stylishly dressed woman named Carmen who didn't look a day under sixty-five. I resigned myself to an evening of being polite. When dessert rolled around, Chiq and Bob got up rather abruptly and said they had to be getting home. "Why don't you two stay on for a while?" said Chiq, throwing Carmen a wink.

My heart sank.

"I know a wonderful place for a nightcap," said Carmen. Well brought up as I was, I went along.

The place we stopped at couldn't have been seedier-looking. A rusty gate creaked. Then another gate. Finally Carmen and I stepped into an astonishing room: walls of crimson velvet, oil paintings of plump, slumbering nudes, amber lights under fringed shades. And lounging about in various stages of undress were the best-looking girls I'd seen in a very long time.

Carmen downed a quick drink, then reached into her handbag. "For you, Peter, dear," she said, handing me an enormous wad of pesos. "Have a good time."

Glancing nervously around, I noticed a guy in a corner, surrounded by girls. To my amazement I recognized him. It was Angier Biddle Duke, a friend from New York.

I walked over. "Angie," I said, "how are you?"

Conversation stopped. Angie peered up at me. Then, through clenched teeth, he said, "Peter, weren't you ever taught *never* to recognize anyone in a place like this?"

Two nights and a day later, I ran out of pesos. I called my stepmother and said, "Chiq, that was the nicest thing you've ever done for me."

"I thought you'd like Carmen," said Chiq.

On my last night in Mexico City, Chiq and Bob took me to Uno, Dos, Tres, the town's answer to El Morocco. Around midnight, I went over to the piano. I had played a few tunes when a man walked up. From the look of him, either he was the bouncer or he was about to sell me his sister.

"I know who you are," he said softly. "You're the son of Eddy Duchin. You play the piano very well. I can help you."

"You can?"

He handed me a card. The name—César Balsa—meant nothing to me.

"Call me when you get out of the Army and you're back in New York," he murmured. "I own the St. Regis Hotel."

=

In October 1960, I got my discharge papers and reported to Fort Dix, New Jersey, for processing out. I landed at Newark Airport with a couple of buddies. On our way to the baggage claim, we stopped for a beer.

The bar was jammed with people who were watching television. On the screen were two men. One looked dark and exceedingly uncomfortable with himself. He was perspiring a lot. The other looked vibrant, graceful, and humorous. The first man I recognized as Richard Nixon. The other was John F. Kennedy, the young American senator I'd met a few years earlier in London.

A few months later, I was in Washington for JFK's inauguration, which took place during one of the worst snowstorms in Washington's history. It was almost impossible to get around, but I'd been dating Pamela Turnure, an assistant to the new First Lady, and Pam had been able to secure one of the last sets of tire chains in the capital, as well as a Secret Service–approved parking permit. She'd even managed to get us seats on a VIP platform at the swearing-in.

Pam and I made the rounds of the balls, plowing through the snow. Sometime after midnight we called it quits. I was helping her into the car when I spotted a hunched figure looking around for a nonexistent cab. It was "Uncle Joe" Alsop, the columnist. "My driver disappeared and I'm bloody frozen!" he said. "Can you give me a lift home?"

It turned out that Joe had invited people over for late-night turtle soup at his house in Georgetown, and the guests had already started arriving when we drove up. He asked us in, and I helped uncork the champagne and ladle out the soup. Around one-thirty, the doorbell rang and in walked Jack Kennedy, looking to unwind. Joe beamed. The rest of us gasped. The party perked up markedly.

My first apartment in New York was in the Carnegie Hall Studios.
I became a regular downstairs at the Russian Tea Room, as were
several Russians, including Rudolf Nureyev.

14

SOCIETY BEAT

The trust fund my father left me had provided just enough to edu-
cate me, keep me clothed, and offer a small allowance. But I had
no means of real support and no direction. The old doors were still
open—Ma and Ave's, Chiquita's, Harry and Axie's—and I went
running back to all of them. During my first months out of the
Army, I devoted myself to seeing old friends, meeting as many new
girls as possible, and waiting for the day when my hair would be
back to its former length.

One day, Ma took me to Toots Shor's for lunch. "Sweetheart,"
she said, "I don't want to interrupt all the fun you're having, but I
think it's about time you got your ass in gear. You need your own
place, and you better start thinking about what you're going to do
with your life."

I nodded sorrowfully.

The conventional thing would have been to get myself a place on the white-bread Upper East Side, as my friends were all doing. But then, through a beautiful, anorexic dancer I was dating, I heard about an apartment in the Carnegie Hall Studios. What could be better than living over the world's greatest concert hall?

My ninth-floor apartment in Carnegie Hall was essentially one big room with twenty-two-foot ceilings, a wood-burning fireplace, a functional kitchenette, and a little flight of stairs that led to a sleeping loft. Huge windows faced north over a flat roof. I bought myself a cheap bed and a pair of bookshelves. From the big house at Arden, Ma chipped in an old refectory table and a set of chairs. Chiq sent up a couch and Dad's favorite rocking chair from her farm in Maryland. Best of all, she sent up his old Bechstein baby grand, the one John Wanamaker had given him when Dad was starting out.

Most of the studios in the tower above Carnegie Hall were used as work spaces by musicians, dancers, and photographers. A few of them had been converted for living. I quickly became friends with two neighbors—the jazz pianist Don Shirley and the cabaret entertainer Bobby Short.

Talk about style: Don, urbane in black from head to toe or an elegant African dashiki; Bobby, the casually tailored gentleman in his houndstooth jackets and handmade shoes. Don and Bobby both worked like hell. Bobby was singing Porter, Coward, Arlen, and Rodgers and Hart at the Blue Angel. Don was playing jazz at places like the Hickory House. Somehow they made it seem as though all they were doing was having a hell of a lot of fun.

Many nights when I crawled home, my phone would ring, and it would be Bobby or Don saying, "How about a nightcap?" I'd lower myself out the window and creep across the roof. There, in Bobby's or Don's apartment at two or three in the morning, would be quite a few of the hippest people in New York, having a ball.

One night before Christmas, I'd arrived home with a girl, ready for the sack, when Bobby called. "Come on over to Don's. We're having a Christmas party."

It was 2:30 and snowing. My date and I climbed out the window and put our heads against the wind. We knocked on Don's window. When it opened, our ears were flooded by a choir of angels. Standing around the piano and belting out "Joy to the World" were Leontyne Price, Odetta, and Martha Flowers, the gospel queen. While we made ourselves invisible in a corner, they went on to "Adeste Fideles," "The First Noel," "Hark, the Herald Angels Sing," "O Little Town of Bethlehem," and "Silent Night." By the time they got to "Go Tell It on the Mountain," nobody in that room had any doubts about the Second Coming.

There was a comforting sense of community in the Carnegie Studios. I'd leave my door open so I could watch the ballet dancers trooping past in their comely, purposeful way. Every day, I had lunch downstairs at the Russian Tea Room, which came to feel like my own dining room. I could depend on seeing friends or famous faces—Leonard Bernstein or Tennessee Williams, or Ruth Gordon and Garson Kanin, who were there every Thursday for *pelmeni*, the dumpling soup that reminded me of Grandma Duchin's kitchen.

I became friends with Sidney Kaye, the restaurant's owner, who took me to a seder at the house of his brother-in-law, the great tenor Jan Peerce, who sang the service. I was knocked out by it. Peerce told me that he'd known my father when they were both starting out—Peerce as a street violinist. To my embarrassment, I had never been to a seder before. I'd heard a bit about the Jewish faith from Aunt Lil and Uncle Ben, but I'd never thought it had anything to do with me. Occasionally, I'd been curious enough about religion to wander into a place of worship, but only to see the architecture or hear the music. I was a mongrel then, and I'm a mongrel today. I've never felt the slightest impulse to align myself with one way of looking at the world. Still, I can tell you that, for warmth and drama, a seder sure beats the Episcopalians.

One of my dearest friends at the Russian Tea Room was a Chekhovian Russian waitress named Nadia. There were two "boys" she favored: "my Pyotr and my Rudy"—me and Rudolf Nureyev. Rudy and I developed a waving relationship across the room as Nadia bustled back and forth, making sure we finished our borscht and blintzes, and tweaking our cheeks for being "good boys." On Russian Easter, she would tap on my door with a Russian Easter cake she'd baked specially for me, and I'd invite her in for a quick shot of iced vodka.

For my first Thanksgiving, I invited twenty-five strays. I called up a caterer and ordered a turkey, all stuffed and ready to pop into the oven. Just before it arrived, my bell rang and my current girlfriend arrived, ostensibly to help out. "Open your mouth," she said cutely.

I did, and she dropped in a little tablet.

"Now swallow."

I did.

"Congratulations, Peter," she said. "You've just taken mescaline. It's going to be an interesting Thanksgiving."

Fortunately, the bird arrived before my head exploded. As I got the turkey into the oven, I began to feel a little weird, getting the odd flash of magenta where it should have been brown. "How the hell do you expect me to get through this?" I said.

"Relax," she said. "I'm starting to feel it, too. God, it's *beautiful!*"

She suddenly turned into a mallard. "Maybe you'd better fly upstairs to the bedroom," I suggested.

The guests arrived. Somehow the drinks were poured and the turkey got cooked and eaten. I was in a nonstop horror movie. Why was everybody bursting into flames or turning into a skeleton? When they opened their mouths, why did worms come out? I was sure that at any minute the mallard would come flying over the banister and land in the sweet potatoes. The weirdest thing was that nobody seemed to notice anything the least bit strange about me. But how would I have known?

$$\equiv$$

In the late fifties and early sixties, all of Manhattan was open to anybody at any hour. After work, people would put on their best duds and hit the town. Live music—music you could really listen to or dance to—was everywhere. All the top hotels had supper clubs featuring great house bands led by pros like Emil Coleman or Ted Straeter. For exclusiveness you went to El Morocco, the Stork Club, or Gogi's La Rue. There was jazz up and down Fifty-second Street and all over the West Village. Tito Puente and Prez Prado were at the Palladium. Later on, you'd taxi over to hear Bobby Short at the Blue Angel, and then cross the street to the RSVP to listen to the Mother of Them All, Mabel Mercer. Or keep on going all the way up to Harlem. At two in the morning, the Red Rooster, Minton's, and Smalls' Paradise were just getting started.

A great friend of mine was the poet, actor, and former champion track star Roscoe Lee Browne. Roscoe was appearing in the legendary production of Genet's *The Blacks* that completely transformed the New York theater by bringing in a whole generation of great and previously little-employed black actors, among them James Earl Jones, Lou Gossett, Cicely Tyson, and Roscoe.

Behind his extravagant manner, Roscoe had a sharp intelligence. Like me, he walked through all sorts of worlds—jazz, theater,

With a friend, the actress Anna Maria Alberghetti,
at El Morocco in 1961.

With Toots Shor and Joe E. Lewis. Toots was enormously
important in my life. He was an old friend of my dad's,
and a warm and generous friend to me.

opera, Harlem, Park Avenue. He was the sort of person I've always admired—self-created and without boundaries. He loved to share his friends, which is another quality I admire. Best of all, Roscoe was pure theater—on about ten different levels at once.

Over lunch the other day, we both got a little nostalgic. "There was so much nightlife in New York back then," Roscoe said, rolling his eyes. "People drank and smoked and stayed up as late as they liked. You could get anything to eat at any hour. Women wore real jewels, and men wore silk. You could even make love in Central Park without getting killed."

"Who the hell did you make love to in Central Park?"

"I'll never tell."

———

Nothing over the years has changed more than the music business. Jazz may be having a resurgence. It's always having a resurgence. But there is almost no place in New York where you can dance to live music. Now, everything's disco—canned and faceless. If I were thinking about starting out in the band business today, I wouldn't do it. Back then, when you decided to become a musician, it wasn't just a job, it was a life.

Of course, doors were open to me because of my name and connections. One call to Bobby Brenner at MCA, and it wasn't long before I had a career, at least on paper. Not that there was anything else on the horizon. Thanks to Hotchkiss, Yale, and the Sorbonne, I had acquired a healthy degree of intellectual curiosity. But that didn't get you a job. Sometimes I dreamed about returning to Paris and leading the Left Bank life. But deep down, I knew I needed more security.

Other times I fantasized about becoming a serious composer. Ma had always tried to steer me in that direction. "For Chrissake," she'd say, "you've been educated for it. Why don't you go to Juil-liard and get serious?" But every time I thought about sitting down and doing it, I'd let something distract me. Writing really good music means creating a universe of one's own in sound. I wasn't sure I had such a universe inside me. And I knew I wouldn't be able to stand the isolation.

I sometimes think I might have made a good symphony conduc-tor. But again, something held me back. Perhaps it was wanting too much to be liked—which is not a good thing when you're standing in front of a hundred brilliant musicians trying to get them all to play it your way. I don't think Toscanini, Szell, Karajan, or Solti ever worried for a second about being liked.

Many people have asked me whether I would have become a bandleader if my father had remained alive. The answer is "Proba-bly not." I'm sure that if my father had been alive and thriving in 1960, I'd have thought more than twice about following in his footsteps. But he wasn't around. As I thought about what I could do with myself when I was twenty-three, I realized that the only thing I had to hang my hat on was his legacy. Not that I wanted to be Eddy Duchin all over again. That was impossible. I simply wanted to use whatever talent and personality I had of my own and make the most of it.

=

If I had any qualms about "selling out" by pursuing a career that others might think frivolous, they were quickly swept aside by Bobby. He had it all figured out. "This is a terrific time for pianist-bandleaders," he said. "Look at Roger Williams and Floyd Cramer. You wouldn't *believe* the records these guys sell. It's MOR—middle of the road. First we launch you with a recording deal. You with some terrific studio guys. Then we cut an album. We get a record promoter—Jim McCarthy's the best in the business. We get a movie contract with Universal. Than we get you a band. Pete, with your name and looks—not to mention talent, of course—it's a piece of cake. Trust me."

"What kind of music do I play?"

"I told you. MOR. Romantic. Melodic. Your dad's kind of stuff, updated."

"Jesus, Bobby, I hate that crap. How about if I do it with a jazz feeling?"

"Forget it. Nobody buys jazz. The name of the game is MOR. Trust me."

I did.

There was something very comforting about this little guy's belief in me. Bobby was a fountain of ideas. Beginning in the winter of 1961, we met regularly in his office to plot my rise in show business. I loved the feeling that I was being molded, just as I had when Bill Kitchen had taught me how to fish or when Ave had showed me how to execute a perfect figure eight on my strawberry roan.

I had a lot to learn. Although I could improvise my way through quite a few pop and jazz standards, I had never consciously developed a style, certainly not one that could be considered commercial.

"Take a few lessons from Ira Brandt," suggested Bobby. "He's one of the best lounge guys in the business."

Me a lounge guy? I winced. But I came to love working with Ira. He was a natty little guy with the pencil-thin mustache of an old-world Jewish tailor. He knew every tune ever written. Twice a week, I'd report to his apartment on Central Park West to learn the right touch for Gershwin, Porter, Berlin, Rodgers and Hart, Jerome Kern, Vincent Youmans, Johnny Mercer, Hoagy Carmichael, Harry Warren, Harold Arlen, Burton Lane, Jule Styne, Cy Coleman, Henry

Mancini, and so on. I learned the accepted chord progressions used by professional musicians. Going through the tunes over and over again with Ira, I learned how to play less percussively, how to sing the melody with the right hand, even in the bass clef, like my father.

It was from Meyer Davis, the dean of society bandleaders, that I learned how to make people get up and dance. Meyer had been a great admirer of my father. When I called him one day and told him what I was up to, he couldn't have been more generous about sharing the tricks of the trade.

"Peter," he said, "when I started out in this business, I was playing for a lot of rich Philadelphia Wasps—Wideners and Wanamakers, people like that. I noticed they all had one thing in common: They had no rhythm. They couldn't waltz. They couldn't rumba. They could hardly fox-trot. One day it occurred to me that at least they could *walk*. I thought, What if I play everything in march tempo? So that's what I did, and it worked. You know why? Because march tempo is the same as the human heartbeat."

Meyer was right. Today, I play all kinds of tempos—slow ballads, waltzes, sambas, rock and roll. But the one that never fails to get them up on their feet is still the old Meyer Davis heartbeat.

Under Ira's tutelage, I practiced various exercises to become more technically fluid. I'd dissect the most familiar standards like a medical student in anatomy class. Ira would have me play "Blue Moon" upside-down, sideways, and backwards. It was the only way, he said, to really get all the possibilities into your fingers. After six months of this, I had mastered some 300 standards, including "Here Comes the Bride" and "Havah Nagilah." Today, I've got about 3,000 tunes in my fingers.

A bandleader sometimes has to play solo background piano during the cocktail and dinner hours, so I started dropping in at the Drake Hotel to hear Cy Walter, the top cocktail stylist in the city.

Cy played the simplest tunes in the most complicated arrangements, everything in sharps and flats. Without injecting any jazz
feeling or deviating much from the melody, he was never perfunc-
tory or boring. With his great technique and inventiveness, Cy
turned everything into a little rococo masterpiece. He was proof
that you could play in the melodic style without being square.

Bobby also urged me to study my father's old recordings. "Not to
copy him," he cautioned, "but to learn why people wanted to listen
to Eddy Duchin all night."

For my taste, Dad's style was too ornate. But as I listened to his
records, I understood why so many people had always said they felt
he was playing only for them. Dad hadn't just played the melody,
he'd played the lyrics, as though he were singing the song in his
head.

≡

The people at Decca Records had done extremely well with the
soundtrack album of *The Eddy Duchin Story* (with Carmen Cavallaro sitting in for my father). I may have been completely wet
behind the ears, but the commercial chances of an album featuring Eddy Duchin's son were too obvious to resist. It also didn't hurt
that Bobby and I were putting together the whole package, including a movie deal. In a matter of weeks, Bobby got me a five-year
contract with Decca, calling for the release of two albums a year.

For an arranger, Bobby hired one of the best in the business.
Henri René was an elegant, classically trained European who had
written for Hollywood, nightclub acts, and recordings. He liked
the idea of working with a neophyte, someone who would be putty
in his hands. For three months, we met at his place or mine, exploring the possibilities of each tune, including what I would play,
note for note.

Listening again to that first album, I wish I'd had the courage to inject more of my own personality and feelings into the arrangements. It might have been too jazz flavored, but it would have been less bland. Even so, *Presenting Peter Duchin* received a lot of radio exposure as well as excellent reviews when it was released in February 1962. It sold surprisingly well—over 100,000 copies. The repertoire included tried-and-true standards, selections from the best musical of the day, Bernstein's *West Side Story,* a pop arrangement of Debussy's "Clair de Lune" (as a lush ballad), and the theme from *Never on Sunday,* the hot art movie of the moment.

All my backup musicians were top studio guys, and Henri's arrangements were tailored to create a style that was intimate but not too personal, bouncy but not too jazzy. The first cut, "Make Someone Happy," written by my friends Jule Styne, Betty Comden, and Adolph Green, got the most airplay. It would become my signature song when I opened at the Maisonette.

=

In March 1961, George Plimpton invited me down to Florida, where he was staying with Harold S. (Mike) Vanderbilt and his wife, Gertrude. George was working on a profile for *Sports Illustrated* of this most distinguished of Commodore Vanderbilt's many descendants. The last of his family to sit on the board of the New York Central, the railway founded by his grandfather, Mike was perhaps the greatest figure in American yachting (he'd successfully captained several America's Cup winners), as well as the inventor of contract bridge, which he had refined from an earlier game called écarté during a long and boring transatlantic crossing in the twenties. He was famously shy, and I was surprised that this tall, straight-backed, quiet man with a scholar's face was so friendly when I arrived at his palatial estate in Lantana, just south of Palm Beach.

My first album was released in February 1962. The first cut,
"Make Someone Happy," became my signature song at the
Maisonette later that year.

Henri René was the arranger for *Presenting Peter Duchin*
and several subsequent albums.

After dinner I found myself in a book-lined den that housed an astonishing collection of pigs made out of every substance—china, stone, metal, precious gems. "Mike was a member of the Porcellian Club at Harvard," whispered George, who had also belonged to the club. "He was obviously quite taken with the symbol."

Mike pulled me aside. "Perhaps you didn't know this, Peter, but we're related."

This was unexpected—and very good—news.

"Well," he explained, "my mother's sister was your great-great-aunt Theresa Fair Oelrichs. Hasn't anybody ever told you about your Newport family?"

"Not really."

Mike remembered my mother well. "She was an interesting woman, with an unusual style," he said, adding cryptically, "She was ahead of her time."

Staying at Mike and Gertie Vanderbilt's was just about the most luxurious experience of my life. Their many servants were scarcely seen or felt. George and I were assigned a valet, a dark, diminutive fellow whom we nicknamed "the Bat" because of his black suit and big, pointy ears. Whenever we dropped our clothes on the floor, the Bat would appear as if by telepathy and whisk them away to be washed and pressed.

One afternoon as we were dressing for tennis, I heard a roar from George's room. I found him on the floor, convulsed with laughter. "You'll never guess what the Bat did," he said. "He found my jockstrap, and he not only took it away and cleaned it but pressed and starched it. It's impossible to put on."

Like Bill Kitchen, Mike was immensely methodical, concerned with doing things *right*. A couple of years later, George and I had lunch with him at his apartment in the River House in New York, and I was surprised when Mike got up from the table, went over to the sideboard, and started tossing the salad. He went at it for quite some time, very deliberately, as though he were performing a chemistry experiment. "Seventeen times," he explained. "That's what my mother always told me about tossing a salad. Seventeen times."

Mike was generous with his knowledge, particularly about contract bridge. George and I knew the rudiments of the game, and Mike took great delight in explaining to us the various conventions he had developed, as well as the defensive strategies, of which he was the acknowledged world master. One rainy afternoon in Palm Beach, he invited us to sit in for a couple who had canceled at the last minute. Our fourth was one of his extremely rich neighbors.

"What should we play for?" said the neighbor.

"How about five cents a point," Mike said.

George and I looked at each other in horror. At that level, we could easily lose our entire net worth in a single game. Noticing our expressions, Mike said, "We'll have the boys play for a tenth of a cent."

By the end of the afternoon, Mike was several hundred dollars in the hole. Waving the invisible, aged butler over, he said, "Charles, would you please go upstairs and get my money?"

"*All* of it, sir?" said Charles, perfectly deadpan.

"Oh, I don't think so," replied Mike with the hint of a smile.

≡

The other night I had drinks with my first wife, Cheray. When I asked her what I'd been like when we met at a dinner party that spring in Palm Beach, I wasn't surprised by her answer:

"I'd heard a lot about you, and you had a perfectly *terrible* reputation as the sort of man who breaks a girl's heart and never calls again. You were exactly what I wanted nothing to do with. But I have to say that I was pleasantly surprised."

A tall, graceful blonde with a clotheshorse figure, Cheray has two qualities I admire: she's a great listener, and she's genuinely down-to-earth. Before Cheray, I had done most of the listening. I had always loved hearing women talk about themselves. Years of coming home to the Harrimans' late at night and finding Ma still up, sipping her vodka on the rocks, puttering around the house, emptying ashtrays and ready to "dish" until dawn, had taught me how to listen. I knew what questions would bring out a woman's confidences, a talent I developed not out of malicious curiosity but as a way, perhaps, of building my own self-esteem.

Except for Sally, I hadn't been terribly interested in women my own age. Once the sex was over, I'd found most of them silly and narcissistic—either too conventional or not worldly enough. So I had dropped them and moved on—without giving a damn about their feelings. Whenever things got messy, or even when they didn't, I split.

Cheray was one of the first women my own age with whom I felt comfortable enough to talk about myself. Turning to her that night on the jasmine-scented terrace in Palm Beach, I opened up. Prodded by her low-key, patient interest, I found myself telling her what little I knew of my family background, as well as my views on art, literature, and politics.

"You were different from the other boys," she reminded me the other day. "You'd been out in the world. Instead of talking about your career or the tennis game that afternoon, you talked about things outside yourself, especially books. At first I thought, Here goes—my turn for the Peter Duchin charm. But you were more than that. You were *interesting*. I even remember the book you were reading: *The Air-Conditioned Nightmare* by Henry Miller."

The morning after that dinner party, I woke up infatuated. At breakfast, I mentioned to Mike that Cheray had invited me to join her at Lyford Cay in Nassau, where she was vacationing with her parents. Mike said, "Why don't you fly over? And by all means, use my plane."

Mike Vanderbilt's private plane wasn't something you turned down. Cheray was waiting for me at the Nassau airport. That evening I met her parents, George and Audrey Zauderer, who greeted me as though I were already part of the family. After dinner, Cheray and I ventured into the center of the island. At a big, open-air nightclub, I jammed with a local band that was playing its own version of rhythm and blues. It was a throbbing, sexy, tropical night, people dancing, swaying, boozing. Cheray sat on the bandstand in a simple cotton dress, barefoot and at home. I had been telling myself that the last thing I wanted was to get involved. But that night, it occurred to me that maybe this was a girl I could get serious about.

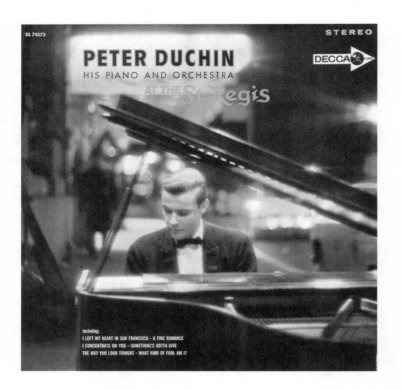

In September 1962, I opened at the Maisonette in the
St. Regis, and suddenly had a career.

15

AT HOME IN THE
ST. REGIS

One night I was taken to dinner at Cole Porter's apartment in the Waldorf Towers by Maria Cooper and her mother, Rocky (Mrs. Gary) Cooper. A terrible riding accident had left Cole a paraplegic, and he lay on a chaise longue, looking damaged and fragile in a silk smoking jacket. He remembered my parents fondly, as well as his old house on the Rue Monsieur, bought by Ginny after the war. Everything was going splendidly until he turned to me after dinner. "Peter," he said, "would you be kind enough to play me a tune?"

My heart stopped. With shaky, sweaty hands, I sat down at his ornate Steinway and played "Night and Day," the first time through in my father's heavily melodic style, the second time with a jazz feeling.

Cole smiled. "That was delightful, Peter. You do have your father's touch."

I didn't believe him.

A few weeks later, I was invited to dinner at the apartment of Mr. and Mrs. Arthur Rubinstein. The great pianist was warm and outgoing, and because his daughter Eva had told him I was starting out on a musical career, he was full of advice. When I asked how aware he was of the audience when he played, Rubinstein replied, "Immensely. To play my best, I *must* have an audience. It's a good idea to play for one person—for me, a beautiful woman. One time in Denmark I played the whole concert to a woman in the back. I played to her as though she were the only person there. Afterward she came backstage. 'Maestro,' she said, 'I was very honored that you played everything just for me.' You see?"

Then came the dreaded moment: "Peter," said the maestro, "why don't you play something for me? I hear you play jazz. I love jazz."

I had no choice. I went to the concert grand in the living room as though to the guillotine and got through a couple of choruses of "How High the Moon."

"Bravo! Bravo!" cried Rubinstein, clapping like a child. "Now I play for you."

Putting down his brandy and cigar, he launched into a majestic Chopin polonaise with the same improvisatory approach I might have used for jazz. He played it like dance music, which it is. And, as if on cue, his wife and children started dancing around the living room. I sat there enthralled by the joy and exuberance. The combination of the beauty of the music and the earthy domesticity of the scene was breathtaking. That's how Chopin should be played.

≡

Being in the spotlight as a performer scared the hell out of me, and when Bobby said it was time to get a band together, I was reminded of how unsure I felt about myself. How would I fare in the critical comparisons with my father? All the bandleaders I most admired—from Count Basie to Ted Straeter—had a persona, a public personality. What was *my* persona?

I had found an old news clip in which my father talked about taking acting lessons to prepare for the films he had appeared in as a bandleader. He said that the lessons also helped bolster his confidence on the bandstand. That my father had felt insecure in public came as a pleasant surprise, and I didn't need pushing when Bobby suggested that I take acting lessons. "If you don't feel self-confident," he said, "you can at least *look* self-confident."

My acting teacher was Wynn Handman, one of New York's most respected younger acting coaches (whom I would later help to found the American Place Theater). In a bare studio, one flight up in an old building on West Fifty-sixth Street, I joined a dozen other students to learn the fundamentals of acting: how to move, how to speak, how to get into character.

I hated it. When Wynn, who was wonderfully soft-spoken and attentive, asked me to stand up and read dialogue, he might as well have been asking me to fly to the moon. My only previous stage experience had been in seventh grade at Eaglebrook, where my turn as a dancing fairy in wings and tutu had brought down the house.

One day, Wynn asked me to read a scene from Molnár's *Liliom* with a shy, fragile-looking student named Mia Farrow.

"Peter," he said, "look into Mia's eyes as you speak. Try to make her *react* to what you're saying."

Gazing into those beautiful eyes, I saw only the reflection of a jerk who didn't know what he was doing. I was totally at sea. Mia spoke her lines sweetly and nearly inaudibly. I lumbered on.

Wynn stopped me. "Peter, what do you think the scene is all about?"

"A man trying to make an impression on a girl, I suppose."

"OK. Try doing *that* to Mia. This time use your own words."

I did, and I began to see what he was talking about: Acting is as much about the actor as about the character. Encouraged, I really came on to Mia. She laughed, and we both broke up.

"That's even better," Wynn said. "Because it's real. That's what you want to be onstage."

In the course of my year in Wynn's classes, I came to enjoy them enormously. I never was much good, but once or twice I felt I'd succeeded in becoming the character. I learned that—paradoxically—you have to lose yourself in order to become yourself. It was exactly the self-confidence I was looking for.

$$\equiv$$

To celebrate the release of my first album, Chiq and Bob invited me to Madrid, where they were living in a fantastic apartment on the Plaza Major. Chiq went to memorable lengths to entertain me. I had done a lot of shooting in my time, but nothing had prepared me for the shooting party we all went to one weekend at a great *estancia* outside Madrid.

I showed up in jeans and sneakers, the Spanish aristos in tailored tweeds and handmade boots. Raising their well-defined eyebrows, they looked down their tapered noses at my American slovenliness.

Everyone had two shotguns and a *secretario,* whose job it was to load and hand you the second gun once you'd emptied the first one. We were seated on camp chairs arranged in a long line, each shooter behind a "butt," or enclosure made of hay and grasses tied together, which had been set up as camouflage. A quarter of a mile in front of us was a medieval army of peasants, some on foot, others on horseback, whose job it was to drive flocks of partridges out of the bushes by banging bells, pots, and pans. Between each butt was a tin shield to keep you from being shot by your neighbors. A darn good thing, too, since I'd never seen people so reckless with firearms as these Spanish aristos. I shot very well, ending the afternoon as number-two gun. Suddenly I was no longer the ugly American.

A few nights later, at a flamenco club in Madrid, Chiquita introduced me to the most beautiful woman I've ever met. While I tried to look cool, Ava Gardner let go with her great horse laugh and checked me out with her almond-shaped eyes. Before long I was coming on to her, and she was coming on to me.

Ava was as real a woman as I've ever known. The pain in her life had outweighed the joy, and she wasn't afraid to show it. Surprisingly, she had no vanity. She needed no jewels, makeup, or entourage. Apparently, she hadn't recovered from her breakup with Frank Sinatra, about whom she talked often and fondly. When we got to know each other, she'd make me go to the piano in her living room and play the songs Frank had sung for her. When I played the beautiful Billy Strayhorn ballad "Lush Life"—her favorite— she'd lean on the piano, sing the lyrics very softly, and cry. Then she'd catch herself and say something like, "That chord is wrong." Or, "You don't phrase it as well as Frank did." I felt both protective of her and awed by her. It seemed inconceivable that one of the world's most beautiful women could be so vulnerable.

She was unpredictable: affectionate and sensual one moment, caustic and confrontational the next. I was half her age, but I must have appealed to her because of my energy, even though it wasn't quite a match for hers. Every night, five nights running, we hit the flamenco clubs. All the musicians and dancers knew her. The moment she walked in, they exploded. Our fling ended abruptly at seven o'clock one morning when her Ferrari spun out of control on a wet country road. While we whirled to a stop in a hay field, my life passed before me. Ava just laughed and laughed.

≡

It was Chiq who called her friend César Balsa in the spring of 1962 and reminded him of the night he'd heard me play in Mexico City. And she came with me when I made my pitch to César at the St. Regis. As coached by Bobby, I said, "You must be really tired of dealing with the managers of all those different singers you have down in the Maisonette. I've got a better idea. Why don't you hire me and a band for the season? You won't have any managers to deal with. I'll bring in all my friends, and they'll bring in all their friends." He went for it—hook, line, and Social Register.

On May 31, 1962, I signed a contract to play with my own band at the Maisonette. It called for me, ten musicians, and a vocalist to perform from September through the following June, six nights a week from 8:00 P.M. to 2:00 in the morning, with Sunday matinee as an option. We would receive $2,439 a week for the first four months; $2,717 for the following four. The St. Regis would pay extra for New Year's Eve, and the hotel could exercise its option for our services the following year, at increased wages.

The fringe benefits were spectacular. I would be given my own suite in the hotel—free. Office space in an adjacent building—free. Dinners at the Maisonette, all the drinks I wanted, and any bottle of wine from one of New York's great cellars—free. And there would be no cover charge for any of my friends who happened to drop in.

It was the last contract personally signed at MCA by Jules Stein. Out of loyalty to my father's memory—not to mention astonishment that I would be starting out at the St. Regis—Jules overruled the objections of one of his top executives, Larry Barnett, who thought I didn't have "what it takes." MCA had just bought Universal Pictures, which had set off an alarm in the U.S. Department of Justice's Antitrust Division. Shortly after I signed my contract, MCA became strictly an entertainment producing and distribution company, and the talent agency was dissolved.

The only thing missing was a band. Bobby was friendly with Otto Schmidt, a sax player and clarinetist in Ted Straeter's orchestra at the Persian Room in the Plaza. Otto, a classy, white-haired veteran, wasn't exactly hungry. But Straeter was about to retire, and he generously suggested that Otto help me get started. In short order, Otto started rounding up musicians for the fall, five of whom came with me for a warm-up gig that summer.

$$=$$

Despite its fancy name, the Mid-Ocean Bath and Tennis Club in Bridgehampton, Long Island, was as nouveau riche as the people who a few years later would turn one of the nicest resort areas on the East Coast into a zoo. Southampton and East Hampton—bastions of Old Money that had been summering on the East End of Long Island since the 1920s—were zoned against such invasions. But Bridgehampton, a sleepy little in-between village with a couple of antique shops, wasn't so well protected. It was there that a guy Otto knew, a real-estate developer named Lou Sacher, was putting up a beach club and a development of condominiums. Bobby and Otto had no trouble selling Lou on the new Peter Duchin Orchestra. With my social connections, he'd get the "right people" in no time. In return, the combo and I would get some badly needed on-the-job training.

That spring, Otto gave me a crash course in bandleading. When I wasn't recording my second album of Henri René arrangements, *In the Duchin Manner,* I was working with Otto in my Carnegie Hall apartment, putting together a book of songs. Unlike jazz or concert bands, successful dance bands play mostly without music, since they don't want to break the flow of the evening by fumbling for the arrangements. Dance band musicians have to carry around thousands of tunes in their heads, along with the fundamental four-part harmonies of each song. Learning the repertoire—a vast, constantly growing body of music—is a task usually accomplished by many years of experience. I found that the best way to memorize songs was to write out arrangements of them, however sketchily. By June, I was still shaky on all but a couple of dozen arrangements. But on the day the painters put the finishing touches on the new Mid-Ocean Club, I opened with my own six-piece band.

We did all our learning in public. My Hampton friends would stop by to lend moral support, and nobody seemed to mind when we played "Night and Day" or "The Lady Is a Tramp" four times in a row. Nor did they complain when we'd follow Rodgers and Hart's "Lover" with a samba, followed by "Let's Twist Again." That we were a work in progress seemed to add to the appeal. Playing requests is a big part of the business, and it became great sport among my friends to ask for the most arcane tunes they could think of. But they couldn't outsmart Otto and the other guys, and I'd stumble along.

≡

A good friend of mine, Geoffrey Gates, a broker with Bache & Company, had rented a beach house with me. It was next to an enormous estate in Southampton owned by Henry Ford, Jr., and his wife, Anne, whose family, the McDonnells, had been around the Hamptons a long time. A jovial roughneck, Henry loved to party all night. He could be incredibly short-tempered and crude, but he was brighter than a lot of people gave him credit for, and he was a lot of fun. One of his endearing traits was that he treated youngsters like me as adults.

Henry was ready for anything. A couple of times, unbeknownst to Anne, I took him to the Hotel James, a funky old establishment on Route 27 with a black clientele and a great rhythm and blues bar in the basement. I made a lot of friends there, and some of them asked me to come by the local Baptist church on Sundays and sit in when they needed a keyboard player. For a half dozen Sundays that summer, I had another learning experience, accompanying the black choir and congregation as they belted out down-home hymns and gospel. It turned out to be enormously useful when, a couple of years later, I had to learn how to play rock and roll.

At dinner one night, Anne Ford mentioned a big party she was planning for the top people in the auto industry, many of whom were flying in from Detroit. Explaining that she'd run out of guest rooms, she asked if I had any suggestions. Jokingly, I mentioned the Hotel James. This broke up Henry, who blew his soup halfway across the table. Anne looked perplexed, but she was used to Henry's primitive manners, and she filed away the name of the hotel. The next morning she booked four rooms at the James, including one for a top General Motors executive.

I would have given anything to have been there the day the big shot pulled up to the James in his limo and was confronted by the sight of all those black people rocking quietly on the rickety front porch. As Henry later told me with enormous glee, the tycoon raced back to the Fords' house and screamed, "What the hell! Is this a joke?" Anne, Henry chortled, "went up the goddamn chimney."

Toward the end of summer, the Fords asked me to play for a party for their younger daughter, Anne, and one of her friends. I was flattered and terrified. Not only would I be fronting a band twice the size of the one in Bridgehampton, but I'd be up there in the spotlight all night long.

"Don't worry, Pete," said Otto, "we can handle it. I'll bring in a bunch of ringers—top guys from Lanin and Davis."

I knew Otto could handle it, but I wasn't sure I could. Although I'd been to countless deb parties, I'd never paid much attention to the music. Most of the time I'd been trying to get the girls into the bushes, not onto the dance floor. In fact, it's always embarrassed me that I've never been much of a dancer. And I didn't have a clue about playing a whole evening. I knew nothing about how to order the tunes, the tempos, or the length of the sets.

Otto said not to worry. He and another musician would call the tunes and decide on the tempos. "I'll give you the key changes with my fingers," he said. "For the flat key signatures they go up—one finger for F, two for B-flat, and so on. For the sharps, they go down. One for G, two for D . . ." He added, "All you have to do, Pete, is look happy, play the right notes. And for Chrissake, don't leave the bandstand. Knowing you, you'll never come back."

=

The night of the party, it felt strange to be putting on my black tie and thinking of it as a uniform. Stranger still was arriving at the Fords' house early and parking behind the tent along with the catering trucks. I had walked into many parties exactly like this one before, but it had never occurred to me that the tents had two entrances—one for the guests, the other for "the help." Tonight, I was the help.

I came in past the pots and pans and liquor and glass cartons. Otto and the other musicians were already there, setting up the bandstand. Otto introduced me around, and a couple of the players remarked that they had seen me at other parties—out front.

One of them, a real old-timer, said he'd once played with my father. Nervously, I took out my little folder of arrangements and put them on the piano. None of the other guys had brought along a single sheet of music.

Thanks to Otto's pacing, the dance floor filled up and stayed that way until two in the morning, when we ended with "Goodnight, Sweetheart." It was like waves. We'd build in tempo and intensity, then subside to something slow and dreamy. Then build again and subside. For the last half hour, we just wailed while the dance floor rocked. I was drenched with sweat and happy to the bone.

≡

Within a few weeks after I'd opened at the Maisonette, the club was mine—my living room, my rumpus room, my dining room, my stage. The critics loved us. The morning after my debut, *The New York Times's* reviewer, Milton Esterow, set the tone: "It seemed as if they could have danced all night. . . . Another Duchin is back in town."

Two weeks later, *Newsweek* reported: "Whether drawn by nostalgia or curiosity, the crowds of young and old New Yorkers pour into the St. Regis Hotel's Maisonette supper club every night to hear Duchin the younger and his eleven-piece orchestra. What they have heard . . . is a dance band with jazz on its mind. Melody and romance are there, but Duchin has added a rhythmic excitement to familiar tunes and a touch all his own."

Among some of Dad's old fans, the jury was still out. The *Newsweek* article began: "Still ruddy from a steam bath, massage and three or four drinks at his downtown club, the old man two-stepped his way to the edge of the dance floor and over to the piano. 'I knew your father,' he told the orchestra leader in a confidential bellow. 'I knew him in the old, old days out at the Central

Park Casino. You know, you're very much like him. But you'll have to go a long way to beat him.' "

We started at nine and played for forty minutes before taking a twenty-minute break, during which we were relieved by a five-piece Latin group. Forty minutes on, twenty minutes off, with a dinner break at eleven. We stopped at two in the morning.

We soon attracted a colorful cast of regulars. There was the businessman who came in every Thursday night with his mistress and every Saturday night with his wife. The first night, he came over and said to me: "Get this straight. You can say hello to me on Thursday, but you make sure you don't ever say Saturday that you saw me Thursday."

There was the high-class hooker, a statuesque brunette with very white skin who came in every night with a different man. We called her—for obvious reasons—the milkmaid. "Peter," she said in her Teutonic accent, "I like your music and I like this place a lot. But you must always act like you never saw me before, OK?" I nodded, and she palmed me a hundred-dollar bill.

Everybody came in, from mafiosi to the Duchess of Windsor. One night Ava Gardner showed up and handed me a tiny cap pistol. "It makes a noise louder than a bull's fart," she said. Backstage, I aimed it at one of the musicians and pulled the trigger. Ava had understated the bull's fart. The victim smeared his white shirt with catsup, staggered out, and collapsed on the dance floor. The place erupted in screams until I appeared and announced that it was all a joke.

There were lots of big tippers in those days, none bigger than the Arab sheikh who came in one evening with a girl out of the kick line at the Copa. As we were ending one evening with "The Party's Over," he reached into his voluminous robes and pulled out an enormous wad of bills, which he proceeded to throw at us like confetti. We accelerated to the last bar, ended with a flourish, and scooped up the cash: more than a thousand bucks in five-dollar bills.

=

The Maisonette staff became my family. Most of them had been hired by Vincent Astor, who had owned the hotel before César. Vincent had put a premium on old-world manners—as did all the top hotels in New York in those days—and the place still had the feeling of a European grand hotel.

There was Rudy, the impeccable, Austrian-accented maître d' who glided through the room like a swan. For fun one night, I asked him if he'd start the band with a wave of his hand. Rudy loved it so much that it became a tradition. Every night at nine, he'd stroll out to the middle of the dance floor and announce, "Time, boys! Time to go!" Then he'd give the downbeat, and we'd launch into "Make Someone Happy."

Not since Chissie and Zellie had anyone looked after my welfare better than Rudy. The royal *we* was his only pronoun, and before my dinner break he'd come over to the piano and say, "Why don't we have the striped bass with *beurre blanc* tonight? It's very fresh. And what are we going to drink? I think we'll enjoy the '53 Montrachet." If two girls I was taking out arrived unexpectedly, Rudy would make sure to seat them as far apart as possible, tipping me off with a wink and a nod. For these and countless other favors, I called him Mother.

Rudy was a walking *Who's Who* of names, faces, and pedigrees. He conferred titles on all the notables. "Peter," he'd say, "the Governor is coming in tonight": he meant Ave. Or, "The Producer"—David Merrick—"is coming. I'm sure he'd appreciate hearing something from one of his shows." Or, "The Artist"—Salvador Dalí—"is in booth number twelve. He'd like you to come over and say hello."

Dalí, who lived in a suite upstairs with his wife, Gala, was a regular. One night, he handed me a manuscript. "Peter," he said, in French, "would you be kind enough to translate into English a little poem I have written?" I waited until I got back to my suite to look at it. A dreadful exercise in pseudopornography about a king greatly given to self-abuse, it was called *"Le Grand Masturbateur."* I never managed to put it into English or any other language, and the subject never came up between us again.

My last sighting of Dalí was a couple of years later, when I was hired by Rebekah Harkness, the dance patroness, to play for her daughter's wedding in Watch Hill, Rhode Island. In one of the surrealist tableaux vivants that had been set up for the guests' amusement, I spotted "the Artist" squirting shaving cream on a group of naked models from a can of Barbasol. I waved at him, but he was so absorbed in what he was doing that he didn't even wink.

Another of my favorites at the Maisonette was the men's room attendant, whom we called Jack the Turk. A stocky, swarthy man with a permanent smile, he looked like the swami on the Fatima cigarette packs. Jack maintained a running feud with Anna, the ladies' room attendant, who was stationed forty feet across the foyer. They pretended not to notice each other, and, according to Rudy, they hadn't exchanged a word in twelve years. No one could figure out why.

Jack, like Rudy, had his *Who's Who* down cold. One night he heard Rudy telling me that my friend Anthony Biddle Duke, whose family had owned the St. Regis before Vincent Astor, had reserved a table for the evening. Jack's smile broadened. When Rudy asked what he was up to, he replied, "You'll see."

During my first break, I went to Tony Duke's table and found him doubled over with laughter. "I've never given anyone a hundred-dollar tip in my life," he said. I glanced up and saw Jack standing by

Salvador Dalí lived in the St. Regis and was a regular
when I was playing at the Maisonette.

the men's room, his grin bigger than ever. Tony explained that when he'd gone inside to relieve himself, he'd found the men's room in darkness except for a pair of candles burning on either side of a urinal. As he was unbuttoning himself, he heard the silky voice of Jack the Turk: "Welcome home, Mr. Duke . . ."

≡

Early on, I realized that what would make us distinctive was *not* to have a particular sound, as did the bands of Count Basie, Duke Ellington, and Lester Lanin. Since I hadn't developed a strong personal piano style of my own, I made a virtue of eclecticism, and it paid off. The Maisonette was usually filled with people of all generations from all over the country. I wrote arrangements of music from various periods; we even used some of Dad's arrangements. Being able to play in all kinds of styles—from swing to rock and roll—is still a hallmark of the Duchin bands.

The bulk of our repertoire consisted of a wide range of show tunes, from the twenties to current Broadway shows. Occasionally we played the theme from a hit movie, as well as a few Top 40 tunes. One of the things that made us popular with young people was that I made a point of adding the latest styles when they seemed appropriate. We may have been the first supper club band in New York to play Ray Charles, the Beatles, and bossa nova. When we first played "I Want to Hold Your Hand," the older people came up and complained that it was too "wild."

≡

My friends poured in. One night Mother (Rudy) announced, "Ma is bringing in the girls." (By then Rudy had become so friendly with Marie Harriman that *he* called her Ma.) "The girls" meant Ginny Chambers, Anita Loos, and Madeline Sherwood. In they came, and by two in the morning they still hadn't ordered anything but soup and drinks. Rudy, who wanted to close up, eyed me meaningfully as I stopped to say good night and see them to their car.

"I'm hungry, girls," Mado Sherwood suddenly announced. She waved Rudy over, and he politely informed her that the kitchen was closed. "What about breakfast?" persisted Mado. "I'd sure like to get back into that kitchen and see if we can whip up some buckwheat cakes. I've made some mean buckwheat cakes in my day. Come on, girls."

We all trooped into the kitchen, where everything was locked up for the night.

"Where's the buckwheat?" demanded Mado.

Rudy said he'd have a look in the cellar. He disappeared and a few minutes later returned with all the necessary ingredients, plus a half dozen bottles of the best champagne in the house. At three in the morning, Ma, Neetsie, Ginny, Mado, Rudy, and I sat down to a breakfast of buckwheat pancakes and Dom Pérignon.

Another night, Jule Styne, the composer of *Gypsy, Bells Are Ringing,* and many other terrific shows, arrived halfway through the first set. With him was a familiar-looking man whom I couldn't place. The way they both kept staring at me made me nervous. During the break, I went over and asked Jule what he was up to. He introduced his friend as the playwright S. N. (Sam) Behrman and asked me to sit down.

"You did fine." Behrman smiled. "You passed."

"I did?"

"We wanted to see if you were good enough to play Gershwin in a new musical we're writing about him. You are. Would you be interested?"

I was more than interested. Dad, who had looked far more like the composer than I did, had almost played Gershwin in the movies. Now I would—on Broadway. I gulped. "You mean I'll have to be there every night?"

"Of course," said Jule impatiently. "And we're thinking of having you play part of one of the big ones—Concerto in F or 'Rhapsody in Blue'—every night. As well as the standards."

They were serious.

Over the next year, Jule, Sam, and I met occasionally to talk about various musical and dramatic ideas. Then Sam died, having completed only a rough draft of Act One. When Jule called after Sam's funeral to say that the project had been shelved for the time being, I felt let down. At the same time, though, I couldn't have been more relieved.

=

Bobby Brenner's master plan was working like a charm. In the spring of 1963, I spent three weeks playing a bit part as Angela Lansbury's young lover in *The World of Henry Orient,* an offbeat film about two privileged Manhattan schoolgirls who stalk the object of their teenage puppy lust, a hilariously narcissistic concert pianist played by Peter Sellers. I was excited about working with the most brilliant comic actor in the movies, but unfortunately Sellers did not appear in any of my extremely brief scenes, and we never met. The filming at Astoria Studios in Queens was unbearable. George Roy Hill, the director, was a pro, and Angela, my leading lady, couldn't have been nicer. But I spent most of the time waiting to be called so I could saunter out and recite lines like "Nice weather we're having."

The World of Henry Orient opened at Radio City Music Hall to excellent reviews, none of which mentioned me except in passing. It was embarrassing to see my name up there on the marquee with those of Peter Sellers and Angela Lansbury. Worse was the sight of myself in one of my brief scenes, emerging from a shower naked from the waist up and ten times larger than life.

Bobby, who had probably arranged the marquee billing, crowed, "It's just the beginning, Pete."

"No, it's not," I said. "It's the end."

That year, my third album, *Peter Duchin at the St. Regis,* came out. Thanks to all the publicity at the Maisonette, it was a big success, selling several hundred thousand copies. I thought the cover was very cool: a shot of me at the piano in front of the hotel's belle époque entrance. At 2:30 one morning, we'd taken a baby grand piano out on the sidewalk, where I was photographed playing Gershwin and Porter until dawn to an amazed assortment of night crawlers.

"Forget the movies," I told Bobby. "This is enough for me."

=

Cheray and I had our ups and downs. We had dated on and off, and my feelings had vacillated between seriousness and panic. She was sexy, and I was more comfortable with her than with anybody else I was seeing. She would clearly make some man a great wife. But did I want a wife? Tentatively we discussed marriage, but when the discussions got real, I took off. Finally, Cheray got fed up and married another guy.

Years later, Jackie Onassis recalled something Cheray had told her about our on-again, off-again, on-again courtship. In the spring of 1962, when her hasty marriage was just about over, Cheray had been in the kitchen about to feed her Yorkshire terrier, Toodles, when she spotted a photograph of me in the newspaper under the doggie bowl. "The moment I saw Peter's face," she told

Jackie, "I burst into tears. Finally, I got up the courage to hear him play in Bridgehampton. He seemed just as thrilled to see me as I was thrilled to see him. That fall we started dating again. Slowly."

I've always liked Jackie's footnote: "Ari," she said of her husband Aristotle Onassis, "loved that story. He called you 'two wonderful children in love.' When I told him how Cheray had burst into tears, *he* burst into tears."

Cheray became something of a regular at the Maisonette—just as my mother had been at the old Central Park Casino thirty years before. Through the fall of 1962 and the following spring, I dated her as well as other girls. I was wondering what to do during my summer break when Geoffrey Gates suggested that the two of us charter a big sailboat and cruise the Greek islands, each with a girlfriend. It sounded pretty darn good to me.

Cheray was my first choice, but I doubted her parents would let her go. She had been brought up so strictly that during her college years she'd been accompanied by her old governess, Miss Fendler, whenever she went for a weekend to a men's college. But to my delight, her parents caved in, and off we went.

The six weeks on that Greek schooner were the longest period of time I'd ever spent with one woman. To my surprise, I liked it. We sailed from island to island, checking out the ruins. When I suggested celebrating my twenty-sixth birthday with a suckling pig, the captain, Geoffrey, and I went ashore, hired a taxi, and drove to a farmhouse where we bought a poor, squealing pig and loaded it into the trunk of the cab. None of us could watch as the animal was slaughtered on the beach. But after it had been slowly roasted over pine and seaweed, and Cheray and I were holding hands under the Greek stars, I felt a contentment I'd never felt before.

That fall, I was at the bar in the Russian Tea Room, having a Bloody Mary with the writer Terry Southern, when Cheray phoned to give us the news that President Kennedy had been assassinated. Like everything else in New York, the Maisonette was closed until after the president's funeral, and during the next numbing days, Cheray and I stayed at her parents' house in Mount Kisco, glued to the television, crying a lot and holding each other.

≡

Inseparable from my feelings for Cheray were my feelings for her parents. In George and Audrey Zauderer, I found a sense of family security I'd previously only known from afar. George was a quiet, serious man of German-Jewish stock who had inherited a small business in real-estate bonds from his father and built it into a sizable fortune through extremely astute investments in commercial properties, mostly hotels. He was meticulous about every aspect of his life. Later, after Cheray and I moved to Westchester County, a couple of miles away from my new in-laws, he never arrived at our place without his gardening clippers, with which he proceeded to prune the deadwood from every bush on our property.

George's homes on Park Avenue and in Mount Kisco (and later in Jamaica) were opulent—a bit too opulent for my taste—but in spite of his wealth, he remained an extremely modest man. The first thing that comes to mind when I think of George is the little brown paper bag in which he carried his lunch every morning to his office on Fifth Avenue, courtesy of his cook, Margaret.

Audrey Zauderer, who came from a well-to-do Jewish family, was a good deal younger than George—she had been sixteen when they married. She was six feet tall and had an immense mane of blonde hair, and she cut a flamboyant figure. She still does. When she dances by, my band affectionately calls her "the behemoth."

As much as George loved reading the newspapers for tidbits about New York politics and finance, Audrey devoured the society

The summer of 1963, I chartered a sailboat with a
friend and we cruised the Greek islands for six weeks.
Cheray Zauderer came with me. It was the longest
period of time I'd spent with one woman.

Cheray and I got married on June 24, 1964. My friend
Bobby Short was in attendance.

columns, most of which were written by good friends. She loved entertaining on a grand scale, which she did with originality and obsessive perfection, always removing the plastic that covered the backs of her French antique chairs before "company" arrived. She only wanted the best of everything for her two daughters, Cheray and Pam—and the same for me. Occasionally, George needed Audrey's nudging to loosen the purse strings, but when he did, it was unconditional. How could I not have loved them?

≡

On June 24, 1964, Cheray and I were married in a civil ceremony at the Zauderers' apartment at 911 Park Avenue. The night before the wedding, Ma and Ave gave the bridal dinner at Eighty-first Street. With a great flourish, Ave produced cases of an ancient *premier cru* claret that had been brought from the cellars at Arden. The labels were fabulous, the color muddy, the taste beyond vinegar. But Ave was so proud of having "driven it downstate," as he put it, that not even Ma had the guts to tell him the wine was undrinkable.

George had come to me about the music for the reception. I'm sure he thought I was going to suggest my band. Egged on by Cheray—and backed by Audrey—I'd said, "What about Count Basie?"

Six hundred people came to the reception at the St. Regis Roof, and Basie never sounded better. The last guests left at three in the morning, and I can honestly say it was the best party I never played for.

≡

George and Audrey gave us two wedding presents—a racehorse and a house. One afternoon in Mount Kisco, Cheray and I went over to the farm where George bred horses. "Choose any foal you like," he said. "I'll pay the costs until he gets on the track." Knowing that the chances were a hundred to one that the horse would ever get that far, we wandered among the newborn foals, holding out apples. Of the seven beasts, only one came over and nuzzled us. We picked him on the spot and named him Mr. Right.

"Not the best way to judge horseflesh," said George.

But Mr. Right couldn't have been better named. Before being retired to stud, he won a slew of races, among them the Woodward Stakes and the Santa Anita Handicap, thrilling George beyond measure and adding significantly to our family coffers.

The Woodward victory inspired the most personal letter I ever got from Averell. Somehow he found time during his negotiations with the North Vietnamese during the 1968 Paris peace talks to write: "I have been waiting impatiently to get the Sunday newspapers [for] a more detailed account of the race . . . particularly the stretch run in which Mr. Right held out against Damascus's drive at the finish. It must have been very exciting."

For his second wedding present, George had suggested a "reasonable" apartment in the city. We had no idea what that meant, so we picked an apartment on Fifth Avenue in the Sixties. It was in a very Waspy co-op whose board of directors turned us down with the explanation that, because of the other tenants' concern for privacy, "entertainers" were not acceptable. I had never been turned down for anything in my life, and it came as quite a shock. The real reason, I suspect, had less to do with the board's distaste for showbiz types—to which Cheray and I hardly conformed—than with the fact that I was half Jewish and she was fully Jewish (though, like me, she had been raised entirely outside the faith). We didn't make an issue of it. In those days one didn't.

Cheray and me with Malcolm X in our apartment on
East Seventy-first Street in New York.

Instead, we found a wonderful house without a board of directors. A charming four-story brownstone with a garden on East Seventy-first Street, it needed everything from wiring to wallpaper. George, a do-it-yourself sort of guy, snapped it up so he could supervise the renovation. I loved the look of patriarchal satisfaction on his face when the last lightbulb was finally installed behind the mahogany bar in the den.

16

PORTS OF CALL

After the presidential election in 1964, we landed a windfall. My pal James Symington, a congressman from Missouri and the son of Ave's old friend Sen. Stuart Symington, was in charge of planning Lyndon Johnson's inauguration. Jimmy had come into the Maisonette one night and to my astonishment asked if I'd be interested in taking care of all the music for the president's inaugural balls.

For the next two months, Otto and I had had our hands full, putting together the entertainment for the dozen-odd balls. It was an immense amount of work, but the benefits really paid off. Suddenly we were on the map, big-time. Every band in the country, as well as many top entertainers, got in touch with Otto and me, hoping to be part of the action. We were now established as the band of choice for presidential events, and ever since then we've been regularly called for inaugurations and state dinners—even the White House weddings of Lyndon Johnson's two daughters.

In the two and a half years I'd been at the Maisonette, the room had quadrupled its business. According to *Time*, the Maisonette had been the "only cheek-to-cheek dance spot in New York, besides El Morocco, to prosper in spite of the discotheques." Led by Le Club and Arthur, Sybil Burton's place, discos had become the rage.

I was a Luddite. Why should anyone pay to dance to canned music? Just as my father had made a national name for himself by touring the country after the Central Park Casino closed, Otto and I decided it was time to take the band on the road. Our first booking was in St. Petersburg, Florida—two weeks at a lounge in a marina called Guy Lombardo's Port of Call.

"Isn't St. Petersburg where everybody is over sixty-five and plays shuffleboard?" I asked.

"Yeah," Otto replied. "Perfect for getting us tightened up before we hit the big time."

By that he meant our next gig—the Gigi Room at the Fontainebleau Hotel in Miami Beach.

In February 1965, Cheray and I packed up our Pontiac station wagon with enough clothing and supplies for eight weeks. With us was Malcolm X, our black Labrador. On the way down to Florida, we stopped for a couple of days of quail shooting at one of the magical places of my childhood, Jock and Betsey Whitney's magnificent antebellum plantation in Thomasville, Georgia.

We approached Greenwood down a spectacular allée of ancient magnolias and towering oaks that dripped with Spanish moss. Three servants appeared at the end of the long, reddish clay drive. One identified himself as the kennel man. I introduced him to Malcolm—minus the X.

In 1965, I took the band on the road, and we've been
playing for parties all over the country ever since
(photograph by Jill Krementz).

"Our dogs sleep on cedar chips, sir," he said. "Will that be suitable for Malcolm?"

"Just fine," I said.

"And does he prefer dry food or ground top round?"

"Either, thank you."

Malcolm growled happily.

Another servant stepped forward. "Any problems with the car, sir?"

"None, thank you."

He climbed into our filthy Pontiac and took it off to be washed, gassed up, and lubricated.

Meanwhile, another servant had silently unloaded the trunk—everything we'd packed for two months. "Madam," he said, disappearing inside, "is expecting you for tea in the drawing room."

Betsey Whitney embraced us at the door. After tea, she led us up the grand staircase to our quarters: two bedrooms sharing a central bath. "It's the suite President Eisenhower loves," she said.

Except for the separate bedrooms, so did we. Proper shooting clothes were hanging in the closets. Everything fit. Several pairs of Gokey boots were there for me to choose from. Our evening clothes had already been pressed and laid out.

I heard a shriek from Cheray's room. "My God," she wailed, "they've even unpacked my makeup—the mascara, powder, everything! I've never been so mortified!" Lined up on her dresser was a gooey platoon of her most intimate belongings.

At dinner, for which everything had been grown or shot on the plantation, Jock regaled us with tales of his Hollywood days, when he had coproduced *Gone With the Wind* with David O. Selznick. Many Jock stories later, we wobbled upstairs. Our beds had been turned down. Out of an atavistic impulse, I rumpled the sheets on my bed before joining Cheray in hers.

The next morning we were roused by a soft knock on the door and the announcement of breakfast. Like a guilty schoolboy, I leapt up, stark naked, and made a dash for my bed. In the bathroom, I stopped. Moving silently about my room were three manservants: one stoking the fire, another setting down a breakfast tray, the third opening the curtains. Turning back to Cheray's room, I was stopped again. Three maids had arrived: one to stoke *her* fire, another to set down *her* breakfast tray, the third to open *her* curtains. While I cowered naked in the john, Cheray curled up in bed, convulsed with laughter.

After two more luxurious days at Greenwood, we sadly said good-bye and set off for St. Petersburg, where we were greeted by an enormous sign: GUY LOMBARDO'S PORT OF CALL PROUDLY PRESENTS PETER DUCHIN AND HIS NEW YORK ORCHESTRA. Y'ALL COME BY, HEAR? Malcolm X, who still smelled pleasantly of cedar chips, didn't raise an eye. Cheray looked deeply mournful.

Many in the opening-night audience arrived clutching canes. We stuck to the golden oldies, and those who could, got up and danced. By ten thirty, the place was empty. "Well," I said to Cheray as we were crawling into bed well before midnight, "at least we'll get a nice rest."

The next day we went out fishing in the bay for trout and redfish, while Malcolm X had a wonderful time on the beach, chasing gulls. When we got back to the marina, we saw a ladder ascending to the sign. It now read: GUY LOMBARDO'S PORT OF CALL PROUDLY PRESENTS PETER DU— While we watched, the U disappeared.

Otto was standing on the dock. "The place has gone bust," he said. "The sheriff's here. Take a deep breath, Pete. We're not getting a dime."

"So what do we do now?" I spluttered. "We've got eleven musicians, all on salary. How are we going to pay them?"

"I've been on the phone. Wayne King has just canceled a horse show in Lake Wales. I said we'd fill in for his band."

"A horse show?"

The biggest annual event in Lake Wales, a town of orange groves in central Florida, took place in an old, peeling riding ring with low barricades and bleachers. After we'd checked into the funky little motel at the edge of town, the phone started ringing with invitations from local bigwigs. One was from a citrus magnate named Snodgrass who asked me to come fishing with him the following morning. It sounded great to me. I arrived at seven to find a large, flat barge, buoyed by oil drums, on top of which stood a wooden shack housing a bar around which Snodgrass and his pals were already sloshing down the bourbon and Bloody Marys.

We pushed off and began casting for alligator gar, a prehistoric bottom fish with alarming teeth and not much fight. It certainly wasn't the kind of fishing I was used to. Having consumed a couple of prebreakfast bourbons, I pulled up several of the vile creatures in the mosquito-infested heat and felt violently sick.

That evening, the bleachers were packed as we accompanied the local equestrians through their paces. Everything was going fine until the loudspeaker announced the favorite event: "And now . . . the Arabians!"

We'd been asked to play something spirited for this part of the show, and I'd come up with the brilliant idea of the theme music from *Lawrence of Arabia*. As I nodded the downbeat, a dozen magnificent white steeds appeared, ridden by rednecks dressed like Peter O'Toole in caftans. The arrangement called for a big drumroll, followed by a really big cymbal crash. We gave it all we had, and the next thing we knew, the horses were jumping out of the ring in search of desert sands. Snodgrass's horse went completely berserk. The last I saw of the orange grove magnate, he was chasing his Arabian steed across the ring yelling, "Stop, you dumb sonofabitch! Stop!"

≡

I've never been so vividly reminded of my sheltered upbringing as I was when we hit the Fontainebleau. Cheray and I gaped at the opulence of this most outrageous of the kitsch palaces lined up along Collins Avenue in Miami Beach: acres of gold on the women, acres of sweating flesh by the pool, acres of flamingo pink architecture in the Gigi Room, where we played for dinner and dancing. But the food was great, and the guests, most of whom were pushing eighty, were having the time of what remained of their lives.

One afternoon we played for a tea dance down by the pool, at which a good many rumbas were danced in the heat of the day. One active gentleman suddenly collapsed, felled by a heart attack. In a flash, two large, well-trained pool attendants scooped him onto a stretcher and whisked him down the walkway past the kitchen, where the garbage was taken out. He had scarcely disappeared when his former dance partner, a lizard-skinned lady in high heels and bathing suit with the energy of Ruby Keeler, snared a replacement. After that, Cheray and Malcolm X spent more and more time in the room.

≡

Having gotten our feet wet in the Atlantic, Otto and Bobby decided we should try the Pacific. Hardly had Cheray and I unpacked in New York than we were off to Los Angeles for a two-month gig at the Ambassador Hotel.

L.A. was nearly as exotic as the Fontainebleau. Mike Romanoff, one of the town's more colorful poseurs, was a regular. One night he brought in Sam Goldwyn and his wife, Frances. During the break, Mike waved me over to meet the mogul. The talk got around to croquet, which was Goldwyn's favorite sport. Turning to me, Goldwyn said, "Mike tells me you're a player. Come over to my place on Saturday."

I wish I could describe what Goldwyn's house was like, but I was never invited inside. Despite evidence of many servants, the only food or drink his croquet guests were offered was a glass of water. "Whatever you like to bring yourself," he had said magnanimously, "you can put in the icebox by the pool."

Goldwyn had leveled a good-size hill on which he had constructed an A croquet course for experts and a B course for beginners and intermediate players. One of the regulars on the A course was a man generally acknowledged as the world's best player, the French actor Louis Jourdan. Louis was even nicer off screen than he had been as the heartthrob in *Gigi* and *Can-Can*. Gates Davison, an old friend of mine from Long Island, was visiting from New York, and he and I were often pitted against Sam and Louis.

Having grown up on croquet courses, Gates and I were a formidable pair. But because of Louis, we were no match for our opponents. Louis wasn't just the greatest shot maker I've ever played against; he had the most uncanny understanding of strategy. His partner's best asset—apart from ferocious competitiveness—was his habit of wearing brand-new shoes that squeaked. Just as Gates or I would be lining up a crucial shot, Sam would come squeaking up to wreck our concentration.

Sam's impatience was monumental. One afternoon we stood there gaping as Louis executed a perfect turn around the course, getting through wicket after wicket with one amazing shot after another. It was taking a long time, and Sam began to fume. "Can't

I grew up playing croquet with Averell Harriman, one
of the most competitive players in the world, but I was
no match for Sam Goldwyn and Louis Jourdan.

you hurry up!" he finally exploded to the man who was winning him the match. While Sam glared, Louis finished the course with painstaking perfection. Like Ave and other men of power, Goldwyn was a terrible loser. After the few times Gates and I won, he didn't bother to congratulate us but walked away in a sulk.

Just the other day, playing a gig in Los Angeles, I ran into Louis. He looked as marvelous as ever, but when I asked how his croquet game was doing, he shook his head sadly and said, "There are no players left."

$$\equiv$$

Sooner or later, one ran into Irving "Swifty" Lazar, whom I had seen on and off since our first meeting in Ginny's living room on the Rue Monsieur. One afternoon I was given the opportunity to witness how the diminutive superagent had earned his nickname. Cheray and I had gone over to Swifty's place for a swim, and we watched in fascination as he arrived at his impeccably kept pool in a billowing terry-cloth robe, armed with a giant aerosol can. Shedding his sandals, he spent the next twenty minutes spraying a malodorous fungicide onto every pore of his elfin feet, as well as on every inch of the surrounding cement. Finally he lowered himself—not very far—onto a chaise longue next to a phone. Sure enough, it rang.

From Swifty's excited responses, I gathered that his caller was telling him about a book that had just been published:

"Who's the author?"

" . . ."

"Never heard of him. It's gonna be hot?"

" . . ."

"If you say so. What's the story?"

" . . ."

"Sounds great. What's the guy's number?"

" . . ."

"Got it."

That call had taken less than five minutes. The next one—to a top executive at MGM—took less than four:

"I have just taken on the representation of a very hot new book by a very hot author. [Gives title and author.] It's going to be very big. Paramount wants it for $400,000, but I know [author] would be much happier at MGM."

" . . ."

"What's the plot? [Swifty gives a thirty-second plot synopsis.] See what I mean? It's dynamite."

" . . ."

"You're offering $450,000?"

" . . ."

"OK, we'll consider it."

The next call was to Paramount.

Same palaver except for one line:

"MGM wants it for $450,000, but I know [author] would be much happier at Paramount."

" . . ."

"You're offering $500,000?"

" . . ."

"OK, it's a deal."

The next call was to the author in New York:

"Hello, this is Irving Lazar, the literary agent, in Los Angeles. I've just finished your [title of novel], and I can tell you that it's one of the greatest books I've ever read. I'm happy to represent you on the movie sale. If you sign with me, I guarantee I can get Paramount for $500,000."

" . . ."

"That's right: half . . . a . . . million . . . dollars. A deal?"

" . . ."

"Good. I'll send my secretary over with the papers."

He lay back, clasped his hands over his little tummy, and blinked owlishly at us through his black horn-rims. I didn't know what to say.

≡

Sam Goldwyn and Swifty Lazar were pillars of the Old Hollywood, which valued shrewdness, respectability, and self-invention. This being 1965, a new Hollywood was making its entrance, one with a premium on talent, irreverence, and self-destruction. One evening, Cheray, Gates, and I—three innocents from the East—got an eyeful at a Fourth of July party thrown by Jane Fonda and Roger Vadim.

I'd known Jane since her college days at Vassar and seen her go through various personalities. In 1965, she was in transit from the American girl who shacks up with the decadent older European man (Brigitte Bardot's director) to the Joan of Arc of the New Left. All the up-and-coming Hollywood crowd had been invited to Jane and Roger's beach house in Malibu. It was a great party, thanks to the presence of a terrific new rock band called the Byrds and a generous supply of mind-altering substances.

Gates, Cheray, and I—none of whom sampled the drugs—wandered around wide-eyed. My only memory of an actual conversation is of the hour I spent squatting on the beach with a very stoned Sal Mineo, who wouldn't stop talking about the imminent arrival of a Pacific fish called a grunion. It never arrived.

≡

It was thanks to Swifty that I encountered another Hollywood legend, one who would have a significant impact on my career. I'd been introduced to Frank Sinatra a couple of times at Toots

Shor's—Toots called him Dago; Frank called Toots Fatso—where his behavior had been completely benign. One night at the old Bistro restaurant in Beverly Hills, I got a dose of the other Sinatra.

Swifty was throwing a party for two clients, Dominique Lapierre and Larry Collins, whose new book *Is Paris Burning?* had just been published. Walking into the Bistro, Cheray and I saw Sinatra having angry words with an older woman. With him was Mia Farrow. Things were getting heated, and when Mia recognized me, she waved us to keep moving. (Later, she told me that the older woman was her mother, Maureen O'Sullivan, who disapproved highly of her relationship with Frank.)

Upstairs was a room full of Hollywood notables, including Lauren Bacall and Jason Robards, Jr., Harry Kurnitz, the Billy Wilders, and our good friend Lennie Dunne, wife of the writer Dominick Dunne. When Frank and Mia walked in, the temperature rose. Drinks became dinner, during which Frank started in on Lennie, saying terrible things about her husband. Various people tried to calm him down—first Betty Bacall, then Swifty.

Eight words out of Swifty's mouth, and Frank blew. Jumping up, he overturned the table of food and drink onto the tiny, fastidious agent. The sight of Swifty's amazement at finding himself half-buried in a sea of Bistro ratatouille has delighted me ever since.

Frank grabbed Mia. "Come on," he said. "Let's get the hell out of this dump!" Just before they disappeared, he stopped at my table. Putting a hand on my shoulder, he said, "Kid, don't waste your time with these bums. You got stardust on your shoulders."

What could I say to that?

≡

Frank became something of a mentor and a pal, and that was the last I ever saw of his dark side. We ran into each other a few years later, when I was back in Miami Beach. This time I was playing at the Doral Hotel, and he was headlining at the Fontainebleau. My last set ended before his, and Cheray and I would often head over to catch the end of his show.

Nobody has ever gotten to the heart of a song so directly and with such authority. Frank makes it all sound effortless, but just try singing along, matching his phrases, and you'll appreciate his astonishing technique. Frank's sense of rhythm and line is infallible—beyond style. There is never anything forced or sentimentalized, just the perfect balance between toughness and tenderness—like the man himself when he wasn't pumped up on booze.

Frank's arrangements have always been incomparable. All the top guys—Nelson Riddle, Gordon Jenkins, Don Costa, Neal Hefti, Marty Paich—produced their very best for him, and, almost uniquely in the business, Frank has always mentioned not only the name of the composer and lyricist of every song he sings but also that of the arranger. One of the ways he's stayed so young so long—as I write this, the man is turning eighty—is by keeping his ears open for the most talented young songwriters and arrangers in the business, people like Jimmy Webb and the late Joe Raposo, to name two out of many.

Being around Frank meant action. Hearing that Don Rickles was opening at a nearby hotel, he got Shecky Greene, the comedian he was working with, Harry Kurnitz, his Sancho Panza for the month, and two or three of his entourage, including Cheray and me, to arrive at the Rickles show, armed with key lime meringue pies supplied by his chief hanger-on, Jilly Rizzo. With Frank in the lead, we walked into the club like a battalion and were seated at the front table.

Five minutes into the show, Rickles launched into his celebrity introductions, beginning with Frank.

Frank hollered, "OK, guys!" and we all stood up and heaved our pies at Rickles, who didn't bother to duck. Then Shecky and Frank jumped onstage with more meringue and finished him off. Rickles loved it, the audience loved it, and we all followed Frank out into the night.

Later in the seventies, after Cheray and I had moved with our kids to the village of Bedford in Westchester County, we got to know Sinatra more privately. We had mutual friends in Bennett and Phyllis Cerf, who had a house nearby in Mount Kisco. Frank often spent weekends there, and we'd be invited over for dinner or lunch.

Away from the limelight and his fellow night crawlers, Frank was great company. I've never heard a better raconteur. Like his singing, his stories were sharp and mellow, perfectly timed. He knew I liked hearing about the days when he was starting out with Tommy Dorsey. What a wonderful oral history of that period his stories would have made if only he had allowed somebody to tape him. George Plimpton, who would have been perfect for the project, begged him, but Frank wouldn't do it.

His temper was matched by his generosity. I knew three or four musicians whose hospital bills he paid without their knowing it. Over the years, he threw several extraordinary gigs my way. In the mid-seventies, he called me up and said, "Peter, how about you and Cheray coming out to my place in the desert for a week? It's Jack Benny's birthday, and I'm throwing a party. I need a pianist around the joint."

"A week?" I said.

"Yeah." Frank laughed. "The guy's eighty."

Out we went to Rancho Mirage, near Palm Springs, for Jack Benny's eightieth birthday. It was my first visit to the southern California desert since I'd arrived in the oxygen tent, which, as things turned out, wasn't all that different from spending a week in Frank's maximum-security compound.

Most of the other houseguests—besides the Bennys, they included Morton Downey, Sr., and his wife, the Milton Berles, and George Burns—were nearly twice our age. The people who dropped in for dinner, including the Walter Annenbergs and Ronald Reagans, were not much younger. Like Arden, Frank's place was totally self-sufficient. However, instead of fishing, riding, shooting woodchucks, or picking vegetables, the daily activities consisted of drinking, eating, sitting by the pool, tottering over to the fabulously equipped health spa for a sauna or massage, talking on the phone to bookies and agents, and telling—rarely listening to—nonstop jokes. Barbara Marx, who had been married to Zeppo, was seeing Frank at the time (they were soon married), and she was a superb hostess, with an extraordinary ability to keep Frank on an even keel.

Being at Frank's was like being in a spa—a very funny spa where the guest of honor, Benny, was a legend and still hilarious at eighty, where the host might whip up a spaghetti dinner at two in the morning, and where no one ever seemed to go to bed. One evening toward sundown, I took a stroll in the elaborate cactus garden. Suddenly I spotted a beautiful hummingbird hovering in the spiky foliage. "Wow!" I exclaimed aloud—and heard the click of a bullet in the chamber of a gun.

I froze. From behind a cactus stepped a tall, armed man in a blue suit.

"Anything wrong, sir?" he inquired.

"Just looking at that hummingbird . . . sir."

"Fine, sir." He lowered his weapon and disappeared behind the cactus.

Turning to see where he'd gone, I spotted the somber figure of Spiro T. Agnew, strolling through the cacti on a path parallel to mine. He had just arrived as a guest and would shortly lose his Secret Service protection after resigning as Nixon's vice president under a cloud of scandal.

Later, when I told Frank about my adventure in the garden, he said, "Jesus, that's all I need! A reputation for shooting hummingbirds!"

Another memorable gig he threw my way was a party hosted by the owner of Caesars Palace in Las Vegas for the first of Frank's many "comebacks" in the seventies. I had been asked to play for a dance after Frank's opening. Preceding the show, one of the hotel's owners was throwing a black-tie dinner in his lush garden in the desert.

At seven in the evening, Cheray and I walked through the vast house, adorned with fake Michelangelos and white and gold furniture, and out onto an emerald lawn festooned with enough blossoms for a Hawaiian luau. With the white-clothed tables circling the pool and the vermeil goblets and plates, it attempted to be a cross between Southampton and Versailles. But the crowd was strictly Vegas: lacquered beehive hairdos and heavy rocks on the women, gold chains and brilliantine on the men. After drinks, everyone sat down for dinner, beginning with champagne and caviar brought by waiters in togas.

It was perfect, except that someone had forgotten to turn off the timer on the sprinkler system. Suddenly, the sprinklers went off. Mascara ran. Beehives tumbled. While everyone shrieked and ducked for cover, the host screamed, "Where the fuck is Juan?"

That line, Frank and I agreed, was the best.

At Frank's invitation, my band played with him at Carnegie Hall in 1982, when he made his first East Coast comeback. He asked us to play a couple of tunes in the first half of the program. Frank, ever the great pro, arrived exactly on time for the afternoon rehearsals. We were all in place with his fabulous book of charts, all set up in advance by his people. Without ado, we went through the songs. He heard all the mistakes—every lapse of intonation or slurred attack—and he wasn't shy about pointing them out, always in the most pleasant, accurate way. He was a dream to work with—the smoothest, most knowledgeable, most secure guy I've ever seen on a stage.

Walking out on that stage that evening, I felt like Lewis Carroll's Alice. It was as though I had suddenly shrunk to find myself inside a glittering gold watch. My gaze went up to the top balcony, to the little door through which I used to sneak in for concerts when I was living in the Carnegie Studios.

My next appearance with Frank was again at Carnegie Hall, as part of the gala 1989 concert held to celebrate the hall's reopening after its renovation. By this time, I had joined the Carnegie Hall board of directors, and I'd been active in the refurbishment. Caught up in the excitement of the event, I didn't have time to be nervous—not until Vladimir Horowitz announced at the last minute that he would join the program in the slot preceding mine. Walking onstage in the wake of the Horowitz ovation, I felt even tinier than Alice. The band and I did our thing, and after I'd finished my bows, I spotted Frank—the next act on—standing at the stage door, chatting with Leonard Bernstein. He was sipping a drink, cool as could be. "You did great, kid!" he said. "Now it's my turn." Out he strolled, and the audience—pillars of New York's classical musical establishment—went crazy.

Watching Frank, I remembered how Mait Edey and I used to sit on Mait's bed at Hotchkiss, listening earnestly to Jelly Roll Morton, Sidney Bechet, Art Tatum, and Dizzy Gillespie. Neither of us owned a single Sinatra recording. In fact, we would have put him down as hopelessly square. It was our loss. That night, I didn't feel the least bit ashamed for not having had the guts to pursue a career in jazz or classical music. By then, I had been a bandleader for more than twenty-five years. I was proud to belong to Sinatra's world.

I must have played five thousand parties.

17

VIEW FROM THE BANDSTAND

Since that first road trip in 1964, I've traveled a lot. In the sixties and seventies, I played about 150 gigs a year. Nowadays, I try to keep it down to about 100 a year. We have to say no to 500 to 600 jobs every year, because I'm busy, I don't want to play them, or the price isn't right.

We've played for the victory parties of presidents, governors, senators, congressmen, and mayors. We've played for senior proms, marriages, wedding anniversaries, birthdays, bar mitzvahs, high school and college graduations, movie premieres, play openings, book publications, and art exhibitions. We've celebrated the openings of airports, performing arts centers, private clubs, hospitals, museums, banks, shopping malls, and auto showrooms. We've played for New Year's Eve parties, Easter parties, Fourth of July parties, Columbus Day parties, Christmas parties, and ego-trip parties of every variety. We've played for more than a thousand charity balls and helped raise millions of dollars for every conceivable cause and disease. We've given concerts in symphony halls, parks, gardens, sports arenas, libraries, and Macy's lingerie department. We've played on cruises from Australia to Bali, Hong Kong to Singapore, Fort Lauderdale to Peru, New York to Bermuda. We've played in forty-six states—never in Alaska, Montana, North Dakota, or South Dakota. Foreign countries? Austria, France, Great Britain, Mexico, South Africa, Panama, Colombia, Canada, Monaco, Italy, Germany, India, the Bahamas, and Bermuda.

My most arduous stretch of traveling was a couple of years ago, when I played a dance in New York on a Thursday night, flew to Paris on Friday night, played a party that began at nine on Saturday night and ended at five in the morning, flew that morning to Frankfurt, where I changed planes and flew to Vancouver, British Columbia, where I hopped on a private plane that took me to an island ninety miles north for a party on Sunday night.

We've played one funeral—for my old friend Gubby Glover, out in Moline.

I keep about fifteen operable tuxedos in my closet, which are replaced by visits to my designer friends Bill Blass and Oleg Cassini. The rest of my rig consists of patent leather Belgian shoes that fit like slippers; black bow ties from Turnbull & Asser that take a long time to fray; pleated white Brooks Brothers shirts that leave a lot of sweat room; suspenders of all patterns provided by my wife or daughter. I hate men's jewelry. I keep my cuffs fastened with those little elasticized twist knots you get at Paul Stuart or Brooks Brothers. I never travel without miniature bottles of Tabasco sauce, which makes airplane food somewhat edible.

Since the Peter Duchin Orchestra changes in size to fit the needs of each job, it's not a fixed aggregate like the groups that played under my father, Glenn Miller, Ellington, or Basie. I draw on a pool of fifty-some musicians, out of which my office forms groups of various sizes that we send out under my name. There's a smaller core of twelve players and two singers whom I consider a family. Finally, there's the hard core—eight of us: a trumpeter, a reed player, a trombonist, a bass player–vocalist, a guitarist-vocalist, a drummer, a synthesizer player, and me.

By now, our musical communication is subliminal and our friendship tight. Besides affection, it's based on countless shared mishaps, which range from late flights and missed connections to lost baggage and lost instruments, screwed-up hotel bookings, unforeseen hurricanes and blizzards, and dealings with service people (as well as occasional clients) who are subhuman. Whenever anything on the road goes perfectly right, my trumpet player and road manager, Tone Kwas, always says, "That's one out of one."

I could write a book on the decline of the travel experience in America. I've joined it a bit myself. When we started out, I insisted that every member of the band wear a jacket and tie on planes. Now I insist only that they look presentable.

Service? I can get teary-eyed thinking about those old Pan Am stewardesses and how much pride they took in their jobs. Nowadays when you step into an airport, you're usually greeted by petulance, arrogance, and indifference to your very existence. Travel used to be a treat. Now it's an ordeal—by far the most difficult part of what I do.

Still, after thirty-odd years of being on the road, I usually have a ball. My audience is there to have fun, too, and it's up to me to help them have it.

My father once told Rocky Cooper that he'd seen "more than one marriage break up on the dance floor." I must be a chip off the old block, because I've never ceased being fascinated by what happens out there. Since I'm always positioned in the middle of the band, right up front, I've got a ringside seat. I've been told that I almost never look at the keyboard. Another thing I unconsciously do when I play is rock back and forth, as though I'm riding a horse. My ear is tuned to the band. My fingers work by second nature, constantly improvising. And always, I'm scanning the crowd. What's the age span out there? The predominant generation? Economic level? Ethnic background? Where *am* I? Every region—New England, the South, the Midwest, the border states, the mountain states, the West Coast—has surprisingly different musical tastes. American party manners are amazingly diverse, too. They range from blasé (Manhattan) to uptight (Boston), wild (New Orleans), sedate (St. Louis), loud (Texas), and narcissistic (Los Angeles). My sense of all this informs what we play, the order we play it, the tempos.

At every job I get dozens of requests, which I'm usually able and happy to fill. I invariably get requests that clash with my sense of the mood. I play them either later or not at all. When someone wants to know why I haven't played his favorite song, I reply, "You mean you didn't hear it? I just played it five minutes ago." Generally he nods dimly and says, "Thank you."

Watching the dance floor, I've seen people fall in love, come to blows, nearly copulate, die. They used to do this in nightclubs, in front of live musicians. Since the sixties, however, the scene has changed greatly. Nightclubs have by and large disappeared. There are very few places anymore where one can go dancing to live music. My band plays mostly at big events now—fund-raisers or private parties.

The behavior of partygoers has changed. People don't dress up as much. They rarely wear their best jewelry. And they have agendas. Thirty years ago, when people arrived at a party, they left their troubles at home. They came in with a certain lightness, a look of expectancy. Today, I see people entering beautifully set rooms looking as grim and self-absorbed as if they were beginning another day at the office. It's not as bad in Europe. There, partygoers still put on something of an air. That amused-looking Italian who has just arrived and is murmuring something in the hostess's ear to make her giggle might have gone bankrupt that morning, but you'd never know it.

In America, parties used to be occasions for pure, innocent fun: five or six hours of release from daily life during which people could be a little more handsome, a little more beautiful, a little more witty, even a little more dangerous with one another. I think of the marvelous costume parties that Joan Payson, Jock Whitney's sister, used to give in Manhasset. The idea of anyone talking business under her tent was anathema.

Thirty years ago, it wasn't unusual for a party to last until three or four in the morning. Arriving at a deb ball, I'd be told by the host to play "until it becomes light"—lovely phrase—"so the kids can see their way to drive home." Nowadays, parties that last beyond one thirty are virtually unheard-of, except in Europe. (At the 1993 ball thrown by my pal Giovanni Volpi for a goddaughter at his palazzo on the Grand Canal, his only instructions were "Don't stop until you can hear the opening of the fish market in the Rialto.")

The music we used to play was much more homogeneous—mostly fox-trots and the occasional waltz or lindy. Today it's mandatory to play in every style, especially rock and roll, which would have been unthinkable at a fancy party before the mid-sixties. From the musicians' standpoint, that's a big improvement.

Many jazz musicians like to play rock because of the rhythm, but most of them have not taken rock seriously enough to learn how to play it properly. They incorporate its rhythm into their jazz style, which is not really the point. It's very hard for a jazz-oriented musician to learn how to play true rock and roll. Rock and roll is squarely on the beat or slightly ahead of it, whereas jazz tends to lag slightly behind the beat. Roberta Fabiano, my lead guitarist and singer, always chides me for trying to interpret rock and roll in a jazz way. She's right. I guess I can't completely lose the jazz feeling. There are very few people who can play both styles authentically. Miles Davis, Herbie Hancock, and others have made notable efforts to fuse the two, but I've never found it convincing. They end up with a hybrid without the urgency of rock or the irony of jazz.

I love rock and roll. When it's good, it's great popular music, as terrific as big-band swing was in its day. I like the energy, the irreverence. And for filling up the dance floor it's foolproof. Everybody gets out there. Rock is almost the only music the under-forty generation knows how to dance to. Generally, the first dance we play at weddings is still a traditional song like "Embraceable You" or "Isn't It Romantic?" But the bride and groom often have a difficult time doing a slow fox-trot. Thanks to reruns of movies on TV and to video rentals, however, "close dancing" may be coming back in vogue. The other night, I played for the senior prom at the St. Paul's School in New Hampshire, and six or seven couples came up and asked for "Cheek to Cheek," "Isn't It a Lovely Day?" and "I'm Old-Fashioned." They danced beautifully to these wonderful old Astaire songs. I've had the same requests from kids in San Antonio.

=

I'm often asked two questions: What was the best party you ever played for? And, What was the worst party?

What's the point in dwelling on the bad parties? Thank God there haven't been too many of them. On the rare occasions when I've felt a malaise in the air (even then, there's always one couple

I've seen people fall in love, come to blows, nearly
copulate, and die on the dance floor.

who seem to be having a great time), the band and I have given our all to rev things up, right up to the last minute. When it just doesn't work, we take it personally.

My list of reasons for bad parties isn't surprising. But here are a few of them:

· The host and hostess hate each other and can't hide it.
· The food and drink are lousy and/or inadequate. The service is rude.
· Most of the guests didn't really want to be there in the first place and can't wait to get home.
· The tables are either too cramped or too spread out; the room is too hot or too cold, too dark or too bright.
· The bandstand was put in the wrong place, and many of the guests can't hear the music.

The best parties?

The most outrageous affair I've ever played for was the quintessential party of the eighties. To celebrate his son's bar mitzvah and his daughter's bat mitzvah, an extremely, newly rich man in the New York real-estate business hired the Cunard Lines' flagship, the *Queen Elizabeth II*, from six in the evening until eight the following morning. For fourteen hours, 600 guests—including everyone the host had ever done a deal with, as well as his children's entire school classes—had the run of the *QE II* as it sailed out of New York Harbor. There was enough food and drink to last a month, including buckets of beluga and Roederer Cristal. There were all-night movies; an all-night beauty salon that was heavily patronized; and all-night gambling tables that opened for business the moment we got beyond the offshore limit. We were one of three full-size bands hired to play in three different lounges. I brought along fourteen musicians. There was also a discotheque. Out-of-work actors wandered around in masks and white makeup, encouraging everyone to have a good time. Everyone did.

For me, the highlight was when the ship stopped as we were pulling out of the harbor so that a helicopter could land. Out stepped Ivan Boesky, king of the shady Wall Street arbitrageurs, in a shimmering white suit and a vulpine smile. He melted into the crowd, and I didn't see him again until the next morning, when the *QE II* docked at a pier in lower Manhattan so that the guests could go off to Wall Street.

Postscript: Not long afterward, Boesky was thrown in jail. The man who had hired the *QE II* for the night—at what must have cost well over a million dollars—lost everything, including his collection of old master Dutch paintings, his fortune, and his wife. The other day I was told by one of the guests that under his white suit Boesky had been wired by government investigators who were trying to get the goods on other Wall Street scoundrels by bugging the kids' celebration.

≡

The most historic parties I ever played had to be the White House weddings in 1966 and 1967 for the daughters of Lyndon and Lady Bird Johnson, Lynda Byrd and Luci. Although the guests included an eye-popping array of America's most powerful, both weddings had the informality and warmth of Texas-style family affairs. At Luci's wedding, we were the first band ever to play rock and roll in the White House; LBJ danced to it as energetically as he did to everything else. (His favorite song was "Hello, Dolly!") Lady Bird Johnson was one of the most gracious, meticulous hostesses I've ever worked with. I was amused that the band was paid by checks from her personal bank account, not her husband's.

Toward the end of Luci's reception, LBJ came over behind the bandstand to say thank you and tapped the leg of the nearest trumpet player. We were in the middle of "When the Saints Go Marching In." Without looking to see who it was, the trumpeter turned and blasted a high A right into the face of the president. The A instantly became a squawk.

≡

The most civilized party: In 1980 the South African diamond king Harry Oppenheimer threw a dinner dance for the birthday of his wife, Bridget, at the home of one of their children in Johannesburg. I've never met a host with more exquisite manners, nor have I ever played a party that was so gracefully integrated among the black and white guests as was this one in what was then still the land of apartheid.

≡

The most musically astute party: In 1992, while my wife and I were traveling in India, our Sikh friend Patwant Singh, a political writer in New Delhi, invited about thirty Indian friends over to his Lutyens-designed house in the Lodi Gardens and asked me to play an old upright he'd borrowed at great effort for the evening. I did two hours of Broadway show tunes—some familiar, many not— and I was amazed that every Indian knew the words to every song, including the verses.

≡

The best after-party party: In the summer of 1974, during Race Week, Cheray and I went up to Saratoga Springs, where I had been hired to play a benefit for the opening of the new Saratoga Performing Arts Center. The following evening we went to Jock Whitney's house for dinner. Betsey Whitney was away, and Cheray and I were greeted by Jock, his crony Shipwreck Kelly, and Fred Astaire. After dinner we all went over to the yearling sales, where Fred, a racing enthusiast, was as entranced by the elegance of the young horses as we were entranced by his elegance in tweed jacket and ascot as he stroked their manes.

Back at the house, we followed Shipwreck into the bar, where Jock poured us snifters of brandy. Fred was reminiscing about my parents, whom he had known casually, when Shipwreck bellowed: "Enough of this crap. Astaire, you gotta helluva pianist here. Sing us a song, goddamnit!"

Fred merely smiled, looked at me, and said, "How about it?"

"Sure," I said nervously. We went over to Jock's piano in the front hall, a big, square room with a wide-planked floor and no rug.

" 'Top Hat'?" suggested Fred. He started snapping his fingers.

From ten until three in the morning, Fred Astaire sang and danced his way through nearly every song from his movies in Jock's front hall. He used Cheray—a terrific dancer—as his Ginger and me as his backup. Before each song, he explained its context in the film, as well as how he and the choreographer had put the number together.

His last song was "One for My Baby." "This is the way Frank sang it," he said—meaning Sinatra, of course—setting a medium swing tempo. He stopped after one chorus and said, "This is the way *I* liked to do it." He put an elbow on the piano and rested his head in his hands. He slowed the tempo way down. With just a couple of gestures and the flicker of his eyes, he conjured up a man who had plummeted from the heights of success to the depths.

Before it was over, Jock, brandy snifter in hand, was crying. Even Shipwreck's eyes were wet. Over his shoulder, I spotted Jock's valet, Eric, and some of the kitchen help, peeking out of the doorway that led up the back stairs.

=

The best guest list: Truman Capote's Black and White Ball, held in honor of *Washington Post* publisher Katharine Graham in the Plaza Hotel in 1966, closed an era of elegant exclusiveness and ushered in another of media madness—the one in which we still live. As Marie Harriman and her pals had done back in the thirties and forties, Capote merged the worlds of old money, literature, show business, Washington, and just plain folks with such diabolical shrewdness that his 500-name guest list instantly became the index of who was in and, by omission, out.

The masked ball was preceded by small dinners orchestrated by Truman's puckish sense of name power (the Henry Fords with the Henry Fondas, the Irving Berlins with the Isaiah Berlins). It began at ten in the Grand Ballroom, paused for a supper of chicken hash and scrambled eggs at midnight, and became one of those very rare New York parties where the dancing is as good as the conversation. The two most memorable moments were Lauren Bacall doing a Fred Astaire number with Jerome Robbins, and Kay Graham being twirled around by a Plaza doorman. At three in the morning, the joint was still jumping.

The Black and White Ball inspired more ink than a British coronation, which was just what Truman had hoped for. With his genius for publicity, he decreed that TV cameras, photographers, and reporters be confined to the lobby. By ten fifteen there were more media out there than guests. Truman had cautioned me not to allow any "professional snoops" to sneak in via the band. On the

Truman Capote's Black and White Ball at the Plaza in 1966 had
the best guest list of any party I've ever played for. Truman arrived
with the guest of honor (above), Kay Graham. Ave and Marie,
below, were among the glittering five hundred invitees.

morning of the ball, I got a call from Earl Wilson, the *New York Post* gossip columnist, asking if I would smuggle him in as one of the musicians. "Meyer Davis once got me into the White House as a trombonist," said Earl. "How 'bout it, Pete? I'll love you forever." I was sorely tempted, but I kept my word to Truman.

=

The most touching party: In the late eighties, I got a letter from a man named Bill Graves in Cincinnati asking me to play for a regatta party that he and his wife were giving at their house near the Ohio River. He said he'd been a great fan of the big bands in the thirties, especially my father's. An amateur pianist himself, he had emulated my father's style and had even made it the subject of his senior thesis in college.

Five of us flew out to Cincinnati, wearing blue blazers and white ducks, and were greeted by our host and hostess. To our surprise, both of them were confined to wheelchairs. Their son, Harry, took me aside and explained that his parents had multiple sclerosis. His father's condition was very precarious, he said, but one of the things that had kept him alive was the prospect of hearing me play in his living room.

During the party, Mr. Graves wheeled himself over to the piano, a pampered old Steinway, as we played the list of classic show tunes he'd requested—Porter, Gershwin, Arlen, and so on. Toward the end of the evening, I asked if he'd like to play a duet with me. His face lit up, and he wheeled himself around to my left and played "Cheek to Cheek" while I improvised in the upper register. Everybody cheered when it was over. Mr. Graves literally wept with joy. We made him an honorary band member, and in the last letter he wrote me before he died, he said that playing Irving Berlin with me that night had made him feel like "a giant."

≡

The best down-home parties: In the early seventies, I was hired to play at a farewell party in San Antonio at which the host and hostess were saying good-bye to their house. Since they didn't believe in taxes, they had given the mansion to the University of Texas and were moving to Uruguay. The centerpiece on each of the hundred tables was a five-pound tin of beluga nesting in a bowl of shaved ice. That night I met two people who would become close friends, Illa and Jim Clement. Illa's uncle was Bob Kleberg, who ran the legendary King Ranch.

Through Illa, I was hired to play at a half dozen family affairs at the ranch, including a wedding, a birthday, and the cattle sales. The atmosphere was old Texas, relaxed and boisterous. The food was laid out on long tables: shellfish from the Gulf, great haunches of beef roasted in open pits, mountains of every conceivable Mexican dish, prepared by the help, who had lived in their own village on the ranch for generations.

The musicians were made to feel not like servants (as they frequently are in New York City) but like guests at the party. From the bandstand, we had an endless view of the Old West. Under the big sky were paddocks with cutting horses, pastures with the ranch's specially bred Santa Gertrudis cattle, and *birds*—from wild turkeys, swirling hawks, and sandhill cranes flying to roost to peacocks who strutted among the guests, occasionally punctuating the music with outraged honks.

≡

My favorite party? In 1983, my booking manager got a call from a Mrs. Blum in Chicago, who wanted to hire me and a twelve-piece orchestra to play at the Palmer House hotel for her and her husband's fiftieth wedding anniversary. Given the size of the band, I expected the party to be held in the grand ballroom. Instead, we were led into a smaller private room, with a capacity for about forty guests. There we were surprised to find one table, set for two.

"It must be for the hors d'oeuvres," I said to the guys as we were setting up on the far side of a small dance floor. "They're probably bringing in the other tables for dinner."

At 7:30, Mr. and Mrs. Blum arrived—two dignified, beautifully dressed people in their late seventies or early eighties. Mrs. Blum took me aside. "I hope you won't mind, Mr. Duchin," she said, "but it's just my husband and myself. During dinner we'd like the piano alone. Could you play 'The Anniversary Waltz' after the first course? After dessert we'd like the whole orchestra to join you for the rest of the evening."

I was worried that the band might fall asleep playing for only two elderly people, but we never sounded better. From 9:00 until 10:30, Mr. and Mrs. Blum danced every dance without a break. At 10:31, they came over to the bandstand. "Thank you, Mr. Duchin," said Mr. Blum. "You've given us the happiest night of our life."

18

THE PRIVATE
SPORT

Perhaps because my own mother and father were more shadows than substance, I had never felt a *part* of another person's flesh and blood until the birth of my son Jason in 1966. Two years later, my daughter, Courtnay, arrived. She was followed a year and a half after that by Colin, my second son. I thought of the five of us as the fingers of a hand. And I imagined a home that would be like a glove: a place with room for everybody to be independent yet joined.

With children, the house in the city was too cramped, too vertical. Cheray and I dreamed of a place in the country, one with a big playroom where each of the kids would have a corner, a big garden for me to muck around in, and plenty of room for animals. In the summer of 1969, we put our brownstone on the market and headed for the hills of Westchester. We first rented a wonderful old stone house in Bedford Village. Two years later, we acquired from the estate of Cheray's uncle a derelict house outside the village on forty overgrown acres a couple of miles down a dirt road. We tore down the old house and built a new one—a mélange of Tudor and modern whose main feature was a forty-five-foot-high living room with a big stone fireplace surrounded by a wall of glass and a sweeping view of woods and meadow.

Because my father had died when he was only forty-one, I'd always been haunted by the feeling that I might not live past my forty-first year, and I was determined to do as many things as possible with my kids before then.

I taught them every sport I knew, throwing baseballs and footballs, kicking soccer balls around the lawn, lobbing tennis balls. I taught them how to swim and how to ride their first bikes. I took them to school on a motorcycle, just as Harry Whitney had taken me. I read them my favorite bedtime books—*The Jungle Book* and Babar stories. I insisted they all take piano lessons, but I was afraid that if I pushed them, they'd get turned off. Instead, to my great regret, they never got turned on.

Together, we went to museums, concerts, plays, and the ballet, to dude ranches in Montana so they could learn how to ride Western style, to game parks in East Africa so they could see great wildlife outside a zoo. I taught my kids how to shoot—first BB guns, then .22s, then shotguns. Most important of all, I taught them how to fish.

=

Cheray had put up no argument when I suggested we take our honeymoon in the wilds of Quebec. We spent the first couple of weeks fixing up a log cabin on a remote lake, a three-hour drive west of Montreal. It was situated on a hundred acres of woods that

Me and my oldest child, Jason, in our cabin
in the Canadian woods.

I'd bought some years before at the suggestion of Donald and Jean Stralem, who owned an enormous property next door. As a wedding present, Donald and Jean had given us plumbing and electricity. Cheray and I furnished the cabin with primitive, local furniture and an old upright from the Zauderers' house in Mount Kisco. With me at the helm of a borrowed tractor, we made a clearing for a front lawn.

To my delight, Cheray loved the isolation and simplicity. She wasn't much interested in fishing in Limmer Lake, but she didn't complain when I disappeared for hours in a rowboat—the same kind of boat I'd had at Arden.

When friends of ours called and suggested we join them for some serious fishing in the northernmost part of Quebec, I was worried that ten days of camping out in a corrugated tin shack, sleeping on wooden bunks in bedrolls, would be asking too much of my bride from 911 Park Avenue. But Cheray said, "Let's go."

The creature comforts were zero, the fishing terrific. We waded in fast water in near-impossible footing. We fished in deeper water from perilously tippy canoes. Because the fish hadn't been spoiled by invaders like us, they gobbled up everything we threw at them. It was instant gratification. I tried to teach Cheray how to cast, but she was happier just sitting in the canoe, walking along the shore, or immersing herself in a good book.

≡

Instant gratification is not what fishing is all about. The first thing fishing does is make you slow down—way down. You can't be any good at it unless you stop everything and begin to look, really *look*—whether it's for terns diving into a stretch of the Gulf Stream (a sure sign of fish below) or that dimple on a slick glacial lake (sure sign of a hungry trout).

Cheray and I built a house in Westchester where we could raise
the kids and let the animals run around.

Slowing down used to come easier, when I was a child at Arden and going fishing was simply part of everyday life. Now, making the transition from bandleader and husband to fisherman requires some effort.

Bill Kitchen taught me everything about the rituals of preparation: first, unscrewing the fly rod case; then, sliding the rod from its cotton sleeve, fitting the parts together, attaching the reel, stringing a line through the guides, deciding on the leader, finally attaching it to the end of the line, either by knotting it to the existing tippet or by tying it to the loop left from the previous outing.

All fishermen know the charge of adrenaline that comes as you approach the water. But the best ones also know to rein themselves in for ten or fifteen minutes. Very quietly, they sit down out of sight in order to read the situation: the flow of the current; the play and hatch of insects; the position of the sun, which is crucial, because you don't want to spook the fish with your shadow; any perceptible movement of fish. Only when he's taken it all in and *thought* about it does the good fisherman feel ready to select the fly and wade in.

There's a story about the legendary fisherman and author the late Lee Wulff, with whom I was lucky enough to fish on many occasions. At an old Canadian salmon camp on the Upsalquich River, the houses were situated on a hill overlooking the "home pool," a hundred-foot stretch of water in which, sitting on the porch, you could actually make out the resting salmon. It was August. Hot and dry. Low water. And none of the fishermen had been able to move even one of the fifteen or more visible fish.

Lee arrived for a couple of days of fishing. They bet him he couldn't catch anything either. "Lee, those damn fish haven't shown any interest in anything we've thrown them," said one of the guys. "John here was talking about using a harpoon. And we've almost run out of bourbon."

Lee sat down on the porch and for about an hour did nothing but look at that pool of fish. Finally, he put together his rod, slipped down the hill, and proceeded to catch—and release—every last salmon. Lee was so meticulous in his scrutiny that once, when the two of us were filming a show for *The American Sportsman* series on the Lairdahl River in Norway, I watched him tie a new fly right on the spot because none of the ones we'd brought had worked.

Like all great fishermen, Lee had a respect for nature that was at once romantic, philosophical, and scientific. How different the sport has become in the last twenty years. These days, everybody who has a little money seems to want to fish. They have to have the latest and newest equipment. They have to spend outrageous sums renting fishing space on the most exotic, faraway rivers—just to say they've been there. They have to build, buy, or hire boats with the latest electronic fish-finding devices—gizmos that take much of the chance out of the sport. They have to compete, as if they're still in the bond market. Thirty-five years ago, when I started tarpon fishing in the Florida Keys, you rarely saw another boat. Silently you poled the flats in solitude. Today it's a traffic jam.

As far as I'm concerned, fishing has nothing to do with competition. It's the most private and personal of sports, and it elevates you to heightened levels of consciousness. Fishing is one of the few sports that can be as pleasurable by yourself as in the company of friends. But they have to be the right friends. Fishing can bring out the worst in people who, in other settings, are above reproach. Suddenly that urbane landscape architect becomes ferociously territorial about *his* pool in the stream. That mild-mannered author of musical tomes becomes a loudmouth braggart. That gray, pinstriped banker, famous for his probity, reveals himself to be a terrible liar, adding pounds and inches to the bass that never was.

A few years ago, my best fishing buddy, the art critic Robert Hughes, and I went to the South Island of New Zealand for giant brown trout. With us was an aristocratic Brit whose company I'd enjoyed for many years. The moment the Brit put on his waders, he underwent a complete personality change, becoming rude, sullen, and standoffish. Perhaps because Bob is Australian and I'm American—and our friend was temporarily not the lord of the manor—he'd lost his bearings. Or perhaps he just wasn't up to the delicate camaraderie that prevails among real fishing buddies.

The kind of fishing I enjoy demands thoughtfulness and good manners. They're not the sort of manners that are dictated by a country club—there's no dress code among fishermen. It's simply a way of behaving that starts out as respect for nature and becomes respect for one another.

Fishing gives you its own time and space. I've surf-cast for bluefish off a Florida beach, five feet away from Ave. I've shared ten miles of a Colorado river with nine others, each of us standing a mile apart from the next, all day long from breakfast to supper. I've done a television show on the White River in Arkansas (pre-Clintons) with the cameras rolling just inches from my shoulder. I've been dropped into a far corner of Alaska by floatplane and left alone for the day with nobody but grizzlies and a guide. I once fished on a stream twenty yards from the Long Island Expressway at the height of the evening rush hour, and I didn't hear a single car.

No matter how different the circumstances are, time disappears when you're fishing, and as the hours pass by unnoticed, it becomes unbearable to think of quitting, even to *think*. The shadows grow long, and you're carried along by the sound of the stream, the repetition of casting, the intensity of focus.

Wives and nonfishermen always ask me the same question: What in God's name do you all do when you're not fishing?

When I sink into the ritual of fishing, everything else fades away.

Quail hunting in Georgia.

There are only a few things that are really essential in a fishing camp: a hearty breakfast; a lemon, some salt and pepper, a can of shortening, a box of matches, and a roll of aluminum foil; a well-stocked bar to come home to; a good supper; and a place to sleep—preferably dry. Conversation is a bonus. There's something about having spent the day alone, walking up and down a piece of water, that frees the tongue to talk about everything under the sun. You don't gossip. You don't feel compelled to confess. Fishing takes your mind to more abstract places. You may be a half dozen guys from different backgrounds, but you find yourselves trying out ideas about the things that really interest you—politics, art, music, history, sports. When anybody brings up something to do with business, I tune out and open a book. I've done some of my best reading in fishing camps. The mind has slowed down.

=

My favorite fishing spot is on the Whale River in northern Quebec. To get there, you fly to Montreal, spend the night, and the next morning pick up the once-a-day flight to Kuujjuaq, an Eskimo village. There you catch a floatplane for the hour's flight to the Whale, cruising low over tundra streaked with caribou trails. The only worry is that you'll miss the return plane to Montreal and have to spend the night in Kuujjuaq, God knows where.

The camp I stay in can fish ten rods comfortably. A good part of its attraction is that most of the fishing can be done by wading or standing onshore, rather than from a boat. Apart from the fish and other fishermen, the only creatures you encounter are gulls, hawks, ospreys, and a real weirdo—the crossbill sparrow. You might see caribou, ambling through the woods or swimming across the stream in their perpetual migration. You might spot a bear, in which case you stay very still.

The weather is eccentric. It can be hot enough during the day to fish in a T-shirt. At night you'll probably need a blanket over your sleeping bag. On my most recent trip to the Whale, I was getting in some last-minute fishing while waiting for the floatplane to fly me to Kuujjuaq, from where I'd embark for Montreal, thence to Detroit, and finally to Kansas City, where I was to play a wedding that night. At eight in the morning, what had been a perfect late August day with temperatures in the sixties suddenly turned into December: A blizzard was followed by a hailstorm with stones the size of jelly beans. An hour of this, and suddenly it was summer again. In came the plane, just in time for me to make my connections. Eight hours later, I was under the tent in Kansas City, strapped into my black tie.

It was on the Whale that I had my greatest day of salmon fishing. It was a cold, slate gray afternoon, with a brisk, northern wind blowing upriver. Perhaps two hours of good fishing light remained before sundown. The night before, one of the fishermen had recommended a pool called "the Ledge." "The water level should be just about right for holding some fish if a run starts coming," he'd said. "It's just beyond a big rocky point. You can't miss it."

I wasn't having any luck where I was when I remembered that rocky point—about a quarter of a mile upstream. I made my way to it along the shore, moving crabwise so as not to spook any fish that might be holding near the bank. When I reached the point, I sat down on a rock to look and dropped the fly just over the water's edge to get it out of the way. While the fly idly bobbed in the stream, I sank into that state of *oneness* that I can achieve only by being near water or listening to Bach.

God knows where my mind was when a salmon, very large, leapt out of the water, dive-bombed my fly, grabbed it in his mouth, and took off. I got hold of the rod just before it would have vanished with the fish, jumped up, and for the next fifteen minutes played him—a bright, silver male that had just come into the river from Ungava Bay. I landed him, released him, and wondered whether there were any more where he'd come from.

Over the next hour and a half, I cast exactly eleven times and hooked a fish every time. I didn't have to walk more than ten yards. I barely got my waders wet. Finally, only because the guide in his motor canoe had arrived and it was getting quite dark did I realize that it was time to quit. Dead tired as I was hobbling into the boat, I've never been so exhilarated. Each fish had presented me with a different challenge. With each landing and release, I'd gone to another plateau of satisfaction. All were bright, strong fish—none less than fifteen pounds. I kept only the last one for supper.

The guide, a son of the camp's owner, said, "How'd you do?"

"There's a brand-new run in the river," I replied.

"It'll be good tomorrow then," he said.

That was all there was to say.

≡

One of my favorite fishing buddies doesn't fish. Driving to my house in Connecticut, I often stop by the only store I enjoy shopping in. (Virtually every other store I've ever been in puts me into a cold sweat.) Harry Whitman has owned The Bedford Sportsman, right across from the railroad station in Bedford Hills, at least since Cheray and I moved out to Westchester. Harry sells everything from flies, rods, waders, and vests to sporting prints and sporting books, old and new. He's even been known to sell a few of the latest compact discs of me and the band. Everything at Harry's is top quality and in seeming disarray—the way a store should be.

Harry sits behind the counter, directly in front of the door—a tall, fair man with reddish hair and a beatific smile. I'm not sure that Harry has ever held a rod except to sell it, but his appreciation of the sport is as deep as that of any fisherman I know. Harry sees fishing as having a great tradition. He knows that every pool, whether it's on the Housatonic or the Lairdahl, contains a thousand stories. Without any stories of his own to tell, he draws to his shop all the best fishermen from a hundred miles around. Like me, they come to buy flies and leaders, or perhaps a magnifying glass and hook sharpener—stuff they'll never use. Or to chew the fat about where they're going fishing next. Or to leaf through first editions of magnificently written fishing books by Norman Maclean, Joe Brooks, and William J. Schaldach. Or simply, as Red Smith put it, to "tackle-fondle."

Ma

19

LOSING MA

It was Otto who called with the news: "It's bad, Peter," he said over the phone. "Marie died last night of a heart attack. You'd better get on the next plane."

It was September 26, 1970, and we were far away. For three days, Cheray and I had been guests of my friend Simon Frazier, the eighteenth Lord Lovatt, at Beauly, his Scottish castle near Inverness. We'd come over for two weeks of stalking stag and fishing for salmon. We'd visited the nearby loch, where Nessie the monster was reputed to reside. We'd begun to unwind.

I took the call in the library, an immense paneled room hung with eighteenth-century French tapestries bordered with fleurs-de-lis. After Otto hung up, my eyes filled with tears. Mindlessly I began counting the fleurs-de-lis. As they got blurrier, I just stood there, holding the dead phone, counting.

Finally, Cheray came in. Giving her the news, I totally lost it. I sank to the floor, turned on my side, grabbed my knees, and rocked slowly back and forth, as I had done as a child when I couldn't get to sleep.

The next day we flew to Washington. Ave was beside himself. Marie had died at sixty-seven. He was seventy-nine and had never expected to outlive her. Immediately he wanted to show us her body. In his Checker town car with its awful springs, we bounced up Massachusetts Avenue to Joseph Gawlor's funeral home. As we entered the dim room where Ma was laid out in an open coffin, I couldn't bear to look. Ave, clutching my arm heavily, said, "Isn't she beautiful! Isn't she beautiful!"

That night we joined the family at the house in Georgetown for dinner, along with Mike Forrestal. While Mike and I planned the funeral music, the others manned the phones. Just before bed, Ave asked Cheray and me to drive him back to Gawlor's. He had something on his mind.

The place was locked up for the night, but after much ringing of the bell, we were let in by a watchman. This time I forced myself to look. Ma was dressed in one of her favorite dresses, but she had on much too much makeup. There were no dark glasses. No Viceroy in a white plastic holder. This woman belonged in Madame Tussaud's. She was a cartoon of Ma.

The sense of loss I felt was physical, as though I were suddenly without a vital organ. Ma had been my best sounding board, my late-night drinking buddy, my bulwark, my conscience. Definitely my last resort. From the beginning she'd watched over me. She'd been in the driveway at Arden when Chissie and I had returned from California. She'd been the life of the party at my graduations, openings, and personal celebrations. She'd stood in the receiving line at my wedding.

During the birth of my first son, she and Ave had come to New York Hospital with sandwiches and vodka and kept an all-night vigil on folding chairs in the corridor. She had always said, "Oh, Averell, why don't we take Peter along?" Late one evening, just a few months ago, the two of us had been sitting around her living room in Sands Point. After too many nightcaps, I had made her cry with my angry outburst: "Why *didn't* you marry my father? You loved him, didn't you?"

Suddenly Ave bent over the coffin. I thought he was going to kiss her. Instead he said, turning to Cheray, "I want her wedding ring. Can you help me get it off?" Cheray gulped, but she raised Ma's left hand and slipped off the ring, one of the many she always wore. Cheray handed it to Ave, who put it in his pocket.

"Let's go now," he said.

I thought he was keeping the ring for himself. But a few days later, at the reception after the funeral, he gave it to Ethel Kennedy. In recent years, Ethel had become one of Marie's best friends, just as Ave had become one of Bobby's before the assassination in 1968. Even so, I was shocked by the gesture. If Ave had wanted to give Ma's ring to somebody, it should have gone to her own daughter, Nancy.

Ethel herself was flabbergasted and at first didn't want to accept it. Recently, when I asked why she had, she replied that she hadn't wanted to offend Ave. "I still wear it," she added. "And I think of Marie every day."

Of Ma's two longest obituaries—one in *The New York Times,* the other in *The Washington Post*—I preferred the latter. Whereas the subhead in the *Times* cast her strictly as Ave's helpmate ("Humor and Hospitality Aided Husband in His Numerous Government Assignments"), the *Post*'s line was all about her: "Art Dealer, Hostess, Witty Grande Dame." I liked it that the obituary cited one of her typical acts of generosity: the time, after JFK's assassination, when she'd given her Washington house to Jackie Kennedy and her two children without a second thought. (The *Post* didn't mention the diplomatic skill she had employed getting Ave to move into a room in the Georgetown Inn for several weeks. As Ma had joked over the phone, "All he does is complain about the goddamn bath being too short!")

Both newspapers misquoted the one-liner she'd thrown at Ave during a particularly dicey stretch of Franco-American diplomacy: "For gosh sakes, Ave, de Gaulle doesn't know his arm from his elbow." How I would have loved hearing her correction of that. Ma had never said "gosh" in her life, and I know she didn't say "arm."

There were two memorial services. The first, in Washington's National Cathedral, was filled with friends from all over, high and low. Marie had commanded extraordinary affection from anyone who had ever worked for her, and I spotted not only all of her own servants, including a few part-timers, but those of her friends, whom she had always greeted like pals.

The second service was held in St. John's, the little Harriman chapel at Arden. It was mostly just family, with the addition of Bob Silvers and George Plimpton, who had taken as much delight in Ma as she had in them. After the service, Ma was buried in a wooded knoll near the chapel in the Harriman family plot, next to Averell's parents and his sister Mary. A space was left on the other side of her grave for Averell.

I received more than a hundred condolence letters, written to me as though I had been Ma's son. And the truth is, I felt I had lost a mother.

After the thousand thank-you notes had been written and the parade of condolence callers was over, Ave went into a deep depression. Even though friends continued to look in on him, he didn't cheer up. I don't think he'd realized how dependent he had become on Marie during the previous ten years.

That winter, he went down to Hobe Sound and rarely went out. When Cheray and I called to ask how he was doing, he plaintively asked whether we might come down for a visit. "How about our spending a few months after New Year's?" I suggested. There was a long pause—possibly to turn up his hearing aid. Then: "Fine, Petey. Come along." It was Ave's way of saying, "I'd love it."

In January, Cheray and I flew down with the kids, the nurse, and Malcolm X to Hobe Sound, where temporary places were found for Jason and Courtnay in the local school. Ave was in worse shape than we'd imagined. He had mastered every sport from polo and croquet to bridge. He had served in more high-level diplomatic jobs than any American statesman since John Quincy Adams. He had matched wits with many of the century's most ruthless leaders, from Stalin to Marshal Tito. Now he was like a helpless child. He was so listless that he could barely watch the evening news.

He talked incessantly about Marie, reminiscing about the trips they'd taken together and the wisecracks of hers that had made him laugh—more now than when she'd said them. He loved telling about the time in Tehran when he'd been sent by Truman to settle the crisis over Mosaddeq's seizure of the British oil concessions. One evening when Ave was off somewhere else, Ma had paid a call on the prime minister. Along with other dignitaries, she was led into his private chambers. There, the father of modern Iran lay in bed, seemingly indisposed. Finally, everyone was dismissed except Ma. Diplomatically, she inquired about the prime minister's health, whereupon he leapt out of bed on his birdlike legs and

Ma and Ave in their living room in New York, with Picasso's
Woman with a Fan over the couch.

lunged at her. This set off a mad chase through the Persian gardens, Mosaddeq in his red silk pajamas, Ma clicking along in her high heels. The detail Ave loved best was the pajamas.

Cheray and I knew he was getting his old self back when he burst into our room one day. "Petey," he said, "I've got something I think you'll find amusing. I've just been going through some of Marie's old things, and look what I found."

It was a tattered photograph of me at the age of two, sitting on the potty with my pants down, smiling as always at the camera. Across the lower half, stuck into the cheap plastic frame, was a torn-off piece of Ave's private stationery with a message scrawled in his own messy hand: "For Peter, With love—for letting me win occasionally at croquet. Ave." Coming from Ave, the gift was astonishing, especially the fact that he'd assembled it entirely with his own hands.

This turned out to be a happy time. Between taking off for one-night jobs with the band, I read a lot, played croquet a lot, fished a lot, and learned how to fly a plane. Not since our horse-and-buggy rides had I felt so relaxed with Ave. We played croquet every afternoon—for Ave, the best therapy in the world. I guess there's nothing like hating to lose to make you feel young again.

=

One morning at breakfast, he said, "Pete, I've been thinking. I can cut off an acre down by the grapefruit grove without hurting the property. I'd love to give it to you and Cheray if you'd consider building a small house on it. It's right on the ocean. Something you and the kids could use from time to time. You know, there will soon be no beachfront property left on the Atlantic coast."

This was more surprising than the photograph. The one subject that nobody—not even Ave's wife or children—had ever been brave

After Ma died, Cheray and I moved down to Hobe Sound
to help Ave through a bad time. Playing croquet was
one of the only things he enjoyed.

enough to bring up with him was anything to do with money or property. Ma had loved going shopping with Cheray, who couldn't get over how timid she was about charging purchases to Ave. One day, long after one of Ma's fur coats had reached a stage beyond repair, they found the perfect replacement at Bergdorf's, a mink for $5,000. As Cheray later told me, "Marie was just terrified. It took everything I had to give her the courage to buy the damn thing and have the bill sent to Averell."

I had always been thrilled to be considered "family" by the Harrimans, but it was a matter of pride for me never to ask Ave for anything. About a year before Ma died, she'd mentioned she wanted to leave me a Degas sculpture in her will, one of the bronze ballerinas with a real tutu. Ave had jumped in and said, "Oh God no, Marie. It's worth far too much. Can't you think of something else?" (Fifteen years later, after Ave died, his widow, Pamela, sold the Degas for several million dollars.) Ma had next suggested leaving me her best Daumier bronze. Again Ave had vetoed it for the same reason. What she did leave me was $5,000 and a small Daumier bronze called *Le Fat Sebastian*. The caricature of a self-satisfied Parisian businessman, circa 1860, still sits on my desk in New York, where it always gives me a chuckle. I'd never dreamed I would be named in any Harriman will, and I was thrilled by Ma's generosity. But I do wish Ave had kept his mouth shut about the Degas.

Now, lonely as he was, Ave was offering me an acre of Hobe Sound oceanfront, a valuable chunk of *his* property. "Great," I said, "we'd love it. But are you sure?"

"Of course I am," he said. "Let's go walk it."

When Ave suggested that we call up an architect, I knew he was serious. He took great pleasure going over the sketches for the modest bungalow we envisioned, offering many suggestions. Thinking I might actually own a piece of this childhood place, I felt a wonderful sense of roots. The fact that I would also be providing Ave company—as well as a built-in croquet partner—in his old age made it even better.

Since the kids would want to use the Jupiter Island Club, I called on Nat Reed and his mother, Permelia, just to make sure there wouldn't be a problem over membership. "Don't be silly," said Nat. "This is your home. The moment you build your house, you're in." A week later, I got a letter confirming it.

20

PAM

Among the first new friends Cheray and I made after moving out to Bedford was a glamorous couple, Leland and Pamela Hayward, who lived in nearby Yorktown Heights at their estate called Haywire. I had first met Pamela when she was still Pamela Digby Churchill, the ex-wife of Winston Churchill's dissolute son Randolph. At the time, I was too naive to spot her as anything other than an attractive, upper-class Englishwoman with a fancy apartment in Paris, to which I'd been taken a couple of times by journalist friends from *Paris-Match*. I was nineteen, living on the barge, and more impressed to have spotted Jean-Paul Sartre and Simone de Beauvoir at the Deux-Magots than I was to be meeting this rather plump, red-haired, milky-skinned woman, even though she'd been the notorious mistress of Aly Khan and Gianni Agnelli and was currently "being kept" by the French banker Elie de Rothschild. Twelve years later, she reappeared as my neighbor in Westchester.

An extraordinary ability to focus on the object (or objects) of her desire—not beauty, wit, imagination, or style—is the secret of the woman who has been called "the courtesan of the century." Pam has always known exactly what she wanted. And, if she doesn't get it, how to move on. Having failed to marry the European potentates on whom she set her sights, she had arrived on the American scene by breaking up the marriage of one of the princes of show business, the agent and producer Leland Hayward, whose wife, Slim, was not exactly a pushover. By marrying Averell not long after Leland died, she would get what she had always wanted: a pile of money. And after Averell died, she would get what she *really* wanted: not just the pile of money but power and position, when President Clinton named her, despite her British origins, U.S. ambassador to France.

Pamela couldn't have been nicer to Cheray and me at first. When she heard we were looking for property to buy around Bedford, she offered to help us look. Two or three times, she drove us around herself. She seemed the perfect wife for Leland. I had met him casually in New York, and though he hadn't had a hit since his smash musicals *Gypsy* and *The Sound of Music* (and, before that, *South Pacific*), his boyish charm, enthusiasm, and nervous energy were still immensely attractive. He seemed besotted by Pam, especially after he suffered a mild stroke in 1970. By then, Cheray and I were among the "young people" asked over for lunch or dinner to "cheer Leland up."

Leland seemed totally dependent on Pam, the way a little boy becomes dependent on his nanny. Like many Englishwomen, Pam

Pam and Ave a few days before their wedding in 1971.

was a terrific nanny. At Leland's urging, she loved to take center-stage after dinner by reading aloud from her favorite book, *The Wilder Shores of Love* by Lesley Blanch, a collection of short biographies of four adventurous women of the Victorian era. One of them was an ancestral relation of hers, Jane Digby, a femme fatale who had scandalized nineteenth-century Europe with her marriages to various princes and barons and her affairs with, among others, Balzac, King Ludwig of Bavaria, and an Arab sheikh with whom she ended her days in a tent.

Although her adventures made good reading, they became less enthralling with each of Pam's recitations. It didn't take much intelligence to realize that we were meant to view Aunt Jane as the woman on whom Pam had modeled herself. We became further bemused when—again at Leland's urging—she would go into one of her potted imitations of Winston Churchill, the ex-father-in-law whose name she couldn't seem to mention often enough.

═

Ave had been a widower for six months when Leland died of a more massive stroke in March 1971. It wasn't long before Pam heard about an upcoming dinner in Washington being given by Kay Graham at which Ave, Pam's old wartime lover, would be present. Truman Capote claimed he persuaded her to call Kay and get herself invited. If so, it couldn't have taken much persuading. According to several of the guests, Pam directed her focus almost exclusively at Ave, even though they were seated back to back—positions she had arranged beforehand in order to heighten the allure.

At Ave's suggestion, Cheray and I and the kids had been spending that summer at the Harriman house in Sands Point. Ave was in Washington most of the week, and he'd shuttle up on weekends. Casually he mentioned having "run into" Pamela at Kay's—too casually, we thought. The moment he'd left for Washington on Monday morning, the phone rang. It was Pam. She wanted us to know *how wonderful* it had been seeing Ave again. And he had *looked* so wonderful. Twenty-four hours later, she called again. This time she said: Wouldn't it be *fun* if she came by some weekend and saw *all* of us?

Why not? Having Pamela as a houseguest would undoubtedly give Ave a lift. I called him to see if it would be all right. I'd hardly opened my mouth when he said, "Great idea!"

A few days later, Pam pulled up in her beige Cadillac. Out she jumped, looking glamorous and indomitable in her English country best. Ave, having just played croquet, shambled over in his ancient seersucker shorts and shabby Brooks Brothers sweater. Their embrace was correct, friendly but not too friendly. Ave ushered her to a guest room at the farthest point from his bedroom, just down the hall from our quarters. Absolutely correct. I followed, carrying two very heavy bags.

That night we all went next door for dinner at the house of Ave's old friends George and Evie Backer. Pam was the belle of the ball, solicitous of everybody, vibrant, filled with stories. Ave had his hearing aid turned up so high it squeaked.

The following night, Cheray and I couldn't join them for dinner, since I had a job to play and Cheray had a long-standing invitation elsewhere.

"Good night, children," said Pam and Ave as we exited, leaving the two of them alone.

It was one thirty when I got back. The house was dark as I went out on the screened porch to pour myself a nightcap. When I switched on the light over the bar, I heard a shriek. There in each other's arms on the couch were Pam and Ave, unbuttoned.

"Jesus wept!" Ave bellowed.

The last thing I saw before turning off the light was Pam pulling her blouse together.

"Sorry," I mumbled, and fled.

I ran to wake Cheray. I'd gotten as far as "You'll never believe" when we heard Pamela tromping very loudly down the hallway. Passing our room, she called out in her best nannylike voice, "Good night, children!" With a decisive click, she closed her door.

We were almost asleep—both of us delighted at Ave's rejuvenation—when we heard a loud crash in Pam's room. I got up, ran down the corridor, and knocked softly on her door. "Is everything all right?"

"Just fine," cooed Pam. "Absolutely fine. No problem. The lamp fell over."

I went back to bed.

The next morning there was a knock on our door. In came Pam, radiant in her pink negligee. Seating herself at the foot of the bed, she said in a conspiratorial half whisper, "Children, you'll never *guess* what happened! Remember that ghastly sound around two thirty in the morning?"

"The lamp?"

"It wasn't the lamp. It was Averell. He fell through the window."

"He *what*?"

"He walked all the way around the outside of the house in his slippers and pajamas. But the poor darling forgot about the screen."

"Is he all right?"

"Of course he is. . . . Well," she added, showing her dimples, "he's a little . . . *bruised*."

Scarcely a month later, on September 27, 1971, Pam and Ave were married very quietly in New York. According to Cheray, who had heard it from the source herself, the clincher had been Pam's telling Ave: "I won't go with you to Washington unless I'm your wife."

It was a year and a day after Ma's death, six months after Leland's. Ave was nearly eighty. Pam, at fifty-one, was twenty-eight years younger. The ceremony was held at St. Thomas More's Church, Pam having converted to Catholicism some years earlier in her attempt to marry Gianni Agnelli.

An hour after the ceremony, they announced the news to more than a hundred friends and a few relatives at the Harriman house on Eighty-first Street. Without a word of explanation from Ave, Cheray and I had not been invited to the wedding—only a handful of people had, as witnesses. We felt a little uncomfortable as we climbed the red-carpeted stairs to the living room.

It was spooky. There was Pam, wreathed in smiles, welcoming everybody. There was Ave with his arm around her. But it was still Ma's room. Her ghost was everywhere. Over there, under the Derain painting, was where we'd hugged after my father's death. In front of the fireplace was where she'd welcomed the guests for our bridal dinner. We had played her favorite card games—bridge, canasta, gin—on the worn maroon leather table in the corner. I thought of the night, still recent, when Ma had given us the house so that we could host a benefit for John Kerry's Vietnam Veterans Against the War. I could hear her husky laugh as she stood at the top of the stairs, watching a dozen disabled veterans playing dodgem in their wheelchairs on the black-and-white marble below.

Pam's timing was brilliant. Ever so subtly, she changed everything. Bit by bit, she redid the houses, sprucing up the best of Ma's comfortably lived-in pieces, jettisoning the things she didn't want around. One day she called Cheray and asked if we'd like to have the Chinese vitrine that had stood in the foyer at Eighty-first Street, as well as the Steinway piano my father had picked out for Marie and Ave years before. We were thrilled to say yes.

When Ma was alive, the Georgetown house was a place where everybody felt instantly at home. After Pamela moved in, you expected the *Architectural Digest* photographer to arrive at any moment. Pam put the decorator Billy Baldwin in charge of creating the stage set in which she would make her ascension in the Washington power scene.

One morning at breakfast after I'd spent the night there, I asked Ave how much Pam was doing to the place. "I don't know," he said, glancing up from the *Times*. "But there's this little man who pops up now and then and talks to me in this sort of English accent. He seems to be a decorator."

"He sure is," I said.

"Who is he?"

"You'll know when you see the bills."

Ave glowered and went back to his *Times*.

Since Ave had always been perfectly content living out of a suitcase, I'm sure he hardly noticed when the Digby family crest—an ostrich with a horseshoe in its beak, supported by two chained monkeys and the unintentionally ironic family motto *Deo Non Fortuna* ("From God Not Fortune")—began appearing on needlepoint pillows, household stationery, and matchbooks. Pam even had the hood ornament on her Cadillac replaced by a chrome ostrich. Another change was the vanity license plate, which read PCH, for Pamela Churchill Harriman. Pam had scrapped Hayward, and even her ancestral name, Digby. But she would never let go of Churchill—even though she had not only divorced Randolph but had the marriage annulled.

Ave may have grumbled about the bills, but he—as Leland had been—was a goner. One day when I idly asked after his health, he replied, "Things are great. Why, do you know that Pam even puts my favorite flower by my bed every morning?"

"Really?" I said. "I didn't know you had a favorite flower, Ave. What is it?"

Ave stammered: "Oh . . . I don't know. But whatever it is, she puts it there every morning."

Pam tarted up Hobe Sound as well. The story of what she did to the garden has become a local legend. It had become Ave's habit after lunch to retire to his room for a couple of hours. One afternoon, the bulldozers and steamrollers arrived the moment he'd disappeared upstairs. Minutes later, they were followed by trees, bushes, shrubs, earth, and sod. When Ave woke up and came down for his afternoon swim, his landscape of thirty years had been transformed. As the story goes, if he noticed it, he never said a word.

Now that Pam and Ave's life was centered in Washington, Cheray and I didn't see much of them, especially after Pam persuaded Ave to sell the house on Eighty-first Street for tax reasons. During the first years of their marriage, the Georgetown house was open to us as a place to stay, as long as we called ahead and made a reservation. But as Pam accelerated the building of her power base, her bedrooms began filling up with people who could be useful to her.

She occasionally suggested I be hired for a party for one of her organizations, but this soon ended. Later, I was told by one of her friends that she'd been put out by the fact that I hadn't given her organization a discount. Such a thing had never occurred to me. Whenever Ma had gotten me a job, she'd insisted I charge the full price, saying, "It's one way Ave and I can help you along."

Meanwhile, the acre of land Ave had promised us in Hobe Sound was never brought up. In any case, it wasn't something Cheray and I thought very much about.

So I wasn't at all prepared for what happened when I found myself seated next to Pam at the Al Smith Dinner, the Archdiocese of New York's annual fund-raiser at the Grand Ballroom in the Waldorf. Casually, as though she were remarking about the weather, Pam mentioned that she and Ave had put Hobe Sound on the market.

Knowing how much Ave loved the place, I was surprised.

"Yes," she went on. "We think we've found a very good buyer for it. And I've found an absolutely super place in Barbados."

Ave looking for shells on a Caribbean beach? I couldn't see it.

"Pam," I said, "I hope you're not including that acre of land as part of the deal."

"What acre?" she said sharply.

"The one Ave promised Cheray and me. You know, down by the grapefruit grove."

Her smile froze. "Is it in writing?"

In the moment I paused to answer, "Of course not," I realized there was nothing more I could say. I glanced over at Ave, who occupied one of the central seats on the speakers' dais. If I had never been able to ask him for anything before, I certainly wouldn't be able to now.

≡

One day without warning, a large box arrived at our door, courtesy of UPS. Inside was every framed picture of me with Ma and/or Ave, or me with Cheray and the kids and Ma and/or Ave, that had occupied a place in the Harriman houses. Her secretary included a brief, explanatory note.

From then on, every time I called Ave to ask how he was doing, or perhaps to meet for lunch, I was never able to speak with him alone. After we'd say hello, Pam would get on the line and footnote the conversation. When Ave and I did meet for lunch, it was never just the two of us. Pam, as I later learned from a former secretary of hers, would have changed whatever appointment she had in order to be there. It wasn't out of fondness for me.

The invitations declined sharply. Now, Cheray and I were included pro forma only at Ave's birthday parties—never to meet any of the politicos Pam collected for one of her lavish dinner parties. Not that I wanted to be at Pam's dinner parties, which seemed to be about nothing but building her power base in Washington. But I missed the calls I used to get from Ma: "Peter, we've got Leonard Bernstein for dinner on Friday. You *must* come for it." And I really missed my friendship with Ave.

≡

By all reports he was thriving under Pam's stewardship. His clothes got spiffier, though I can't imagine how Pam got rid of those ancient Brooks Brothers sweaters. She even built him something he would never have built for himself—a proper, perfectly manicured English croquet course at Haywire. Raising the subject of our altered relationship would only have confused and upset him—the last thing I wanted to do. By the time the seventies had turned into the eighties and Pam had begun laying the groundwork for her next adventure as fund-raiser par excellence for the Democratic party, I was seeing very little of Ave.

The house in Hobe Sound was sold, along with my acre. As Ave became increasingly deaf—and, before long, increasingly blind—he was transported into new domains that were entirely of Pamela's creation, arriving in their private jet. Weekends they spent an hour's drive away from Washington at Willow Oaks, a many-acred equestrian property in Middleburg, Virginia, that Pam had transformed at untold expense into a showplace. They wintered in Mango Bay, their fairy-tale hideaway in Barbados, which had been built by the British set designer Oliver Messel largely out of coral. Ave had clearly moved on.

21

ENDINGS

The past is constantly being recycled back into my life to delight, depress, or haunt me. Faces I haven't thought of in years suddenly pop up at the piano to reminisce about some long-ago night or request a favorite tune. I still get letters from people telling me about the ancient, unforgettable evening when they danced to my father's orchestra. I'm constantly revisiting houses, lawns, clubs, halls that may have changed drastically over the years but are still filled with memories.

Rummaging through old cardboard boxes the other day, I came across a scrap of paper I hadn't seen in years. It was a note, hastily scribbled by Jackie Onassis to Cheray and me, that had been left on the bureau in our stateroom on the *Christina*, the Onassis yacht on which we took three cruises in the seventies. We had come aboard at sunrise in Casablanca and been greeted in typical Jackie style: "Promise that you will do what you feel like doing today," she wrote. She suggested that we sleep all day and have meals sent to our room, or go out in Casablanca with an escort from the yacht, or loll around on the deck. "All that matters is that you are happy." Ari kept "crazy hours" and he had decided long ago that his guests need not try to adjust to his schedule or anyone else's.

Rereading Jackie's note, I thought back to the last "state" funeral I'd gone to: the memorial service held in St. Ignatius Loyola Roman Catholic Church in New York City after Jackie's death in the spring of 1994. Listening to the music, the readings, the eulogies and prayers, I tried to keep the stalwart image of Jackie clear before me. Soon, I found a still point. Seated next to her husband, Luther Hodges, Jr., about a dozen rows ahead of me, was Cheray. Gazing at her, I thought about how important our friendship with Jackie had been to both of us.

She had been an indestructible thread. Although I'd met and liked her casually before, our friendship had really begun during Bobby Kennedy's presidential run in 1968, for which Cheray and I had energetically campaigned. The day before Bobby was killed at the Ambassador Hotel in Los Angeles, we'd been out in California, making appearances and speeches and hosting a discussion group after the debate with Eugene McCarthy, which Bobby had won handily. We'd returned to New York certain that there was no stopping him now.

Somehow Bobby's death, coming after the assassinations of his brother and Martin Luther King, Jr., was the hardest to take. As I think back over all the muddled agendas of our subsequent leaders, Bobby—because of the clarity of his caring—remains for me our greatest political loss.

"I've always felt an outsider . . ." Jackie said to me. "Haven't you?"

After the service for him in St. Patrick's Cathedral, Cheray and I were part of the cortege on the train from Pennsylvania Station to Union Station. The feeling after Jack Kennedy's death had been shock and disbelief. The feeling on that train was utter despair. We who had worked for Bobby had become extremely close. Losing him like this had made us speechless and sick. The tracks were lined with mourners, and the trip seemed to take forever.

It wasn't just our work for Bobby that had brought us close to Jackie. Her mother and my mother had both gone to the Spence School in New York and had been good friends. A few months before she died, I had lunch with Jackie in her New York apartment. We talked a lot about this book, which I was starting to write, and she was happy to share what she could about her own past. "Peter," she said, "you're about to embark on a very difficult journey. I could never do a book like this. It would be too painful."

When I asked if she had any memory of my parents, she replied, "Only indirectly. But I'll never forget the night my mother and father both came into my bedroom all dressed up to go out. I can still smell the scent my mother wore and feel the softness of her fur coat as she leaned over to kiss me good night. In such an excited voice she said, 'Darling, your father and I are going dancing tonight at the Central Park Casino to hear Eddy Duchin.' I don't know why the moment has stayed with me all these years. Perhaps because it was one of the few times I remember seeing my parents together. It was so romantic. So hopeful."

Moments later, she said, "You know, Peter, we both live and do very well in this world of Wasps and old money and society. It's all supposed to be so safe and continuous. But you and I are not really *of* it. Maybe because I'm Catholic and because my parents were divorced when I was young—a terribly radical thing at the time—I've always felt an outsider in that world. Haven't you?"

"Yes and no," I replied.

Smiling, Jackie added, "That's not a bad place to be."

What had really cemented our friendship was the time Cheray and I testified on her behalf in the suit she brought against Ron Galella, the photographer who had been making her life hell with his stalking. In the late sixties, after Jackie had moved into her apartment at 1040 Fifth Avenue, the three of us would often meet for a movie, followed by dinner at a neighborhood restaurant. We'd begin the evening with a drink at her place, and by the time we'd step out into her lobby, the locusts would be there in full force, swarming around the awning. As she walked unfalteringly into the flashbulbs and shouts of "Hey, Jackie, over here!" her only armor was her dark glasses and frozen smile.

Having been pushed and yelled at by Galella more than once when we found ourselves blocking his prey, Cheray and I had something to contribute to the trial. From that point on, we were old pals.

Our times together on the *Christina* were memorable not only for the staggering luxury and ease of life onboard—the attentions of the fifty-six crew members (two chefs, one French, one Greek; the availability of boats to take you skin diving or fishing and a helicopter to take you ruin looking); the immense library of movies; even the stools in the bar, upholstered with the skin of whales' penises—but for the pure, simple joy of being with Jackie and Ari.

Before his only son, Alexander, died in a plane crash a few years later, Ari was great, magnetic company. He loved to argue and tell stories all night long. He treated Jackie with a tenderness bordering on reverence, and she clearly adored him. After the death of his Alexander, Ari changed completely. He became moody, short with people, and impossible to live with. They separated.

Jackie wasn't the sort of person who expected anything in return, but I suppose I more than paid her back while skin diving one

Cheray and I (upper right) worked for Bobby Kennedy
in the 1964 campaign.

morning in the Aegean with her son, John. After taking a couple of lessons in the art of scuba, John—then a strapping teenager—and I had descended to perhaps a depth of forty feet when I noticed he was struggling with the mouthpiece of his oxygen hose, which had stopped supplying air. I swam over and motioned him to ascend. While the two of us slowly made our way to the surface—he, showing amazing cool—I shared my oxygen with him, trading inhalations on my mouthpiece.

Jackie was one of the first people I told about the most painful event in my life—the breakup of my marriage to Cheray in 1981. A great listener, she gently suggested that if any good came out of this divorce, it might be that I would learn how to deal with living alone. It was something about which she knew a great deal.

Cheray and I had had seventeen full years together. We had raised our three children, created homes, taken care of animals, and shared countless adventures. In 1977 we'd all gone on a safari through the game parks of East Africa. Nothing can make the concept of "nuclear family" more real than sleeping *en famille* for ten days in tents in the Serengeti, listening to elephants thundering by in the night and waking up to a lion eating a freshly killed gazelle for breakfast.

Cheray had been the perfect bandleader's wife. I couldn't have built my career without her. For years she had traveled everywhere with me, staying up to the bitter end, even though she hardly ever drank more than a glass of wine. She had always made an effort, even when she'd found herself at a table of strangers at a charity ball—the worst part of being a bandleader's wife.

But in my perpetual motion, I'd lost sight of her. After the travels with the band had long since become understandably tedious for her, after the children had begun to leave home for boarding

Life on the *Christina* with Jackie and Ari
was luxurious and joyous.

school and gain their own feet, after her father died, she momentarily lost direction. She felt isolated in the country, and I was pig-headed in refusing to move back to the city. I wasn't sensitive enough to stop and understand how to help her—as she had helped me. When she moved out, I had never felt so alone.

Brooke and me.

22

SECOND TIME

AROUND

It seems to me that my second wife, Brooke, and I were fated for each other. Certainly the connections in our lives have been too numerous and strange to be merely coincidental. For example, during our recent visit to Rosecliff, the Newport mansion built by my great-great-aunt Theresa Oelrichs, we were astonished to discover hanging in a corridor on the second floor a stunning portrait of Maisie Plant Hayward, Brooke's step-grandmother. A woman who'd inherited an immense fortune by marrying old Commodore Morton Plant shortly before he died, she was decked out in an evening dress and an opera-length string of pearls the size of pigeon's eggs. Brooke was thrilled. "That's the famous strand of pearls!" she exclaimed. "Maisie traded the Plant mansion on Fifty-second Street and Fifth Avenue to Cartier for those pearls. Utter madness!"

I first realized there was a weird thread connecting our lives when I read in Brooke's memoir *Haywire* that as a child she had named a pet squirrel Mr. Duchin. That was in 1945, when Brooke was eight. When I asked her why on earth she'd named the squirrel Mr. Duchin, she explained that, back in the early forties, her father had insisted that she and her brother and sister learn to play the piano. Hoping to provide inspiration, Leland and his wife, Maggie—the actress Margaret Sullavan—invited over their pal Eddy Duchin, who happened to be passing through Los Angeles on his way to his warship in Hawaii. The musical inspiration didn't stick, but the name did. A few years later, when Brooke's parents moved east to a farm in Connecticut, she acquired a baby squirrel that had fallen out of a maple tree and been rescued by her mother. Brooke remembers that Mr. Duchin would ride around the house on her bare shoulders and that her father would yell, "Get that goddamn rodent out of here!" "One day," she recalls, "the dreaded eleven-year-old son of the neighboring farmer came around, picked up the squirrel, and swung him around by the tail like a lasso. Mr. Duchin escaped and fled back to the maple tree, never to be seen again."

Our lives touched again after my father's death, when Chiquita sold the house in Manhasset to Leland and his then-wife Slim, who was a friend of Chiq's. Brooke and I had both loved that house, and in the early eighties we paid it a sad farewell visit just before it was torn down to make way for a housing development.

The first time we actually met was in 1957, when I'd returned to Yale from my junior year in Paris. Brooke had left Vassar to marry a classmate and friend of mine, Michael Thomas, the novelist and columnist. They lived in an off-campus apartment, where I went occasionally for dinner because her cooking was a whole lot better than mine. I remember Brooke as a very pretty, smart, funny girl. She remembers me as "extremely conspicuous": "With your green loden cape and long hair flying in the wind, you cut quite a swath, intentionally or not. First, the fact that you'd spent your junior year on a barge in Paris was very romantic. Second, you were an orphan. You were exactly the sort of person my mother and father would have wanted me to marry—wild but polite."

The summer after Yale, I occasionally glimpsed Brooke—then very pregnant—dancing with Michael at the odd party in Southampton.

In February 1961, when I was living above Carnegie Hall and preparing to record my first album, I got a call from Danny Selznick, the son of David O. and my father's old flame Irene.

"Peter," said Danny, "I've got the perfect girl for you: Brooke Hayward."

"But I know Brooke Hayward," I replied. "She's married."

"Not anymore," said Danny.

Several nights later, Danny and Brooke slogged through a New York blizzard, bearing Chinese food to my studio. Brooke recalls that I barely greeted them as I sat at the piano, practicing arrangements and wearing a "dreamy expression." She and Danny stood there and ate all the Chinese food. After an hour, they left. As Brooke was going out the door, I said, "Why don't you give me a call sometime?" Needless to say, she didn't.

I had more or less forgotten about her until the summer of 1965, when Cheray and I were in L.A. and we ran into each other at Jane Fonda's Fourth of July party. Now Brooke was married to Dennis Hopper, the actor, and a few nights later we were invited to their house for a party. It was a collection of very hip guests—among them, Terry Southern, Tony Richardson, Rudi Gernreich,

Ed Ruscha, Peter Fonda, and Jack Nicholson. I arrived wearing a blazer and tie—very disappointing to Brooke. "Your wild, poetic look had vanished," she says. "You'd gone back to the conservative side of your upbringing. I remember Cheray in one of those mid-sixties sleeveless dresses with three strands of pearls—very Jackie. The two of you were the only squares in the room."

She's right. But as far as Cheray and I were concerned, square was just fine.

Five years later, Brooke and I ran into each other again at her father's Westchester estate. Having recently divorced Dennis, she was back in Leland's good graces. That summer she was dating the screenwriter and actor Buck Henry, and one afternoon Cheray and I invited them over to our rented house in Bedford.

Brooke remembers thinking: "It was all so suburban. Lots of children and lots of dogs. Very tennis oriented and lots of *noise*."

Right again. And I wallowed in it.

Reading *Haywire* cast Brooke in a new light for me. She had written a remarkable book, honest and graceful, about the collapse of her brilliant family. With devastating understatement, she'd painted her stepmother Pamela as the formidable adversary I had come to see for myself. I felt a great kinship with Brooke—she was like a long-lost sister. And she was a survivor. One night, I spotted her having dinner at "21" and sent the waiter over with a fan note. She was, she recalls, "extremely touched."

Four years passed. I'd been hired to play for the opening of the Meyerhoff Collection, a new museum of contemporary art in the rolling hills outside Baltimore. The entire New York art world showed up, including Brooke. She looked great—lots of wonderful long hair. At some point, she came over and sat on the piano bench next to me. I usually hate it when women do this, but that night I didn't mind.

It was the first time Brooke actually observed me as a band-leader. "I felt I was finally seeing you as you really were," she says. "You were good at it, and you looked terribly happy doing it."

A year later, my marriage broke up. Toddie Findlay had lent me temporary digs on the third floor of her house in the East Sixties, and I was having a bad time of it. For a month, I did little but lie in bed and stare at the yellow walls, trying to figure out what had gone wrong. Then I erupted, dating every girl that came along—all sizes, types, and ages. Reading in the columns about whom I'd been with and where started to bug the hell out of me. One day I went through my address book, looking for the name of a woman who was independent, artistic, and attractive—in that order. I stopped at the *H*'s.

The first thing Brooke did when I called to invite her to dinner was ask why my marriage had ended. Was there another woman? I replied—truthfully—that in seventeen years of marriage I'd never once been unfaithful.

"You've got to be kidding," she said.

"I'm not."

"Then what happened?"

"Cheray claims she has to find herself."

"Oh God! Not *that* shit!"

That made me laugh. I repeated my invitation.

"No thanks," she answered, explaining that her policy was never to have dinner with a man until he was divorced.

I suggested lunch. She said that would be fine. What about today?

"All right."

At the restaurant, Brooke told me she was living in a loft on lower Fifth Avenue. It sounded interesting, and she offered to show it to me. As she recalls, "The first thing you said when you walked in was 'Very nice, but where's the piano?' I thought that was kinda cute."

I noticed shelves with lots of musical tapes.

She said, "I'm afraid I only have classical music, which will probably bore you."

I drew myself up. "My dear," I said, "in case you've forgotten, I *majored* in music. I think I know a bit more about classical music than *you* do."

She threw me a look.

We had lunch the next day and again went back to her loft. Again, our only exchange was verbal—not even a kiss. As I was leaving, I blurted out another invitation—this one to Swifty Lazar's Academy Awards party in Los Angeles.

"Are you *mad*?" she said. "It'll get in the papers and ruin what's left of your domestic situation."

I decided to bag Swifty's.

At the end of the week, I took my three kids off skiing to Vail. We had hardly settled into our condominium when the doorbell rang. There was my old friend and Brooke's ex, Michael Thomas.

"Don't shoot," he said. "I'm only the messenger. I just got here with my kids, too. Brooke's sent you this care package."

It was a double-cassette tape of Verdi's Requiem, conducted by Herbert von Karajan. Attached was a note: "I thought you might need a little uplift."

Three times a day, for the next ten days, I phoned Brooke in New York. Because I felt guilty calling when the kids were around, I got up at seven. While the garbage truck was making its rounds, I pushed through the snow to a pay phone on the corner. At noon, while the kids were having lunch, I called from the restaurant on top of the mountain. Just before bed, it was back to the goddamn phone booth. Each call took not less than an hour. That was our courtship.

You can learn a lot about another person from thirty hours of heart-to-heart phone conversation. Thanks to the 2,000 miles between us, we were able to reveal ourselves with an intimacy and sense of safety we could never have had if we'd been in the same room, face to face.

On my last night in Vail, I said simply, "See you soon."

The next evening I took a cab straight from the airport to Brooke's loft. When she opened the door, I was loaded down with ski equipment and duffel bags. All I said was "Here I am."

And so I moved in. One day, after I'd been there a couple of weeks, I casually remarked, "You know what? I really miss a piano."

"There's only room for an upright," said Brooke.

The next day she went out and sold her "one valuable possession"—an early Warhol painting of a Campbell's soup can. With the proceeds, she bought me a piano.

I would have been happy with a much cheaper model, but Brooke hates anything but the best. As she explained: "If we have to have a piano, it better be a Steinway."

=

In the fall of 1985, I phoned to tell Ave of my impending marriage. Luckily, the call was answered by one of Ave's nurses, who got him on the phone alone.

"Great, Pete!" he said. "Who's the lucky girl?"

"Brooke Hayward," I said, trusting that he wouldn't have even heard of *Haywire*, in which Brooke had accused Pamela of stealing a valuable string of pearls left to her by her mother.

I was right. "That's wonderful!" said Ave. "When can I meet her?"

We were talking about getting together when Ave interrupted

me: "Wait a minute. Pam's just walked in. Let me put her on the phone."

There was no escape.

"Peter, what good news!" said that beautifully practiced voice. "Who's the lucky girl?"

"Um . . . Brooke Hayward."

Pam didn't skip a beat: "That's terrific! Where *is* Brooke? I want to call and congratulate her."

Here's how Brooke remembers getting the call:

"The last time Pamela and I had talked was in May of 1976, when I was in Los Angeles, holed up at the Chateau Marmont and editing the final version of *Haywire*. Somehow she'd found me. We had barely spoken since my father's funeral service, for which she had not invited me or my brother, Bill, to speak—something I'd found unforgivable. The moment I heard her voice, my heart began to pound.

" 'Hellooo, Brooooke?'

" 'Yesss . . .'

" 'Brooke, it's Pamela.'

"If she could play it, so could I: 'Why, Pamela, how *are* you?'

" 'Fine. . . . Oh by the way, I understand you've written this book . . .'

" 'Yes.'

" 'What's it called?'

" '*Haywire.*'

"Silence. Then: 'Why?'

" 'Well, Pamela, it's a triple entendre: Everyone in my family is crazy. My father's cable address was "Haywire." And Haywire was the name of his house.'

"There was a long silence. Then small talk. Then we hung up. A few days later, a friend called from New York and said, 'You're not going to believe this, but Haywire is no longer Haywire. Pamela's had the name taken off the matchbooks, the stationery, everything. It's now called Birch Grove.'

"Now I was hearing that voice again:

" 'Brooooke. I want to tell you how *thrilled* I am with the news. We just *love* Peter so. The Governor is *so* excited. I'm going to put him on the phone.'

"No, I thought: I don't know him. But it was too late. Averell got on the line and in his deaf way yelled, 'You're marrying the most wonderful man!' Then Pam got back on and said, 'We're going to give you a wedding present. Five hundred shares of Union Pacific stock!'

"I was dumbfounded: It was as though nothing had ever happened."

=

In the spring of 1986, Pam invited Brooke and me to her estate in Middleburg for what would be the last time I saw Ave alive. He was failing from what turned out to be liver cancer, and Pam, thoughtfully, had called and said, "I think you should see him fairly soon."

Brooke and I flew to Washington and took a cab to the Harriman house on N Street. Pam gave us a tour of the premises. Conspicuous in the living room were two familiar works of art. One was van Gogh's magnificent *White Roses*, which had been purchased at Ma's suggestion back in 1929 and given as a wedding present to her and Ave by Ave's mother. The other was the Degas ballerina.

The façades Brooke and Pamela maintained all the way out to Middleburg never cracked. Listening to Pam's inquiries about Brooke's children and her life in New York, one would never have guessed at the depths of ill feeling they concealed. What a phony, I thought. Or, as Brooke later remarked, "Pam's the consummate pro."

Willow Oaks was splendid. Pam took Brooke by the arm as she led us around the beautifully kept lawns and showed off the stables and cottages. As usual, she talked about her possessions—her house in Barbados, her champion show horses (one of them named Governor), and the nineteenth-century paintings of the Hudson River she'd recently acquired. Along the way, she dropped the names of important guests who'd been down to see Ave.

I was stunned by the sight of him. He was such a shrunken image of the tall, commanding old Ave. Even though he had state-of-the-art hearing aids stuck in his ears, we could make only the most rudimentary conversation, and that by shouting. He was wearing a lime green silk jacket draped over his shoulders, and most of the time he sat staring sightlessly out the window.

Lunch was just the four of us sitting at a very formal table laid with fine linen, old silver, and at least three wineglasses each. Pamela kept saying, "Ave, eat your lunch. Ave, finish up your bran wafer. It's good for you." A good English nanny coaxing her charge.

After lunch, Ave and I said our good-byes in the driveway, kissing each other as we had always done.

"Pete, it's been great seeing you."

"Good-bye, Ave."

Pamela, before getting into the Cadillac, had the last kiss. She was now taller than Ave, and she planted it right on top of his ninety-four-year-old head. I watched as he moved very slowly off to the swimming pool, leaning on his butler.

On the way back to Washington, I asked Pam if Ave had ever mentioned the subject of death.

"No," she said. "We never talk about it."

"I guess he thinks he'll never die."

"I think you're right," said Pam.

A month or so later, Brooke and I were in Salzburg for the music festival when Pam called:

"Peter, I don't want to spoil your vacation, but Averell has taken a turn for the worse. He hasn't very long."

"Should I come back now?"

"No. I'll be in touch. But I'd like you to be a pallbearer."

I said I'd be honored.

Pam's secretary called several days later. "The Governor's gone," she said. "The funeral will be in St. Thomas's Episcopal Church in New York."

We arrived the next afternoon—it was July 28, my birthday—and that evening Pam held a wake at the apartment of her friend Kitty Carlisle Hart, my colleague on the New York State Council on the Arts. It was a room I'd been in many times for dinners and Arts Council meetings, and it felt odd to be here for this. Although most of Ave's grandchildren were present, there was little sense of family. The affair was catered by New York's top caterer, and I couldn't help thinking that in the old days the food would have been *Ave's* food, cooked by *his* staff.

The next day at noon, St. Thomas's was packed with 900 family members, state and national politicians, diplomatic colleagues, journalists, and society figures. I was a pallbearer, along with Ave's five grandsons and Pam's son, Winston. At the end, everyone stood and sang "The Battle Hymn of the Republic"—an eerie echo of the funeral nearly twenty years earlier in St. Patrick's Cathedral across the street, when Andy Williams had sung the same anthem in honor of Bobby Kennedy.

Then I piled into a limo for the procession across the George Washington Bridge, up the Palisades Parkway, through Harriman State Park, and into Arden. At various points we passed squadrons of New York State troopers, standing in formation along the road, saluting the Governor's hearse.

===

There were about sixty of us standing around the open gravesite next to Ma's stone on the knoll opposite the little chapel of St. John. Fanning ourselves in the boiling heat, we watched as the casket was lowered halfway into the grave, while the Episcopal bishop of New York, Paul Moore, Jr., led the prayers and gave the blessing.

How fitting, I thought, that Ave should end up next to the woman who had been through so much with him during his long career. And how generous of Pam, who looked every inch the Dignified Widow, to put him there.

Afterward, we all went up to the big house for a lunch—same fancy caterer as the night before. Now that the place had been given to Columbia University as a conference center, the great reception hall bore no trace of the family living room in which I had once asked Marie Harriman if I could call her Ma. But standing with Ave's daughters, Mary and Kathleen, and looking out over the immense, still unspoiled vista of woods and hills, I felt again that enchanted safety which the forests of Arden had always given me.

My reverie was shattered when Mary remarked, "You know, Ave's not going to be buried next to Marie."

"What do you mean?"

"I mean it was all a show. Ave's going to be buried down by the lake. Pam says it's what he wanted."

"But that's nonsense! I'm sure Ave would have wanted to be buried in the family plot, near his mother and next to Marie. The lake is four miles away."

"Well, according to Pam, a couple of years ago they were walking by the lake one evening when Averell said how lovely it would be to be buried there, just the two of them side by side."

"That sounds like Pam, not Ave. I can't imagine him coming out with anything so sentimental. I certainly can't imagine him talking about death."

"I can't either," said his daughter.

It was shocking that Ave would not be buried in the family plot. After we had witnessed the blessing, Ave's casket was returned to New York, where his body lay for two months on ice at the Frank Campbell Funeral Home while the lakeside site was readied to receive him. When reports of the deception hit the papers, more than one distinguished mourner was furious at having come all the way up to Arden for what turned out to be a sham burial.

After this, I wasn't surprised to hear that Ave had left virtually his entire fortune, including all the houses and art, to his widow. People like Pam don't settle for half. Curiously, she never thought to send me even the smallest memento of Ave's—no set of cuff links, tie clasp, anything. She'd finally gotten it all for herself—even his bones.

Brooke was right: a consummate pro.

Brooke and me and the birds, Pedro and Igor,
in the garden in Connecticut.

23

PIANO ROLLS

Eight years ago, Brooke and I bought a small property in Litchfield County, in northwestern Connecticut. It used to be a very rural area, but now is thought of as sort of chic. Our life there is just the opposite. We rarely go out.

I find it painful to wrench myself away from the country and go back to the city. The minute I drive up the dirt road to our house my cares evaporate—exactly the way they do when I'm alone fishing. Fishing and gardening: two great old passions of mine that go back to my childhood at Arden. Brooke has built a huge birdcage on the deck for our two parrots. Pedro, a macaw, and Igor, a caique, are our only pets now. I don't like the idea of having a dog in the city, although we miss having more animals around.

When Brooke and I first saw the property, we took along a friend who thought the house was so undistinguished that he advised gutting it and making it into one big room. Brooke was all for that idea, but I balked. I like walls and definition. I won that one, but it was only the beginning. The grounds were a disaster. The driveway had to be moved. Ten acres of trees had to be thinned out. The poison ivy growing up to the front door had to be killed. The pond was a mud hole that had to be dredged.

Gradually, what started out as a cleanup became a serious horticultural adventure as we fecklessly created one garden after another. We planted the banks of the pond with irises, rushes, arrowheads, and cattails. At last count, we have planted more than two hundred trees, from apples, evergreens, and birches to weird things like dawn redwoods and aralias—not to mention four hundred ornamental shrubs. Brooke grandly calls it her "arboretum." She points and I plant. For a pianist I'm surprisingly indifferent to the state of my hands, which usually look like a Russian peasant's, my fingers covered with dirt and cuts. Before I perform at night, I have to scrub away the day's work from under my nails.

So much of my life is spent either on the road or in hypersocial situations that when I get to the country I rarely go out except to the market. In the city I run my midtown office like a visiting pasha. I'm on the boards of various cultural institutions, including the Chamber Music Society of Lincoln Center and American Ballet Theatre. For the past decade I've basked in the reflected glory of Kitty Carlisle Hart as vice-chairman of the New York State Council on the Arts. Although I've been an activist for all sorts of political causes—I still think of myself as a liberal—I've come to believe that the most critical thing to fight for is support for the arts. So I'm involved up to my eyeballs.

I tried to instill in my kids a similar appreciation for the arts and a sense of civic involvement. I also encouraged them to be as independent as possible. One of the biggest differences between me and them is that they're not following in anyone's footsteps, which is just fine with me. As of this writing, Colin, the youngest, was deep-sea diving in Indonesia, gathering coral for cancer research. Jason, the oldest, is an actor who teaches theater to underprivileged kids. Courtnay is a graphic designer in Seattle, and just bought a little spread of her own in Montana next to a great trout stream.

≡

Recently I received in the mail a batch of old news clips about my parents that I'd ordered from the Hearst organization. Leafing through them one morning, I was staggered to find a small, barely legible picture accompanying a New York *Daily News* article about my birth in July 1937. It showed my mother, still alive at the Harbor Sanitarium, holding me in her arms: the first time I had ever seen a picture of the two of us together.

Betty Walsh, my secretary, called the *News* archives and ordered a print. A few days later, a stiff brown envelope arrived. Inside wasn't the photograph we'd asked for but another one dated from the same time. This picture was even more staggering. In it were not only my mother and me but my father, kneeling at our bedside and gazing raptly at us. Standing in the background were my godmother Ginny Chambers and my grandmother "Mammy" Oelrichs. There was nothing to read from that picture but hope.

A few nights later, I drove out to Long Island for one of my favorite annual gigs, an outdoor concert in the Old Westbury Gardens. It's an event I've been doing for more than twenty years in a setting I've known for even longer—the old Phipps estate, on whose grounds I'd often played as a child. Like so many of the great relics of more privileged times, the gardens and house are now a tourist attraction, open to anybody who can afford the modest price of admission.

It was a beautiful July evening—the perfect temperature—and I knew exactly how it would go. The lawn would be packed with picnickers of all ages, from infants who had never heard of Peter Duchin to octogenarians who would totter up to the bandstand and tell me about the time they'd danced to my father's music. We'd begin with a little Dixieland, then go into a bit of Fats Waller, then our Astaire medley, then a couple of Beach Boys hits . . . and four generations would be on their feet, dancing every which way as the lights came on in the huge ivy-covered mansion at the top of the lawn.

Then, as a climax, would come the fireworks, exploding in the sky above us. We'd swing into "Stars and Stripes Forever" and "America, the Beautiful," and everybody would be crowded around the bandstand, clapping and singing along.

The village of Glen Cove is just down the road from Old Westbury, and before the concert I decided to stop off at a store to look for a secondhand piano for a friend. It's a place called The Piano Exchange.

I'd met the proprietor before, an intense, wiry fellow named Rick Smith. He was wearing jeans and a plaid shirt, and he had the look of a serious antiquarian—not your typical piano salesman—as he took me around the showroom, where I tried out a couple of unremarkable Steinways and Mason & Hamlins. Then he said, "Let me show you some real pianos."

It was astonishing: Beyond the showroom was a warehouse the size of an airplane hangar—a vast, Dickensian curiosity shop of used pianos in every shape, size, color, and style from a Rococo instrument that Haydn could have played to a sleek Art Deco num-

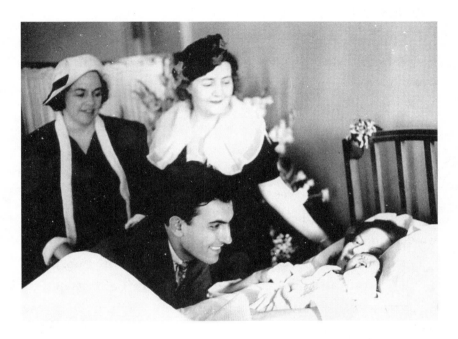

The only picture ever taken of my mother and me together.

ber that looked like something you could drive away in. A musty storeroom in back was filled with piano rolls: bin after bin of them, stacked floor to ceiling.

"I think I've just about got 'em all," Rick said.

He probably did. Scanning the labels, I saw every name from Rachmaninoff and Busoni to Jelly Roll Morton and George Gershwin himself.

"Let me play you something," he said, pulling down one of the rolls. "Let's see if you can guess who it is."

I followed him through a catacomb of pianos. There in a dark, dust-filled corner was a Victorian, walnut-cased instrument—"the best reconditioned player piano in the world," said Rick. He inserted the roll into the holder, pulled down the first sheet like a window shade, and flipped the switch.

I recognized the melody as "Painting the Clouds with Sunshine," an old Harry Warren standard from *Gold Diggers of Broadway*. It was a rather square, upbeat tune, played in a jaunty, no-nonsense style. I was wondering why on earth he'd put this on when I felt myself breaking out in goose bumps.

It was my father. I watched the black and white keys bouncing up and down. I followed the melody as it switched registers, the bass line as it tripped along. Obviously Dad had loved playing with crossed hands.

A strange calm came over me. I could see him sitting at the keyboard in his white tie and tails, smiling his broad smile. The rest of the guys were out on their cigarette break and Dad was taking requests. The ladies had rushed to the piano, where they gathered like butterflies to call out tunes. I could even see my mother standing behind him, lightly touching his shoulder. Pretty soon, the dance floor would fill up.

AFTERWORD

One of the first things people ask me about *Ghost of a Chance* is whether or not in writing it I experienced a catharsis. The answer is yes. It changed me. And I didn't expect that. According to close friends, family, and associates, I behave differently now. They say I am mellower and more philosophical than before. My band tells me that I'm easier to work with—which makes me wonder how horrible I must have been pre-book.

The most curious, and unanticipated, result of writing the book—at least for me—was that I discovered that I could actually spend a series of days and nights totally alone without a sense of foreboding. In fact, I now look forward to being by myself in my place in Connecticut—playing the piano, gardening, reading, or just listening to music. Of course I had spent a certain amount of time alone in the past, wandering around the woods at Harriman when I was a child, or practicing the piano in somber basement rooms when I was a teenager. Later, when I was on the road with the band or in some wilderness fishing camp, I had been alone in a personal sense. But I had never sought out solitude; in fact, I consciously avoided being alone if possible.

I assume that these changes have come about because I finally fitted together the many pieces of the puzzle that constituted my past. For the first fifty-five years of my life, I had totally repressed all painful events from my childhood. Then, as I was slugging through the research for this book, Brooke, who had been through it all before when she wrote *Haywire*, suggested that it might be a good idea to find a shrink who would be able to help me sort out any emotional problems that might arise from all this digging into the past. Even though at the end of my first session ever with a psychiatrist, the doctor, a highly regarded Freudian, announced that I was not remotely in need of therapy, I wanted to continue, and I asked him if he would mind if I brought Charles Michener, my co-author, to a few sessions. Charles could take notes and maybe also frame the necessary questions better than I could. "Highly unusual, but an interesting idea," the psychiatrist said. And thus an unusual three-way conversation began.

To satisfy my wife, I even went to a psychiatric hypnotist in order to jog what Brooke kept calling my "repressed memory." This was a fascinating experience, but I didn't follow up on the hypnotist's instructions to practice self-hypnosis. The TV screen he wanted me to see in my mind never appeared. In the end, it was the occasional visits to the shrink, coupled with incessant prodding from Charles and Brooke, that forced me to face the losses that studded my past. Now I feel that a great weight has been lifted.

=

The responses I've gotten from readers of the book have been astonishing and gratifying. Apart from all the people who've come up to the bandstand to talk to me about it, hundreds of strangers have written letters saying that they were moved to write because of a particular memory of my parents, or of Ma and Ave, from many years ago. A lot of the men who wrote had run into my dad during the war, when he was serving in the Navy in the Pacific. They remember him playing the piano in some bar on some island. Or perhaps they had gone on shore leave with him and had a few beers. Many have said how upset they were to read that Dad never talked to me about his experiences, and they wanted to make up for it by telling me what they remembered of him in combat, or as an officer onboard ship.

Almost all the letter writers have expressed nostalgia for something valuable and unique that has disappeared from American life—something to do with glamour, with good manners, and a sense of fun. Many of the correspondents seem to mourn the loss of Society—the kind with the capital *S*—which is a word that you don't hear much anymore. I do hear it from time to time, because I'm often told that I'm what's known as a "Society bandleader." Just the other day a young journalist asked me what that meant. I shook my head and replied, "Frankly, I don't have the slightest idea anymore."

ACKNOWLEDGMENTS

My thanks to my co-author and doppelganger Charles Michener go without saying. Barbara Brenner was of invaluable assistance early in this project. Sharon DeLano, my editor, has been superb throughout.

My stepmother, Chiquita, and her husband, Robert Everitt, were invaluable sources, as were Rita (Chissie) Chisholm; my oldest friend, Maitland Edey; Jacqueline Onassis, who gave me the courage to start the whole thing; my dear Aunt Lil; my "sister" Nancy Lutz; and of course my ex-wife, Cheray Hodges.

The following people generously added their memories to mine: Helen Edey, Toddie Findlay, Hector Diaz, Herbert B. Swope, Jr., John Richardson, Robert Silvers, Eddie Morgan, George Plimpton, Thomas Guinzburg, Francine du Plessix Gray, Bobby Brenner, Harvey Ginsberg, Dorothy Hirshon, Roscoe Lee Browne, Irene Selznick, Danny Selznick, Dr. William Cahan, Ann Sardi Gina, Henry Kissinger, Marian Goodman, Axie Whitney, Charles Baskerville, Slim Hyatt, Jean Warnecke, Maria Janis, and Rocky Cooper.

Thanks to the Fisks and the Mortimers for confirming that my old gate key still works at Arden; Dr. Peter Neubauer, for helping me figure out a few things about myself; Paul Miller, of the Preservation Society of Newport County, for his guided tour of Rosecliff and the information about my mother's family; Dorothy and Dr. Yilmaz Durudogan, for kindly showing me through the house on Kay Street; my guitarist and vocalist Roberta Fabiano, my trumpet player Tone Kwas, and the other members of my band for their help and support; John Guare for suggesting the title; my agent, Al Lowman, for putting the project together; Rick Smith, of the Piano Exchange in Glen Cove, Long Island, for giving me that extraordinary day; Ann Schneider, photo researcher *extraordinaire*; and my assistant, Betty Walsh, for her tireless help and good humor.

Finally I'd like to thank my wife, Brooke, whose relentless good counsel and sound advice throughout the painful process earned her the nickname "the Goad."

INDEX

Adenauer, Konrad, 66–67

Agnelli, Gianni, 320, 325

Agnew, Spiro, 275

Alsop, Joseph, 213

Ambassador Hotel, 265, 332

American Ballet Theatre, 356

American Place Theater, 235

American Sportsman, The, 301

Amram, David, 172

Arborgast, Fred, 67–68

Arcadia, 112–14, 203

Arden House, 13, 21, 53–55, 80,
    109, 255, 274, 312, 351–53

Armstrong, Lil Hardin, 130

Armstrong, Louis, 48, 128, 130,
    135

Aron, Raymond, 171

Astaire, Adele (Lady Cavendish),
    102

Astaire, Fred, 102, 139, 284, 289,
    290, 358

Astor, Vincent, 102, 245, 246

Ayres, Lew, 102

Bacall, Lauren, 271, 290

Bach, Johann Sebastian, 135, 138,
    188, 197

Backer, Evie, 90, 323

Backer, George, 90, 323

Baker, Chet, 172

Baldwin, Billy, 326

Ball, George, 96

Balsa, César, 4, 5, 6, 212, 238, 245

Bardot, Brigitte, 139, 270

Barnett, Larry, 238

Barrymore, Diana, 25

Barrymore, John, 25

Barthelmess, Richard, 102

Baruch, Bernard, 44

Barzun, Jacques, 171

Basie, Count, 133, 235, 248, 255,
    281

Baskerville, Charles, 26–28

Beatles, 248

Beaton, Cecil, 22, 30–33, 155

Beauvoir, Simone de, 171, 319

Bechet, Sidney, 130, 172, 277

Beethoven, Ludwig van, 188, 190

Behrman, S. N. (Sam), 249–50

Beiderbecke, Bix, 128, 130, 135

Belafonte, Harry, 196

Benchley, Robert, 45

Bennett, Constance, 102

Benny, Jack, 102, 273, 274

Bergen, Edgar, 102

Berlin, Irving, 290

Berlin, Isaiah, 290

Bernstein, Leonard, 217, 226, 276, 329

Berry, Chuck, 153

Black and White Ball, 290–92

Blacks, The (Genet), 219

Blanch, Lesley, 322

Blass, Bill, 280

Bloch, Ray, 204

Blum, Mr. and Mrs., 293–94

Boesky, Ivan, 287

Bogart, Humphrey, 102

Bond, Lionel, 55, 57, 60, 109

Boulanger, Nadia, 185

Bowles, Chester, 176

Bradley, Ned, 138

Brandt, Ira, 223–24

Brant, Bayard, 44

Brenner, Bobby:
    Peter Duchin's career aided by, 196, 221, 222–23, 225, 234, 235, 238, 239, 250, 251, 265
    recording deals made by, 196, 225

Brisson, Frederick, 102

Brisson, Rosalind Russell, 102

Brooks, Joe, 307

Brown Brothers Harriman, 88–89

Browne, Roscoe Lee, 219–21

Bundy, McGeorge, 148

Burton, Sybil, 260

Byas, Don, 172

Byears, Billy, 172

Byrds, 270

Cahan, William, 11

Capone, Al, 64

Capote, Truman, 290–92, 322

Capra, Frank, 102

Carmichael, Hoagy, 103

Carnegie Hall, renovation of, 276

Carnegie Hall Studios, 216, 217

Cassini, Oleg, 280

Cast of Thousands (Loos), 9–10

Castro, Fidel, 205, 207

Cavallaro, Carmen, 225

Cavendish, Adele Astaire, Lady, 102

Central Park Casino, 43–44, 45, 47, 243–44, 252, 260, 334

Cerf, Bennett, 96, 273

Cerf, Phyllis, 96–97, 273

Chamber Music Society of Lincoln Center, 356

Chambers, Brose, 39, 99, 108, 165, 166, 171, 189

Chambers, Ginny, 108, 194
    cultural interests of, 166, 167, 188–89
    family background of, 166–67
    as godmother, 6, 357
    as hostess, 166, 167–69, 171, 174, 176, 188, 192, 268
    Paris home of, 150, 151, 160, 165–66, 167, 180, 233

Peter Duchin's career and, 6, 152, 248–49

Chaplin, Charles, 102

Charles, Ray, 248

Chase, Thurston, 117–18, 119, 133

Chisholm, Rita C. (Chissie), 11–19, 22, 36, 55, 63, 310

Chopin, Frédéric, 48, 136, 204, 234

Christina, 331–32, 335

Churchill, Pamela Digby, *see* Harriman, Pamela Digby Churchill Hayward

Churchill, Randolph, 69, 70, 319, 326

Churchill, Winston, 69, 199, 200, 319, 322

Clarke, Kenny, 172

Clement, Illa, 293

Clement, Jim, 293

Clinton, Bill, 302, 320

Club Saint-Germain, 187

Cohn, Harry, 154

Coleman, Emil, 219

Collins, Larry, 271

Colony Restaurant, 10

Columbia Pictures, 153, 154

Columbia University, 352

Comden, Betty, 226

Considine, Bob, 116

contract bridge, 226, 229

Cooper, Gary, 67–68, 102, 110, 176, 233

Cooper, Maria, 233

Cooper, Rocky, 110, 233, 281

Copland, Aaron, 185

Costa, Don, 272

Crawford, Alan, 55, 64, 101, 109

Crawford, Joan, 102

Crazy Horse Saloon, 182

croquet, 44, 86–88, 266–68, 315

Crosby, Bing, 102, 103

Cukor, George, 102

Curtis, Edward S., 21, 54

Dalí, Gala, 246

Dalí, Salvador, 245–46

Daly, John, 116

Daumier, Honoré, 317

Davis, Meyer, 224, 292

Davis, Miles, 34, 130, 170, 172, 284

Davison, Gates, 266, 268, 270

Decca Records, 225

de Cuevas, Elizabeth, 181, 183

Degas, Edgar, 317, 349

de Havilland, Olivia, 102

de l'Isle family, 181

Denckla, Paula, 131–32

Derain, André, 155, 325

Digby, Jane, 322

Dillon, Douglas, 39

DiMaggio, Dominic, 105

DiMaggio, Joe, 104–5, 110, 115, 116, 138

discotheques, 260

Dodds, Baby, 130

Dodds, Jimmy, 130

Domino, Fats, 153

Doubleday, Nelson, 39–40

Duchin, Brooke Hayward Thomas
Hopper (Peter Duchin's second
wife), 351
book on family written by, 344,
347, 348
childhood of, 342, 344
early marriages of, 342–43, 344
family background of, 140,
341–42
homes of, 342, 345–46, 347, 348,
355–56
Pamela Harriman and, 344,
347–50, 353
Peter Duchin's relationship with,
342–47
physical appearance of, 344

Duchin, Cheray Zauderer (Peter
Duchin's first wife), *see* Hodges,
Cheray Zauderer Duchin

Duchin, Chiquita (Peter Duchin's
stepmother), *see* Everitt, Chiquita Wynn Duchin Heap

Duchin, Colin (Peter Duchin's son),
133, 295, 357

Duchin, Courtnay (Peter Duchin's
daughter), 295, 313, 357

Duchin, Edwin Frank (Eddy) (Peter
Duchin's father), 99–124
as bandleader, 4, 47–48, 161,
222, 235, 334

Bechstein piano given to, 47, 216

biographical film on, 5–6,
153–54, 225

career of, 35, 43, 45–49, 115,
160, 161, 195, 235, 249–50,
260, 281

celebrity of, 35, 103–4, 110, 144

childhood of, 41–43

death of, 97, 105, 119–24, 132,
159–60, 296

family background of, 29, 40–41,
49, 50, 122, 124, 159, 217,
334–35

fatherhood of, 13, 15, 17–19,
35–36, 50–51, 82, 100, 103–5,
108–9, 112, 114–17, 119–20,
132–33, 159, 357

in films, 47, 235, 249–50

first marriage of, 10–11, 29–30,
33, 34, 49, 112

Hayward family and, 342

Hollywood party cohosted by, 5,
101–3

Irene Selznick and, 101–2

Marie Harriman's relationship
with, 19, 76–78, 108, 311

military service of, 19, 35–36,
99–100, 101, 103, 109, 114,
121, 342

musical arrangements by, 248

Peter Duchin's career and, 4, 5,
48, 151, 161, 196, 212, 222,
225, 235, 238, 243–44

physical appearance of, 30, 33,
35, 40, 45, 249, 360

piano style of, 35, 45, 48–49,
133, 151, 160, 224, 225, 233,
292, 360

radio programs of, 35, 47

recordings made by, 47–48, 151,
225

second marriage of, 50, 107–8,
109, 110, 115

signature song of, 48, 204

Duchin, Frank (Peter Duchin's
grandfather), 41, 49

Duchin, Jason (Peter Duchin's son),
295, 313, 357

Duchin, Lillian (Peter Duchin's
aunt), 40, 41–43, 44, 49–50,
122, 124, 217

Duchin, Marjorie Oelrichs (Peter
Duchin's mother):
in childbirth, 9, 10–11
childhood of, 26, 334
death of, 11, 22, 30, 33, 34,
143
family background of, 9–10,
22–23, 25, 26, 228
film portrayal of, 153–55
jobs of, 26, 155
magazine article by, 28–29
marriage of, 11, 29–30, 49
motherhood of, 30–31, 357
physical appearance of, 22, 28,
30, 31, 155

Sun Valley lodge decorated by, 26,
91–93

Duchin, Peter:
in acting class, 235–36
agents for, 196, 221, 238
in Army jazz group, 208–11
arts organizations promoted by,
235, 351, 356–57
as bandleader, 4, 7, 223, 224,
234–35, 238, 239–40, 241–45,
337, 344–45, 357–58; *see also*
Peter Duchin Orchestra
birth of, 6, 9–11, 143, 357
at boarding schools, 110, 117–19,
120, 125–33, 134–39, 159–60
career choices of, 149–50, 161,
188, 195–96, 221–24
childhood of, 3, 4, 11–22, 31–33,
35–36, 38–39, 40, 50–51,
53–64, 71–73, 79–86, 89–93,
100–101, 103–45, 159–63,
300, 315, 352, 355, 357
on classical music, 135, 136, 149,
185–86, 188, 189–90, 234,
346
early musical interest shown by,
17
education of, 71, 117–18,
134–35, 136–38, 152, 167,
184, 185, 197, 221
family background of, 22–26, 29,
40–41, 49–50, 217–18, 228,
256, 341

fatherhood of, 173, 296, 346; *see also* Duchin, Colin; Duchin, Courtnay; Duchin, Jason

favorite musicians of, 128–31, 133, 149–50, 153, 160, 172, 186–87, 210, 224–25, 234, 235, 272, 276–77, 289

film appearance by, 250–51

first marriage of, 38; *see also* Hodges, Cheray Zauderer Duchin

fishing enjoyed by, 38–39, 55, 60–62, 90–91, 135, 142–43, 205–6, 263, 264, 296, 298–307, 355

foreign travels of, 68, 139–40, 150, 158, 160–61, 170, 198, 199–201, 207–8, 236–37, 252, 288, 302, 309, 331–32, 337, 351

guardians for, 105, 184–85

health of, 11, 12–14, 17, 18

homes of, 174–75, 186, 192–93, 216, 253, 256–58, 273, 295–98, 315–18, 320, 339, 344, 355–56

income of, 153, 162, 175, 184, 215, 238

in jazz groups, 149, 208–11

on jazz music, 150, 160, 172, 187–88, 223, 283–84

in military service, 5, 198, 199, 203–8, 211, 213

music studies of, 100–101, 115, 119, 134–36, 138, 149, 150, 167, 185–88, 222, 223–25, 241

in Panama, 5, 205–11

in Paris, 150–52, 158, 160, 162, 163, 165, 167–93, 196, 319

performing enjoyed by, 135, 210–11, 345

physical appearance of, 158, 196, 280, 343, 344, 356

piano style of, 126–28, 136, 149–50, 151–52, 182, 186, 210, 212, 223–25, 233–34, 237, 248, 282, 284

politics of, 97, 148, 190, 207–8, 325, 332–34, 356

professional debuts of, 3–7, 151–52, 204, 240, 243

recordings made by, 186, 222–23, 225–26, 236, 239, 251

religious attitudes of, 126, 218

reviews of, 243, 250

on rock and roll, 153, 241, 283–84

in school Dixieland bands, 128, 135

second marriage of, *see* Duchin, Brooke Hayward Thomas Hopper

social life of, 141–42, 171–73, 176–84, 199–201, 213, 216–21, 226–31, 240–41, 266–70,

272–75, 320, 331–32, 335,
342–44
at Yale, 97, 105, 133, 147–50,
153, 193, 196–97, 342
Duchin, Tillie Baron (Barashevsky)
(Peter Duchin's grandmother),
40, 41, 50, 124, 217
Duke, Angier Biddle, 212
Duke, Anthony Biddle, 246–48
Dunne, Dominick, 271
Dunne, Lennie, 271
Dyer, Nina, 182–83

Eager, Allen, 172, 186–88
Eaglebrook School, 110, 117–18,
132–33
École Normale de Musique,
185–86
Eddy Duchin Orchestra, 4, 47; *see
also* Duchin, Edwin Frank
Eddy Duchin Story, The, 5–6,
153–54, 225
Eden, Anthony, 86
Edey, Anne, 160, 192–93
Edey, Beatrice, 144
Edey, Helen, 142, 143–44, 158,
161–63
Edey, Kelly, 144
Edey, Maitland, Jr., 147
family life of, 142–44
first marriage of, 158, 160, 175,
192–93
hunting opposed by, 145

musical interests of, 128–31,
135, 172, 277
Peter Duchin's friendship with,
120, 125–26, 128–31, 132,
136, 139, 142, 145, 150,
158–61, 192–93
physical appearance of, 125, 158
Edey, Maitland, Sr., 142–43
Edey, Marion, 144
Elizabeth Club, 147–48
Ellington, Duke, 248, 281
Emerson, Margaret, 107, 108
Evans, Bill, 210
Everitt, Chiquita Wynn Duchin
Heap:
background of, 107
first marriage of, 108
fourth marriage of, 211
homes of, 342
as hostess, 211, 212, 236, 237
Peter Duchin's career and, 5, 236,
238
physical appearance of, 5, 107,
109, 144
second marriage of, 50, 107–8,
109, 110, 115, 119, 120, 122,
153
as stepmother, 5, 105–7, 109,
112, 114–15, 117, 121, 132,
133, 140, 141, 163, 175, 184,
195, 205, 215, 216
third marriage of, 140, 141, 211
Everitt, Robert, 211, 212, 236

Fabiano, Roberta, 284

Fair, James Graham, 22

Fairbanks, Douglas, Jr., 102

Fargeon, Eleanor, 166–67

Fargeon, Herbert, 166

Farley, James, 116

Farrow, Mia, 235–36, 271

Fauré, Gabriel, 185–86

Fauré, Hubert, 181

Findlay, Toddie Wyman, 38, 39, 40, 345

Fitzgerald, Geraldine, 102

Flacco (Slim) (Panamanian deejay), 210

Flowers, Martha, 217

Fonda, Henry, 102, 290

Fonda, Jane, 270, 343

Fonda, Peter, 344

Fontaine, Joan, 102

Fontainebleau Hotel, 260, 265, 272

Ford, Anne (daughter), 241

Ford, Anne McDonnell (mother), 240, 241, 290

Ford, Henry, Jr., 240–41, 290

Forrestal, James, 148

Forrestal, Mike, 148–49, 310

Fox, Felix, 41

Francis, Kay, 102

Frazier, Simon, 309

Gable, Clark, 102

Galella, Ron, 335

Gardner, Ava, 237, 244

Garside, Charles, 138

Gates, Geoffrey, 240, 252

Genet, Jean, 219

Gernreich, Rudi, 343

Gershwin, George, 47, 99, 249–50

Gieseking, Walter, 210

Gigi Room, 260, 265

Gillespie, Dizzy, 130, 277

Gish, Lillian, 102

Gleason, Jackie, 196

Glover, Gubby, 38, 280

Gogh, Vincent van, 349

Goldsmith, Gill, 180, 189

Goldsmith, James, 180

Goldsmith, Teddy, 180, 189

Goldwyn, Frances, 266

Goldwyn, Samuel, 102, 266–68, 270

Goodman, Benny, 130

Goodman, Ed, 96

Goodman, Marian, 96

Gordon, Ruth, 217

Gossett, Lou, 219

Graham, Katharine (Kay), 290, 322, 323

Grant, Cary, 5, 102, 153

Grappelli, Stéphane, 172

Graves, Bill, 292

Graves, Harry, 292

Gray, Francine du Plessix, 150–51

Green, Adolph, 226

Greene, Shecky, 272, 273

Greenwood, 260–63

Griswold, A. Whitney, 197

Guinzburg, Harold, 89

Guinzburg, Tom, 89

Gurney, Dick, 134, 138

Guy Lombardo's Port of Call, 260, 263

Halle, Kay, 70

Hancock, Herbie, 284

Handman, Wynn, 235–36

Harkness, Rebekah, 246

Harriman, Averell, 79–97, 105

    beachfront property offered to
        Duchins by, 315–18, 328

    childhood of, 85

    death of, 349, 350–53

    family background of, 14, 94

    as fan of Eddy Duchin, 45

    fatherhood of, 82

    finances of, 88–89

    frugality of, 93–94, 315–17

    homes of, 13, 38, 53, 54, 60,
        79–80, 86, 89–90, 91–93, 110,
        121, 133, 315, 316, 322,
        325–26, 327, 328, 329–30,
        349, 350

    as host, 108, 109, 255, 351

    personal staff of, 39, 79, 83–84,
        90

    Peter Duchin's career and, 6, 327

    Peter Duchin's youth and, 14, 19,
        55, 68, 79–86, 91–93, 97, 110,
        116, 120–21, 131, 132, 133,
        193, 223, 325, 328

    physical appearance of, 6, 79, 80,
        91, 323, 329, 350

    political career of, 6, 9, 53,
        66–67, 68, 70, 76, 79, 85,
        96–97, 148, 200, 204, 208,
        256, 311–12, 313

    railroad background of, 14, 26

    second marriage of, 26, 66–67,
        69–70, 76, 310, 311–12,
        313–15, 349

    social circle of, 44, 90, 94–97,
        102, 350

    as sportsman, 44, 85–88, 140,
        302, 313, 315, 329

    as stepfather, 75

    third marriage of, 320, 322–30,
        347–48, 350, 352–53

    on Vietnam War, 96–97

Harriman, E. H., 54, 94

Harriman, Kathleen, 54, 82, 352

Harriman, Marie Norton Whitney,
    63–78

    art collected by, 70–71, 93, 155,
        317, 349

    death of, 309–10, 311–13, 315,
        317, 325

    Eddy Duchin's relationship with,
        19, 76–78, 108, 311

    family background of, 64, 166

    first marriage of, 64–66, 69, 70, 76

    grave of, 312, 352

    homes of, 13, 38, 54, 89, 91, 110,
        121, 133, 216, 325–26

as hostess, 96, 108, 109, 155,
158, 255
Marjorie Duchin's friendship
with, 9, 22, 26, 154–55
as mother, 71, 73–75, 76, 142
near blindness of, 64, 70, 167
personal staff of, 39, 64, 66, 90,
312
Peter Duchin's career and, 6, 215,
221–22, 327
Peter Duchin's youth and, 13, 14,
50, 55, 63–64, 68, 101, 105,
110, 121, 131, 132, 133, 152,
195, 198–99, 200, 230, 328,
352
physical appearance of, 64, 144,
155
second marriage of, 26, 69–70,
86–88, 93–94, 312
social circle of, 90, 96, 102, 166,
248–49, 290
speaking style of, 64, 66–67, 312,
313
travels of, 68–69, 313–15
Harriman, Mary, 54, 82, 352–53
Harriman, Pamela Digby Churchill
Hayward, 319–30
Averell Harriman's relationship
with, 69, 320, 322–30,
350–51, 352–53
early marriages of, 69, 70, 319,
320–22, 326
family background of, 322, 326

finances of, 317, 320, 353
homes of, 319, 325–26, 327, 328,
329–30, 348–49, 350
physical appearance of, 319, 323,
352
in political world, 320, 326, 328,
329
son of, 351
as stepmother, 344, 347, 348,
349
as U.S. ambassador to France,
320
Harriman State Park, 351
Harrison, Rex, 102
Hart, Kitty Carlisle, 351, 356
Hart, Moss, 44, 153
Hawkins, Robert, 138
Hawks, Howard, 102
Haynes, Rick, 148, 149
Hayward, Bill, 348
Hayward, Brooke, *see* Duchin,
Brooke Hayward Thomas
Hopper
Hayward, Leland, 102, 140, 319,
320–22, 325, 327, 342, 344,
348
Hayward, Maisie Plant, 341–42
Hayward, Margaret Sullavan, 342
Hayward, Pamela Digby Churchill,
see Harriman, Pamela Digby
Churchill Hayward
Hayward, Slim, 320, 342
Haywire (estate), 319, 329, 348–49

Haywire (Hayward), 342, 344, 347, 348

Hayworth, Rita, 102

Heap, Chiquita Wynn Duchin, *see* Everitt, Chiquita Wynn Duchin Heap

Heap, Morgan, 140–41, 211

Hearst, William Randolph, 102

Hefti, Neal, 272

Hellinger, Mark, 102

Hemingway, Ernest, 110, 169, 176

Henie, Sonja, 102

Henry, Buck, 344

Hepburn, Audrey, 171

Hill, George Roy, 250

Hindemith, Paul, 147, 185

Hines, Earl (Fatha), 131, 160

Hitchcock, Alfred, 102

Hobe Sound, 38–39

Hodges, Cheray Zauderer Duchin, 94, 317

    family background of, 252, 253–55, 256

    homes of, 96, 253, 256–58, 273, 295–98, 306, 315, 320, 322, 328, 339, 344

    as hostess, 96, 344

    Marie Harriman's death and, 310, 311, 313

    motherhood of, 337–39

    on Pamela Harriman, 324–25

    Peter Duchin's career and, 252, 337

    Peter Duchin's relationship with, 229–31, 251–53, 262–63, 337–39, 345

    physical appearance of, 230, 344

    political involvement of, 332, 334

    on road tours, 260, 263, 265, 272, 288, 337

    social life of, 262, 268, 270, 271, 272, 273, 275, 289, 309, 319, 320, 323, 327, 331–32, 335, 343

Hodges, Luther, Jr., 332

Holiday, Billie, 130

Holman, Libby, 49

Honegger, Andrée, 185–86, 188

Honegger, Arthur, 185

Hope, Bob, 102

Hopper, Dennis, 343, 344

Hopper, Hedda, 102

Horowitz, Vladimir, 7, 276

Hotchkiss, 134–35, 136–38, 148

Hotel James, 241

Houseman, John, 102

Hughes, Howard, 102

Hughes, Robert, 302

Humes, Harold L. (Doc), 176

Huston, John, 102

Hutton, Barbara, 102

Huxley, Aldous, 14

In Search of History (White), 85

In the Duchin Manner, 239

Jack the Turk (Maisonette staff
    member), 246–48
Jaffe, Leo, 153
jazz:
    improvisation in, 187–88
    Latin music and, 210
    in Paris, 172, 187
    rock and roll vs., 283–84
Jeanne (cook), 90, 91
Jenkins, Gordon, 272
Johnson, James P., 131
Johnson, Lady Bird, 287
Johnson, Luci, 287–88
Johnson, Lynda Byrd, 287
Johnson, Lyndon B., 97, 259, 260,
    287–88
Johnson, Van, 102, 153
Jones, Gloria, 171
Jones, James, 171, 176
Jones, James Earl, 219
Jourdan, Louis, 266–68
Jungle Book (Kipling), 51
Jupiter Island, 38
Jupiter Island Bath and Tennis
    Club, 38, 318

Kanin, Garson, 217
Kaufman, George S., 44
Kaye, Danny, 102
Kaye, Sidney, 217
Kelly, John (Shipwreck), 145, 289,
    290
Kennedy, Ethel, 311

Kennedy, Jacqueline Bouvier, 173,
    251–52, 312, 331–32, 334–37,
    344
Kennedy, John F., 6, 39, 68, 148,
    173, 213, 253, 312, 334
Kennedy, John F., Jr., 337
Kennedy, Robert F., 311, 332–34,
    351
Keogh, Tom, 190
Kerr, Deborah, 176–78
Kerry, John, 325
Khan, Aly, 176, 320
Kilgallen, Dorothy, 5
King, Martin Luther, Jr., 148, 332
Kipling, Rudyard, 51, 56
Kitchen, Bill, 53, 55, 57–62, 71, 79,
    88, 101, 109, 118, 223, 228,
    300
Kleberg, Bob, 293
Korda, Sir Alexander, 102
Kriendler, Bob, 205
Kuhn, Walt, 71, 121
Kurnitz, Harry, 178, 271, 272
Kwas, Tone, 281

Landowska, Wanda, 138
Lanin, Lester, 248
Lansbury, Angela, 250, 251
Lapierre, Dominique, 271
Lardner, Ring, 44
Latham, Hugh, 196
Lazar, Irving (Swifty), 178, 268–70,
    271, 346

LeRoy, Mervyn, 102

Little Richard, 153

Livanos, George, 199, 200, 201

"Lonesome Blues," 128–30

Loos, Anita (Neetsie), 9–10, 11, 13, 14, 15, 103, 171, 188–89, 248–49

Loudon, John, 139

Lovatt, Simon Frazier, Lord, 309

Lupino, Ida, 103

Luter, Claude, 172

McCarthy, Eugene, 332

McCarthy, Jim, 223

McClain, John, 5, 102

McCloy, John J., 171

McGovern, George, 97

McGrath, Robert, 205

Maclean, Norman, 307

MacMurray, Fred, 103

Mainbocher, 151, 152

Maisonette, 4, 6–7, 226, 238, 243–49, 252, 253, 260

"Make Someone Happy," 7, 226, 245

Mango Bay, 330

Mankiewicz, Herman J., 103

Mankiewicz, Joseph L., 103

Manning, Nancy, 7

Marie Harriman Gallery, 71

Marshall Plan, 66, 70

Martin, Mary, 151–52

Marx, Barbara, 274

Marx, Harpo, 103

Marx, Zeppo, 103, 274

Matthiessen, Peter, 176

Maxwell, Elsa, 103

Mayer, Louis B., 101, 103

MCA (Music Corporation of America), 195–96, 221, 238–39

Mercer, Mabel, 219

Merrick, David, 245

Messel, Oliver, 330

Meyerhoff Collection, 344

Mid-Ocean Bath and Tennis Club, 239, 240

Milland, Ray, 103

Millay, Edna St. Vincent, 142, 144

Miller, Glenn, 281

Mineo, Sal, 270

Monk, Thelonious, 130, 182

Montgomery, Robert, 103

Moore, Paul, Jr., 352

Morgan, Eddie, 179–80, 181

Morgan, Helen, 49

Morton, Jelly Roll, 128, 131, 277

Mosaddeq, Mohammed, 313–15

Moses, Robert, 47

Muir, John, 94

Murphy, George, 103

Musée de Cluny, 170

Music Corporation of America (MCA), 195–96, 221, 238–39

New York State Council on the Arts, 351, 356

Niarchos, Stavros, 199

Nicholson, Jack, 344

nightclubs, decline of, 282

Niven, David, 103

Nixon, Richard, 213, 275

Norman, Patricia, 48

Norton, Beulah, 64

Norton, Sheridan, 64

Novak, Kim, 153–55

Nureyev, Rudolf, 218

Odetta, 217

Oelrichs, Blanche (Michael
    Strange), 25–26

Oelrichs, Charles, Jr., 26

Oelrichs, Charles DeLoosey, 22, 24

Oelrichs, Hermann, 22–23

Oelrichs, Marjorie (daughter), see
    Duchin, Marjorie Oelrichs

Oelrichs, Marjorie Turnbull
    (mother), 4, 9–10, 26, 33,
    357

Oelrichs, Theresa Fair, 22–24, 228,
    341

Old Westbury Gardens, 357–58

"Ol' Man Mose," 47–48

Onassis, Alexander, 335

Onassis, Aristotle, 199, 252, 332,
    335

Onassis, Jacqueline Bouvier
    Kennedy, 173, 251–52, 312,
    331–32, 334–37, 344

"One for My Baby," 289

Oppenheimer, Bridget, 288

Oppenheimer, Harry, 288

O'Sullivan, Maureen, 271

Paich, Marty, 272

Paley, Babe, 119

Paley, Jeffrey, 115

Paley, William, 119

Panama, U.S. military in, 205–8

Paris Review, 175, 176, 178, 181,
    190

Parker, Charlie, 130, 187

Parker, Dorothy, 44

Payson, Joan, 283

Peck, Gregory, 103

Peerce, Jan, 217

Perruchin, 210

Peter Duchin at the St. Regis, 251

Peter Duchin Orchestra:
    eclectic repertoire of, 248, 283,
        284, 358
    number of musicians in, 281
    party entertainment provided by,
        241–43, 279–94
    presidential entertainments han-
        dled by, 259–60, 287–88
    signature song of, 7, 226
    start of, 238, 239, 240
    on tour, 260, 263–65, 272, 275,
        279–82, 337
    vocalists for, 7, 284
    see also Duchin, Peter

Peterson, Oscar, 210

Peyre, Henri, 197

Phillips (Sands Point caretaker), 90, 91

Phipps, Diana, 173–74

Phipps, Harry, 172–74

Phipps, Nonie, 115

Phipps, Ogden, 172

Piano Exchange, 358–60

Picasso, Pablo, 21–22, 71

Plant, Morton, 341

Plimpton, George, 175, 176, 179, 186, 226, 228–29, 273, 312

Porter, Cole, 103, 165–66, 233–34

Powell, Bud, 149–50, 172, 182

Power, Tyrone, 103, 153

Preminger, Otto, 103

Presenting Peter Duchin, 226

Presley, Elvis, 153

Price, Leontyne, 217

Pryor, Samuel, 38

Puente, Tito, 219

Queen Elizabeth II, 286–87

Rachmaninoff, Sergei, 49

Raposo, Joe, 272

Rathbone, Basil, 103

Reed, Joseph Verner, 38, 39

Reed, Nat, 39, 318

Reed, Permelia Pryor, 38, 318

Reisman, Leo, 43, 45

René, Henri, 225, 226, 239

Richardson, Tony, 343

Richter, Sviatoslav, 210

Rickles, Don, 272–73

Riddle, Nelson, 272

Rizzo, Jilly, 272

Roach, Hal, 103

Robards, Jason, Jr., 271

Robb, Lynda Byrd Johnson, 287

Robbins, Jerome, 290

Robertson, Cordelia Biddle, 28

Robinson, Edward G., 103

rock-and-roll music, 153, 241, 283–84

Romanoff, Mike, 102, 103, 265–66

Romero, Cesar, 103

Roosevelt, Franklin D., 9, 11, 94

Roosevelt, James, 174

Rosecliff, 23–24, 341

Ross, David, 135

Rothschild, Elie de, 320

Rothschild, Pauline, 171

Rubinstein, Arthur, 139, 210, 234

Rubinstein, Eva, 234

Rudd, Roswell, 135

Rudkin, Mark, 175

Rudy (Maisonette staff member), 245–46, 248, 249

Ruscha, Ed, 344

Russell, Rosalind, 102

Russian Tea Room, 217–18

Sacher, Lou, 239

St. Cyr, Johnny, 130

St. Regis Hotel:
  Maisonette supper club in, 4,
    6–7, 226, 238, 243–49, 252,
    253, 260
  owners of, 4, 212, 246
Sardi, Ann, 66
Sardi, Vincent, 66
Sartre, Jean-Paul, 319
Schaldach, William J., 307
Schloss, Dr., 12, 13, 17
Schmidt, Otto, 7, 239–40, 242,
    243, 259, 263–64, 265, 309
Schneider, Abe, 153
Schwarzkopf, Elisabeth, 189
Scott, Randolph, 103
Scully, Vincent, 197, 200–201
Sefton, Lady (Foxy), 188–89
Sellers, Peter, 250, 251
Selznick, Danny, 101, 343
Selznick, David O., 101, 103, 262,
    343
Selznick, Irene Mayer, 101, 103, 343
Selznick, Jeffrey, 101
Shaw, Irwin, 176–79
Sheridan, Ann, 103
Sherwood, Madeline, 66, 67,
    248–49
Sherwood, Robert E., 44, 66, 67
Shirley, Don, 216–17
Shor, Baby, 105, 109
Shor, Toots, 5–6, 103, 104–5, 109,
    115–16, 121–22, 133, 270–71
Shore, Dinah, 196

Short, Bobby, 216–17, 219
Silvers, Robert, 312
  Army service of, 176, 203
  background of, 175–76, 179
  barge shared by, 176, 179, 186,
    190, 192
  Paris Review run by, 175, 176,
    178, 180, 181
Simon, George, 48
Sinatra, Barbara Marx, 274
Sinatra, Frank, 103, 237, 270–77,
    289
Singh, Patwant, 288
Slim (Flacco) (Panamanian deejay),
    210
Sly, Albert, 134, 135, 136
Smith, Red, 307
Smith, Rick, 358, 360
Solal, Martial, 172
Southern, Terry, 252, 343
South Pacific (Rodgers and Ham-
    merstein), 151, 320
Spence School for Girls, 26, 334
Spiegel, Sam, 103
Stablemates, 211
Stafford, Jo, 7
Stalin, Joseph, 86, 94
Starr, Kay, 7
Stein, Jules, 238
Stewart, James, 5, 102
Straeter, Ted, 219, 235, 239
Stralem, Donald, 105, 119, 132,
    142, 153, 175, 184–85, 298

Stralem, Jean, 105, 119, 132, 298

Strange, Michael (Blanche Oelrichs), 25–26

Strayhorn, Billy, 237

Styne, Jule, 226, 249–50

Sullavan, Margaret, 342

Sullivan, Ed, 204

Sun Valley, Idaho, 26, 110–12

Swift, Archibald, 128

Swope, Betty, 44

Swope, Herbert Bayard, Jr. (Ottie),
 44–45

Symington, James, 259

Symington, Stuart, 259

Syncopators, 135

Tatum, Art, 131, 160, 210, 277

Taylor, Deems, 44–45

Taylor, Samuel, 153

Thomas, Michael, 342–43, 346

Thompson, Rex, 6

Thomson, Virgil, 185

Thyssen, Heinrich von, 182

Tracy, Spencer, 103

Truman, Harry S., 66, 70, 148, 313

Turner, Lana, 103

Turnure, Pamela, 213

Union Pacific Railroad, 14, 26, 89,
 349

Universal Pictures, 238

Urban, Joseph, 44

Urtreger, René, 187

Vadim, Roger, 270

Vanderbilt, Alfred, 107

Vanderbilt, George, 112–13, 114

Vanderbilt, Gertrude, 226, 228

Vanderbilt, Harold S. (Mike),
 226–29, 230–31

Vanderbilt, Lulu, 113, 113

Vanderbilt, Virginia Graham Fair, 23

Vanderbilt, William K., Jr., 23

Van Zuylen, Gaby, 181, 192

Van Zuylen, Teddy, 180, 181, 192

Vaux, Calvert, 43, 44

Vickers, Hugo, 30

Viertel, Peter, 176

Vietnam War, 96–97, 325

Volpi, Giovanni, 200, 283

Walker, James J., 43–44

Waller, Fats, 131, 358

Walsh, Betty, 357

Walter, Cy, 224–25

Wanamaker, John, 45–47, 216

Wanamaker, Mary Louise, 47

Wanger, Walter, 103

Waring, Fred, Jr., 128

Warner, Jack, 103

Warren, Earl, 116

Warren, Harry, 360

Wasserman, Lew, 103

Webb, Clifton, 103

Webb, Jimmy, 272

Welles, Orson, 175

Werblin, Sonny, 195

Whale River, 304–6

"What's the Matter with American
    Men?" (Oelrichs), 28–29

Whitaker, Popsie, 5

White, Stanford, 23

White, Theodore H., 85

White Ball, 23

White Roses (van Gogh), 349

Whitman, Harry, 306–7

Whitney, Axie, 141–42, 189, 215

Whitney, Betsey, 119, 151, 174,
    260, 262, 289

Whitney, Harry, 75, 117, 141–42,
    149, 189, 215
  death of, 73
  in family relationships, 73–76
  Peter Duchin's childhood and,
    71–73, 90, 91, 148, 296

Whitney, John Hay (Jock), 103, 119,
    145, 151, 260, 262, 283, 289,
    290

Whitney, Kate Roosevelt, 145, 151,
    174

Whitney, Nancy, 50, 51, 71–76, 78,
    170, 179, 311

Whitney, Sonny, 66, 69, 71, 76

Who Tells Me True (Strange), 24–26

Wilder, Billy, 271

Wilder Shores of Love, The (Blanch),
    322

Williams, Andy, 351

Williams, Tennessee, 217

Willis, Malcolm, 134, 136

Willow Oaks, 330, 350

Wilson, Earl, 292

Wilson, Teddy, 130, 160

Woman with a Fan (Picasso), 21–22

Woodlawn Cemetery, 33–34

Woollcott, Alexander, 45

World of Henry Orient, The,
    250–51

Wulff, Lee, 300–301

Wyman, Dwight Deere, 38

Wynn, Ed, 47

Wynn, Keenan, 103

Wynn, Montgomery, 108

Yale University, 147, 196, 197

Yalta Peace Conference, 94

Young, Lester, 139, 172, 187, 188

Zanuck, Darryl, 103, 176

Zauderer, Audrey, 231, 253–56,
    298

Zauderer, George, 231, 253–56,
    258, 298

Zellie (governess), 22, 36, 50,
    56–57, 59, 84, 100–101, 109,
    169

Ziegfeld, Florenz, 44

Collection of Peter Duchin: pages 2, 16 (top and bottom left), 27 (bottom), 37, 42 (top), 58, 77, 87, 95, 98, 111, 123, 127, 129, 137, 157, 164, 168, 202, 214, 227 (top), 232, 303 (top), 314; Lester Glassner Collection/Neal Peters: pages 8, 16 (bottom right), 32; Cecil Beaton, courtesy of Sotheby's London: page 20; the Preservation Society of Newport County, Newport, R.I.: page 27 (top); J. N. Erhart/Collection of Peter Duchin: page 42 (bottom); U.P.I./Bettmann: pages 46 (top), 220 (top), 291 (top); Archive Photos/Frank Driggs Collection: page 46 (bottom); Courtesy of Alexandra E. Whitney: page 72 (bottom); Alfred Eisenstaedt, *Life* magazine © Time, Inc.: page 92; Jim O'Grady/U.P.I./Bettmann: page 106; Photofest: page 156; Courtesy of *The Paris Review*: page 177; Philip Pillsbury/Collection of Peter Duchin: page 191 (bottom); Frank Black/U.S. Army Photo/Collection of Peter Duchin: page 209; Bill Mark/Collection of Peter Duchin: page 220 (bottom); Globe Photos: page 227 (bottom); Bela Cseh/Collection of Peter Duchin: page 247; Geoffrey Gates/Collection of Peter Duchin: page 254 (top); Ronald Sarno/Collection of Peter Duchin: page 254 (bottom); Henry Grossman, *Life* magazine © Time, Inc.: page 257; D. Coleman Glover/Collection of Peter Duchin: pages 267, 316; Henry Grossman: pages 278, 285, 299; A.P./Wide World Photos: pages 291 (bottom), 308, 321; Cheray Hodges/Collection of Peter Duchin: pages 279, 338; *Look* magazine: page 303 (bottom); Oscar Abolafia: page 333; Patrick A. Burns/NYT Pictures: page 336; Ellen Graham: page 340; Richard Felber: page 354; Courtesy of *The News*, New York's Picture Newspaper: page 359.

PETER DUCHIN was born in New York City in 1937. His father was the celebrated bandleader Eddy Duchin, one of the most important figures of the big-band era. His mother, Marjorie Oelrichs, the daughter of a socially prominent Newport and New York family, died a few days after he was born. Duchin grew up at Arden, the upstate New York residence of Averell Harriman and his wife, Marie, who had been a close friend of his mother's. He was educated at Eaglebrook, Hotchkiss, and Yale. In 1962, after a stint in the army, Duchin made his professional debut as a bandleader at the Maisonette in the St. Regis Hotel in New York. He soon became one of the preeminent pianists and bandleaders in the country, and he and his orchestra have continued to be popular and sought-after. His organization, Peter Duchin Entertainment, supplies music for more than 600 events each year. Duchin is vice-chairman of the New York State Council on the Arts and serves on the boards of many cultural institutions, including American Ballet Theatre, the Chamber Music Society of Lincoln Center, Friends of the Vienna Philharmonic, the Spoleto Festival USA, the Glimmerglass Opera, and the Citizens Committee of New York City. He is married to Brooke Hayward, and has three children. He and his wife live in New York City and Connecticut.

CHARLES MICHENER, formerly the senior editor for cultural affairs at *Newsweek,* is now a senior editor at *The New Yorker* and the music critic for *The New York Observer.*

ABOUT THE TYPE

This book was set in Fairfield, the first typeface from the hand of the distinguished American artist and engraver Rudolph Ruzicka (1883–1978). Rudolph Ruzicka was born in Bohemia and came to America in 1894. He set up his own shop, devoted to wood engraving and printing, in New York in 1913 after a varied career working as a wood engraver, in photoengraving and banknote printing plants, and as an art director and freelance artist. He designed and illustrated many books, and was the creator of a considerable list of individual prints—wood engravings, line engravings on copper, and aquatints.